PURITANISM

OPPOSING VIEWPOINTS®

Other Books in the American History Series:

The American Frontier
The American Revolution
The Bill of Rights
The Cold War
The Great Depression
Immigration
Slavery

PURITANISM

O P P O S I N G   V I E W P O I N T S®

David L. Bender, *Publisher*
Bruno Leone, *Executive Editor*

Teresa O'Neill, *Series Editor*
John C. Chalberg, Ph.D., professor of history,
    Normandale Community College, *Consulting
    Editor*

William Dudley, *Book Editor*
Teresa O'Neill, *Book Editor*

AMERICAN HISTORY SERIES

285.9
Pur

01676

Cover photos: North Wind Picture Archives

Library of Congress Cataloging-in-Publication Data

Puritanism : opposing viewpoints / William Dudley, book editor; Teresa O'Neill, book editor.
  p.   cm. — (American history series)
  Includes bibliographical references and index.
  ISBN 1-56510-082-4 (alk. paper) — ISBN 1-56510-081-6 (pbk. : alk. paper)
  1. Puritans—New England—History. 2. Puritans—New England—History—Sources. 3. New England—Church history. 4. New England—Church history—Sources. 5. New England—History—Colonial period, ca. 1600-1775. 6. New England—History—Colonial period, ca. 1600-1775—Sources. I. Dudley, William, 1964- . II. O'Neill, Terry, 1944- . III. Series: American history series (San Diego, Calif.)
BX9354.2.P87   1994   93-28918
285'.9'0974—dc20   CIP

© 1994 by Greenhaven Press, Inc., PO Box 289009,
San Diego, CA 92198-9009
Printed in the U.S.A.

"America was born of revolt, flourished in dissent, became great through experimentation."

Henry Steele Commager, American Historian, 1902-1984

Contents

	Page
Foreword	9
Introduction	15

Chapter 1: The Vision and the Voyage

Chapter Preface	26
1. An American Colony Would Have Many Practical Benefits *John White*	28
2. An American Colony Would Serve the True Christian Church *John Winthrop*	35
3. A Puritan Vision of the New Colony *John Winthrop*	44
4. A Separatist Vision of the New Colony *John Robinson*	52
5. God Has Blessed New England *William Stoughton*	57
6. God Has Withdrawn His Blessing from New England *Increase Mather*	62

Chapter 2: Dealing with Religious Dissent

Chapter Preface	68
1. Roger Williams's Banishment Was Not Justified *Roger Williams*	70
2. Roger Williams's Banishment Was Justified *John Cotton*	75
3. The Antinomians Are Destroying the Community *Thomas Welde*	82
4. The Antinomians Are Following the Spirit of God *Anne Hutchinson et al.*	92
5. Immigration to Massachusetts Should Be Restricted *John Winthrop*	105
6. Immigration Restrictions Are Unfair *Henry Vane*	110

7. The Puritans Should Be More Tolerant   112
   Richard Saltonstall

8. The Puritans Are Not Too Intolerant   115
   John Cotton

Chapter 3: Creating a Godly Community

Chapter Preface   121

1. Political Leadership Should Be Restricted to Church Members   123
   John Cotton

2. Political Leadership Restrictions Should Be Lifted   129
   Robert Child et al.

3. Economic Exploitation Harms the Community   136
   John Winthrop

4. Making a Profit Does Not Harm the Community   140
   Robert Keayne

5. Stricter Laws Are Needed   146
   The Massachusetts General Court

6. Stricter Laws Have Limited Effectiveness   153
   William Bradford

Chapter 4: Puritans and Native Americans

Chapter Preface   157

1. Puritan Treatment of Indians Is Justified   160
   John Cotton

2. Puritan Treatment of Indians Is Not Justified   163
   Roger Williams

3. Killing Indians Is Justified by God   165
   Edward Johnson

4. The Indians Should Be Treated Charitably   168
   Samuel Sewall

5. A Missionary's View of Indians   170
   John Eliot

6. A Captive's View of Indians   177
   Mary Rowlandson

Chapter 5: Crises and Renewal

Chapter Preface   189

1. Witches Should Be Condemned   192
   Cotton Mather

2. "Witches" Have Been Unfairly Prosecuted   200
   Thomas Brattle

3. The Witch Trials Reflect the Spirit of God   208
    Increase Mather
4. The Witch Trials Reflect a Lack of Faith in God   213
    Robert Calef
5. The Great Awakening Offers Hope of True
   Religious Revival   218
    *An Assembly of Pastors of Churches in
    New England*
6. The Great Awakening Offers Errors in
   Religious Thinking   225
    *Pastors of the Churches in the Province of
    Massachusetts Bay*
7. Religious Fervor Should Be Praised   229
    Jonathan Edwards
8. Religious Zealotry Should Be Avoided   242
    Charles Chauncy

Chapter 6: Historians View the Puritans
Chapter Preface   252
1. The Puritans Saw Themselves as a Model
   for the World   255
    Perry Miller
2. The Puritans Did Not See Themselves as a
   Model for the World   269
    Theodore Dwight Bozeman

For Discussion   283
Chronology   288
Annotated Bibliography   294
Index   303

Foreword

Aboard the *Arbella* as it lurched across the cold, gray Atlantic, John Winthrop was as calm as the waters surrounding him were wild. With the confidence of a born leader, Winthrop gathered his Puritan passengers around him. It was time to offer a sermon. England lay behind them, and years of strife and persecution for their religious beliefs were over, he said. But the Puritan abandonment of England, he reminded his followers, did not mean that England was beyond redemption. Winthrop wanted his followers to remember England even as they were leaving it behind. Their goal should be to create a new England, one far removed from the authority of the Anglican church and King Charles I. In Winthrop's words, their settlement in the New World ought to be a model society, a city upon a hill. He hoped his band would be able to create a just society in America for corrupt England to imitate.

Unable to find either peace or freedom within their home country, these Puritans were determined to provide England with a living example of a community that valued both. Across the hostile Atlantic Ocean would shine the bright light of a just, harmonious, and God-serving society. England may have been beset by sin and corruption, but Winthrop and the colonists believed they could still save England—and themselves. Together, they would coax out of the rocky New England soil not only food for their tables but many thriving communities dedicated to achieving harmony and justice.

One June 8, 1630, John Winthrop and his company of refugees had their first glimpse of what they came to call New England. High on the surrounding hills stood a welcoming band of fir trees whose fragrance drifted to the *Arbella* on a morning breeze. To Winthrop, the "smell off the shore [was] like the smell of a garden."

This new world would, in fact, often be compared to the Garden of Eden. In it, John Winthrop would have his opportunity to start life over again. So would his family and his shipmates. So would all those who would come after them. Victims of conflict in old England hoped to find peace in New England.

Winthrop, for one, had experienced much conflict in his life. As a Puritan, he was opposed to Catholicism and Anglicanism, both of which, he believed, were burdened by distracting rituals and distant hierarchies. A parliamentarian by conviction, he despised Charles I, who had spurned Parliament and created a private army to do his bidding. He believed in individual responsibility and fought against the loss of religious and political freedom. A gentleman landowner, he feared the rising economic power of a merchant class that seemed to value only money. Once Winthrop stepped aboard the *Arbella*, he hoped conflict would not be a part of his American future.

But his Puritan religion told Winthrop that human beings are fallen creatures and that perfection, whether communal or individual, is unachievable on this earth. Therefore, he was presented with a dilemma: On the one hand, his religion demanded that he attempt to live a perfect life in an imperfect world. On the other hand, it told him that he was destined to fail.

Soon after Winthrop disembarked from the *Arbella*, he came face-to-face with this maddening dilemma. He found himself presiding not over a utopia—an ideal community—but over a colony caught up in disputes as troubling as any that he had confronted in his English past.

John Winthrop, it seems, was not the only Puritan with a dream of perfection, with a vision of a heaven on earth. Others in the community saw the dream differently. They wanted greater political and religious freedom than their leader was prepared to grant. Often, Winthrop was able to handle this conflict diplomatically. He expanded, for example, participation in elections and allowed the voters of Massachusetts Bay greater power.

But religious conflict was another matter because it was a conflict of competing visions of the Puritan utopia. In Roger Williams and Anne Hutchinson, two of his fellow colonists, John Winthrop faced rivals unprepared to accept his definition of the perfect community. To Williams, perfection demanded that he separate himself from the Puritan institutions in his community and create an even "purer" church. Winthrop, however, disagreed and exiled Williams to Rhode Island. Hutchinson presumed that she could interpret God's will without a minister. Again, Winthrop did not agree. Hutchinson was tried on charges of heresy, convicted, and banished from Massachusetts.

John Winthrop's Massachusetts colony was the first, but far from the last, American attempt to build a unified, peaceful community that, in the end, only provoked a discord. This glimpse at its history reveals what Winthrop confronted: the unavoidable presence of conflict in American life.

American Assumptions

From America's origins in the early seventeenth century, Americans have often held several interrelated assumptions about their country. First, people believe that to be American is to be free. Second, because Americans did not have to free themselves from feudal lords or an entrenched aristocracy, conflict is often considered foreign to American life. Finally, America has been seen as a perpetual haven from the troubles and disputes that are found in the Old World.

John Winthrop, for one, lived his life as though all of these assumptions were true. But the opposing viewpoints presented in the American History Series should reveal that for many Americans, these assumptions were and are myths. Indeed, for numerous Americans, liberty has not always been guaranteed, and conflict has been a necessary, sometimes welcome aspect of their life. To these Americans, the United States is less a sanctuary than it is one more battleground for old and new ideas.

Our American landscape has been torn apart again and again by a great variety of clashes—theological, ideological, political, economic, geographical, racial, gender-based, and class-based. But to discover such a landscape is not necessarily to come upon a hopelessly divided country. If the editors desire to prove anything during the course of this series, it is not that America has been enlivened, enriched, and even strengthened by exchanges destroyed by conflict but rather that America has been between Americans who have disagreed with one another.

Observers of American life, however, often see a country in which its citizens behave as though all of the basic questions of life have been settled. Over the years, they see a generation after generation of Americans who seem to blithely agree with one another. In the nineteenth century, French traveler Alexis de Tocqueville called the typical American a "venturesome conservative." According to Tocqueville, this American was willing to risk money in the marketplace but otherwise presented the drab front of someone who thought, dressed, and acted just like everyone else. To Tocqueville, Americans were individualistic risk takers when it came to playing the game of capitalism but were victims of public opinion (which he defined as the "tyranny of the majority") when it came to otherwise expressing themselves.

In the twentieth century, sociologist David Riesman has registered his agreement with Tocqueville. He has defined the modern American as "other-directed." Perhaps willing to leap into the economic arena, this American is unwilling to take risks in the marketplace of ideas. The result is either silence or assent, either because this person is unsure of his or her own beliefs or because the mass media dictate beliefs—or a bit of both. The other-directed American is fearful of standing apart from the crowd.

The editors of this series would like to suggest that Tocqueville and Riesman were too narrow in their assessment of Americans. They have found innumerable Americans who have been willing to take the trouble to disagree.

11

The American Individual

Thomas Jefferson was one of the least confrontational of Americans, but he boldly and irrevocably enriched American life with his individualistic views. Like John Winthrop before him, he had a notion of an American Eden. Like Winthrop, he offered a vision of a harmonious society. And like Winthrop, he not only became enmeshed in conflict but eventually presided over a people beset by it. But unlike Winthrop, Jefferson believed this Eden was not located in a specific community but in each individual American. His Declaration of Independence from Great Britain could also be read as a declaration of independence for each individual in American society.

Jefferson's ideal world was composed of "yeoman farmers," each of whom was roughly equal to the other in society's eyes, each of whom was free from the restrictions of both government and his fellow citizens. Throughout his life, Jefferson offered a continuing challenge to Americans: advance individualism and equality or see the death of the American experiment. Jefferson believed that the strength of this experiment depended upon a society of autonomous individuals and a society without great gaps between rich and poor. His challenge to his fellow Americans to create—and sustain—such a society has itself produced both economic and political conflict.

A society whose guiding document is the Declaration of Independence is a society assured of the freedom to dream—and to disagree. We know that Jefferson himself hated conflict, whether personal or political. His tendency was to avoid confrontations of any sort, to squirrel himself away and write rather than to stand up and speak his mind. It is only through his written words that we can grasp Jefferson's utopian dream of a society of independent farmers, all pursuing their private dreams and all leading lives of sufficient prosperity.

This man of wealth and intellect lived an essentially happy life in accord with his view that Americans ought to have the right to pursue "happiness." But Jefferson's public life was much more troublesome. From the first rumblings of the American Revolution in the 1760s to the North-South skirmishes of the 1820s that ultimately produced the Civil War, Jefferson was at or near the center of American political history. The issues were almost too many—and too crucial—for one lifetime. Jefferson had to choose between supporting or rejecting the path of revolution. During and after the ensuing war, he was at the forefront of the battle for religious liberty. After endorsing the Constitution, he opposed the economic plans of Alexander Hamilton. At the end of the century, he fought the infamous Alien and Sedition Acts, which limited civil liberties. As president, he opposed the Federalist court, conspiracies to divide the union, and calls for a new war against England.

Throughout his life, Thomas Jefferson, slaveholder, pondered the conflict between American freedom and American slavery. And from retirement at his Monticello retreat, he frowned at the rising spirit of commercialism that he feared was dividing Americans and destroying his dream of American harmony.

No matter the issue, however, Thomas Jefferson invariably supported the rights of the individual. Worried as he was about the excesses of commercialism, he accepted them because his main concern was to live in a society where liberty and individualism could flourish. To Jefferson, Americans had to be free to worship as they desired. They also deserved to be free from an over-reaching government. To Jefferson, Americans should also be free to possess slaves.

Harmony, an Elusive Goal

Before reading the articles in this anthology, the editors ask readers to ponder the lives of John Winthrop and Thomas Jefferson. Each held a utopian vision, one based upon the demands of community and the other on the autonomy of the individual. Each dreamed of a country of perpetual new beginnings. Each found himself thrust into a position of leadership and found that conflict could not be avoided. And each lived long enough to face and express many opposing views. Harmony, whether communal or individual, was a forever elusive goal.

The opposing visions of Winthrop and Jefferson have been at the heart of many differences among Americans from many backgrounds through the whole of American history. Moreover, their visions have provoked important responses that have helped shape American society, the American character, and many an American battle.

Is the theme of community versus the individual the single defining theme in American history? No, but it is a recurring theme that provides us with a useful point of departure for showing that Americans have been more rambunctious and contentious than Tocqueville or Riesman found them to be, that blandness has not been the defining characteristic for all Americans.

In this age of mass media, the danger exists that the real issues that divide Americans will be, at best, distorted or, at worst, ignored. But by thinking honestly about the past, the real issues and real differences have often been of critical, even of life-and-death, importance to Americans. And they continue to be so today.

The editors of the American History Series have done extensive research to find representative opinions on the issues included in these volumes. They found numerous outstanding opposing viewpoints from people of all times, classes, and genders in American history. From those, they selected commentaries that best fit the nature and flavor of the period under consideration. Every attempt was made to include the most important and relevant viewpoints in each chapter. Obviously, not every notable viewpoint could be included. Therefore, a bibliography has been provided at the end of each book to aid readers in seeking out for themselves additional information.

The editors are confident that as this series reveals past conflicts, it will help revitalize the reader's views of the American present. In that spirit, the American History Series is dedicated to the proposition that American history is more complicated, more fascinating, and more troubling than John Winthrop, Thomas Jefferson, Alexis de Tocqueville, or David Riesman ever dared to imagine.

John C. Chalberg
Consulting Editor

Introduction

"John Winthrop's 'city on a hill' was never a place of total harmony. Many divisions existed in the early years of the Massachusetts Bay Colony and persisted as the colony grew and matured."

On a cold winter day in February 1674, the Reverend Increase Mather launched into the first of the powerful sermons that would assure him a place of importance in the city of Boston and in the history of Puritanism. It was a jeremiad, or a warning sermon. This style of sermon, named after the brooding Old Testament prophet Jeremiah, summoned an angry God who was prepared to visit great troubles on his people. Titled "The Day of Trouble Is Near," Mather's sermon painstakingly built a case for God's decision to punish his wayward flock for their sins. In Mather's dark view, troubles were coming for the Puritan faithful, designed by God to help the people realize that the "last times," meaning the end of time, were near.

Mather quoted Matthew: "Ye shall hear of wars and rumors of war. . . . For nation shall rise against nation, and realm against realm, and there shall be pestilence, and famine, and earthquakes in divers places. All these are but the beginning of sorrows." Mather had already convinced himself that these "sorrows" constituted a definite sign of the imminent arrival of the last times. Now he had to convince his listeners. Leaning toward them as he spoke, he asked: "What do we hear of this day, but wars and rumors of wars?"

Mather's goal was to raise the collective level of insecurity among his listeners. He feared that too many were already living in "sinful security," which a ministerial colleague had defined as the "great Disease of the last times." As far as Increase Mather was concerned, that disease was rampant among the once-righteous of New England. He therefore devoted the bulk of his sermon to convincing the assembled that even they—perhaps especially they—were not beyond the reach of God's punishment.

But the Reverend Mather was not finished. It was not enough that his audience grow insecure. They had to feel guilt and shame

15

as well. Toward that end, one rhetorical question followed another: Is there not oppression amongst us? Are there no "biting Usurers" in all of New England? Why have people given up on family prayer? How is time being spent instead?

Mather answered his own final question. "We have changed our Interest. The Interest of New England was religion, which did distinguish us from other English Plantations. . . . Now we begin to espouse a Worldly Interest and so choose a new God." The people, he said, were spending their time pursuing and worshiping this new God—money. Who in Boston could deny this? No one. The city's north end was rapidly filling up with merchants and other agents of the God of commerce. The once-pristine waterfront was already lined with docks, warehouses, and shipyards.

As each month passed, more and more ships were being built in local shipyards. More and more ships were being outfitted by Boston merchants. And more and more Bostonian ships were plying the seas in search of goods and profits. All this unholy activity left Increase Mather concerned about the future of the Puritan experiment and determined to communicate that concern, especially to those who were neither as guilt-ridden nor as frightened as he thought they should be.

"Signs have appeared," he pressed on, and he quoted Isaiah: "Thou Shalt be visited by the Lord of hosts with Thunder and with Earthquakes . . . with storm and tempest, and the flame of a devouring fire."

"Hath it not been so with us?" he asked. "We have been visited with terrible Thunders and Lightnings."

The sermon had arrived at its frightening climax. With images of towering thunderclouds Mather moved his audience under a dark "cloud of blood." Within the next few minutes he repeated that phrase several times. Then, just as suddenly as he had terrified his listeners, he offered them a tantalizing release: "This is Immanuel's land." Increase Mather had finally arrived at the conclusion of the Puritan jeremiad. Gone was every reference to a wrathful God wreaking vengeance on His wayward Puritans. Instead, corrupt Boston once again was "Immanuel's land [where] Christ by a wonderful Providence hath dispossessed Satan."

A Little Nation of Godly People

A calmer Mather laid before his audience the central image of seventeenth-century Puritanism. New England was once again an isolated refuge, a "city on a hill." New England was "a little Nation" of godly people. Despite the errors of their ways, they were still the Lord's children. The Covenant between God and His children, though badly frayed, remained intact. Because of this covenant, Mather confided, the Lord might punish them, but he would not destroy them:

> God hath culled out a people . . . which he hath also had a great favour towards, and hath brought them by a mighty hand . . . over greater than a Red Sea, and here hath he planted them. . . . Shall we think that all this is to destroy them within forty or fifty years? Destruction shall not as yet be [because] God cannot finde it in His heart to destroy us.

By the mid-1670s, when he preached this sermon, Increase Mather had every reason to believe that what was left of his Puritan world merited destruction. By this point in the history of the Puritan experiment, Boston was a bustling hive of economic activity. The Puritan ministerial class had been supreme in the early years of the colony, but a Puritan merchant class had begun to assert its own power well before the end of the seventeenth century. For the sons and grandsons of the first Puritans in the New World, dreams of achieving the good life here and now had begun to displace the desire to live a godly life in preparation for life in the hereafter.

Increase Mather himself was a son of a Puritan founder. Richard Mather had arrived in New England in 1635. Already an ordained Anglican minister, he was under suspension in England for his Puritan practices. Once in Massachusetts, the elder Mather put those practices to work to maintain the purity of his new community. He eventually passed this sense of vigilance over the Puritan way of life on to his son. And with it he passed his sense of anxiety as well.

Puritans were forever beset with bouts of anxiety. Belief in the Calvinist doctrine of predestination did not build confidence about one's place in the next world. Good Calvinists believed that God alone held an individual's ultimate fate in His hands. Moreover, everyone's personal fate had been predetermined before they appeared on earth. The whole matter of salvation was, as Richard Mather had once put it, "as if by lot."

According to Calvinist theology, there was no certainty in—and no logic to—God's behavior. God's selection of the saved was, in the final analysis, His alone to make—and a secret as well. Not only was it impossible to change God's mind, but it was out of the question for even the most devout to know His mind.

Increase Mather accepted the tenets of Calvinism, and he knew that each member of his flock was preoccupied with his or her uncertain future. Therefore, the prospect of personal salvation was always a part of the standard message in what Mather called his "sacramental" sermons. If people in his audience had not yet come to Christ, he wanted to extend the consoling promise of salvation once they had done so: "Awake thou that sleep and rise from the Dead, and Christ shall give thee light." Mather's good

17

news was that Jehovah's wrath was always tempered by Christ's love. Mather asserted, "Christ as mediator is the father of the new world". . . and the hope of Puritan New England.

Days of Trouble

By early 1675 Increase Mather had evidence that more "days of trouble" were at hand. In the nearby town of Plymouth three Wampanoag Indians were on trial for murder. The victim was also an Indian, John Sassamon. One of few Indians to have studied at Harvard College, Sassamon had also served as the English-speaking secretary to the leader of the Wampanoags, Metacomet, known to the English as King Philip (after Philip of Macedon). As if to solidify his standing among the New England colonists, Sassamon left Metacomet to join a Christian Indian village. While a member of that community during the winter of 1674-1675, he informed Puritan leaders in Plymouth that various Indian tribes, including the Wampanoags, were preparing to wage war on white New England. Not long after this he was murdered. A witness subsequently identified Sassamon's killers and by June 1675 all three had been convicted and executed.

A few days after the executions, the Wampanoags attacked the frontier town of Swansea. What came to be known as King Philip's War had begun. At that point the English probably outnumbered the Indians in New England by more than two to one. No doubt the Wampanoags and their Indian allies were at least vaguely aware of this discrepancy, influencing their decision to act before it was too late.

But it was already too late. A half-century of relative peace had given the English a solid foothold in the New World. And technological superiority assured the English that they would not be easily dislodged.

For their part, the Indian warriors of the 1670s were adept at using the colonists' own technology against them. The Indian fought with musket and steel tomahawk. So armed, fighting one-on-one, the Indian soldier could hold his own against the English adversary. But the Indian community and the Indian leadership knew that their society was in no position to sustain an open war against a more numerous and better armed foe. Hence, they unleashed a series of sporadic attacks on isolated white settlements during the summer and fall of 1675.

On October 13 the Massachusetts General Court put the colony on a war footing. Reeling from guerrilla attacks, the court finally drafted Articles of War to supersede the regular laws of the colony. As a result, the military commissioners in Boston, not the local town fathers, now made all the crucial decisions. No longer were the small towns and villages of Massachusetts isolated, self-

18

contained "cities on a hill." No longer was Boston *the* "city on a hill." And no longer was Massachusetts an example of perfection achieved in the New World, a collection of harmonious "peaceable kingdoms" scattered throughout the colony. The Puritan experiment suddenly stood in great danger of unraveling completely. No one was more aware of this possibility than Increase Mather.

Mather saw the war differently than the military commissioners. It was not a simple matter of achieving victory by moving troops here or there. Nor was it a question of implementing a certain military strategy. To Increase Mather, the war was God's instrument for punishing New England Puritans—and his opportunity, once again, to warn his wayward followers.

If his fellow Puritans wanted to defeat their Indian foes, Mather was convinced that they first had to come to terms with God's purpose for the war. He delivered his unwelcome message in October 1675, when it was his turn to give the weekly afternoon lecture to the citizens of Boston. Had he not predicted this disaster nearly a year earlier in his sermon "The Day of Trouble Is Near"? Were these Indian attacks not a call from God to the Puritans to repent their sins? Was the accompanying terror not a just reprisal visited upon Puritans who had gone astray? New England had sinned, and King Philip's War was God's punishment for those sins.

"Provoking Evils"

Mather charged his people with an excess of worldliness and pride, harmful experimentation with new fashions, disobedience to superiors, price gouging in the marketplace, and a general decline in godliness. In partial response to Mather's catalogue of sins, the General Court passed an omnibus statute labeled "Provoking Evils" which meted out various punishments for the Mather-defined sins.

New dress codes registering objections to "naked breasts and arms" and to "superfluous ribbons, both on hair and apparell" were devised to counteract the "evil of pride in apparell"—or lack thereof.

"Provoking Evils" also moved against the sale and abuse of alcohol. Mather had long opposed drunkenness. Now he managed to enlist the General Court in his war against alcohol. Under the new edict, residents of towns with taverns were forbidden to enter them. Only travelers, the General Court declared, were permitted to frequent these dens of evil.

In response to Mather's concerns, the General Court also ordered both merchants and workers to abstain from charging exorbitant prices for goods and services. Finally and most importantly, "Provoking Evils" turned to another Mather frustration: declining church attendance on the Sabbath. Mather especially wanted chil-

19

dren to be present at church services. To encourage this holy practice, the General Court ruled that parents were to be fined (or the children whipped) for any inexcusable absence. Once inside the meetinghouse, churchgoers of all ages and ranks now found the doors locked behind them so that no one could leave the service before its completion.

With "Provoking Evils" on the books, Increase Mather was confident of victory over the real enemy. And who was that enemy? Not King Philip and his armed followers. The real enemy was the misplaced pride which had displaced simple asceticism in the lives of too many Puritans.

Mather's efforts to return his people to virtue revealed his disdain for military strategies and diplomatic alliances. His war was an internal war, a war each Puritan had to fight against his or her own sinful nature. But not all Puritans were willing to follow Mather's sober-minded lead. Before the end of the year, in fact, Mather found himself the target of Puritan critics who disdained his tirades against Puritan sinfulness. Among those critics was the governor of Massachusetts. John Leverett. When he was elected to the governorship in 1673, Leverett anticipated a peaceful capstone to a long political career. But he soon found himself a beleaguered wartime leader. The lives of countless men and women suddenly rested on his decisions. As far as he was concerned, the real enemy was King Philip, not wayward Puritans, and the real battlefields were in and around numerous Massachusetts towns and villages, not in the hearts and minds of his fellow Puritans. Governor Leverett's patience for Reverend Mather's rhetoric therefore proved limited indeed.

As Leverett was losing his patience, Mather was losing his audience, because white New England seemed to be losing the war. By early February 1676, Indians were launching attacks against Puritan communities within fifty miles of Boston. By the end of the month there were reports of Indian warriors within ten miles of the city. By mid-April refugees were streaming into Boston.

May 3, 1676, was election day in Boston. Following tradition, the townspeople were to gather early that day to hear a sermon appropriate for the occasion. The customary message was political. So was the choice of the preacher. The town fathers deliberately snubbed Increase Mather. Instead, they turned to William Hubbard of Ipswich. One of the earliest graduates of Harvard, Hubbard was a Leverett contemporary and a Leverett compatriot. Like the governor, he saw the war in practical terms. The task at hand was to defeat King Philip, not to demean Massachusetts Puritans.

Like Mather, Hubbard railed against pride. But he defined pride differently. "Spiritual pride," not prideful dress or prideful swagger, was eating away at New England. Yes, God was angry with New England, but the real source of His anger was what Hubbard called "secret heart evill." And who best exemplified this subversive brand of "evill"?—the holier-than-thou Increase Mather.

The leaders of the General Court were so pleased with Hubbard's words that they appropriated funds to have the sermon printed and distributed. When it was published, William Hubbard dedicated it to Governor John Leverett.

Mather felt compelled to respond. For over a week he ignored his other work, including his history of the war against King Philip. Writing day and night, he produced *An Earnest Exhortation to the Inhabitants of New England*. Where Hubbard had sought to explain the war in rational terms, Mather reverted to his apocalyptic world view. To him the war remained separate from troop movements and supply lines and well within the celestial realm of a punishing God. The founders of the colony had established a godly community, he wrote, and John Winthrop had presided over it. But by the 1670s, the godly community had disappeared.

Not even victory in the Puritan war against the Indians could convince Increase Mather of the righteousness of the Puritan cause or of its eventual rehabilitation. Not even the death of King Philip at the hands of a fellow Indian could persuade him that New England Puritans had finally and forever escaped the stinging hand of a wrathful God.

More Signs of God's Wrath

The following November witnessed another foreboding sign from the heavens. With a military victory barely won, the citizens of Boston faced a new danger: fire. From the streets of the city, Mather and his family watched their own home explode in flames. Despite a cold November rain, at least seventy other homes were consumed by the blaze that struck the city on what Mather called this "fatal and dismall day." To Increase Mather, the fire was more than an occasion for personal depression; it was yet another warning to the Puritan community to mend its errant ways.

Once again he accused the magistrates of permitting New England to fall into sin. And once again the rulers of New England and their ministerial allies charged Mather with an excess of zeal. Two years later the same pattern was repeated as the colony debated the meaning of a devastating smallpox epidemic.

Within the city of Boston, no family could claim complete immunity, though Increase Mather thought he would be safe. While in Ireland in 1659 he had contracted a light case of the disease—enough, he hoped, to exempt him from its deadly work. But in the terrifying summer of 1678, his entire family stood exposed.

As it turned out, the Mather family was lucky. Only Maria, the

eldest daughter, was stricken seriously enough to warrant genuine concern for her life. But she survived, and the family remained intact.

Her anguished father prayed for that result day and night. He
also prayed for his flock and his city. But by early November 340
Bostonians (perhaps ten percent of the city's population) had perished in the epidemic. Fifteen-year-old Cotton Mather watched
"coffins crossing each other" in the streets of the city. He also
counted corpses: "38 in one week—6, 7, 8, or 9 in a day."

At the same time, his prominent father was agonizingly counting
souls; he was in torment over the state of the soul of New England
Puritanism. The epidemic seemed yet another dreadful warning
hurled forth by a displeased God. Borrowing from the Book of
Revelation, Mather preached to the decimated ranks of his followers that "we have seen the red Horse amongst us. . . . Now there is
a pale Horse, and his Name that sits thereon is Death."

Once again Increase Mather was in his element, even as his
community was in turmoil. Once again he was at the center of
controversy. And once against the Puritan leadership balked at
accepting his apocalyptic vision.

A World at Odds with Itself

Clearly, the Puritan world of the 1670s was at odds with itself.
On one side stood the Increase Mathers, who were convinced that
the Puritan experiment had lost its way. On the other side were
the John Leveretts and William Hubbards, who thought there
must be a middle way for a people of God who were also a people searching for prosperity. In Increase Mather's mind, however,
the good Puritan had only one legitimate search: the search for
ultimate happiness in the next world.

Puritans always worried about achieving balance in their lives.
John Winthrop had worried about this when the Massachusetts
Bay Colony was founded. Increase Mather was beyond the point
of worry. By the 1670s he despaired that all sense of balance had
disappeared from the lives of a people awash in commerce.

Puritans were also committed to achieving harmony in the lives
of their local communities. This goal had been announced when
Puritanism was first planted in the stony soil of New England. A
despised minority in old England, these Puritans hoped to establish a like-minded community of God-fearing believers a world
away from persecution. They dreamed not only of moving from
minority to majority status, but of creating a society without any
minorities, whether theological or political, sociological or ideological, ethnic or racial.

But John Winthrop's "city on a hill" was never a place of total
harmony. Many divisions existed in the early years of the Mas-

sachusetts Bay Colony and persisted as the colony grew and matured. These divisions deepened as Massachusetts entered a precarious middle age.

Even before Winthrop and company left England there were disputes. What was to be the ideal relationship between old England and new? Was the proposed colony to sever all ties to England or serve as a model for its eventual reform? Should the colonizers include non-Puritans? And when it came down to it, just who was a true Puritan?

Once Massachusetts was established, controversy and contention did not disappear. In the 1630s the trial of Anne Hutchinson and the banishment of Roger Williams raised anew the dilemma of defining the true Puritan. Ostensibly, the issue in each case was theological. Could a Puritan be saved by God's grace or by the performance of good works? Hutchinson condemned the latter as a violation of strict Calvinism, only to have Winthrop accuse her of claiming to be in direct communication with the Almighty. In truth, not only theology but politics and power played a role in her conviction and ultimate expulsion from the colony. Her views challenged the supremacy of Puritan ministers. In addition, because she was an outspoken woman, she was an affront to every Puritan male.

Roger Williams earned his ticket to exile by insisting that he was the only true Puritan. Lurking always within Puritanism was the temptation to presume that oneself alone was the most saintly of saints. In Williams's case, saintly humility was transformed into a king of arrogance as he advertised himself as the purest of the pure. Such arrogance could not be tolerated, according to John Winthrop. Puritans had separated from the Church of England, but the ultimate goal was to reform England and its religion, not abandon it. Nor should his Puritan community be filled with individuals who had separated themselves from one another as Roger Williams had done.

It was Increase Mather's lot to rail against a different kind of separatism. He was concerned with a Puritan people who had separated themselves from their God through their worship of commerce.

The calamitous events of the 1670s supported Mather's contention that God's anger was working against his faithless people. King Philip's War, the Boston fire of 1676, and the smallpox scourge of 1678 all furthered the apocalyptic vision percolating in Mather's mind. The larger result of Mather's efforts to bring his people back to God, however, was greater division within a community ostensibly built around principles of harmony.

While the search for harmony was an important part of the Puritan story, its achievement was seldom a feature of the Puritan landscape. John Winthrop found it an elusive goal at the outset. A century later, the Great Awakening preacher Jonathan Edwards would be just as frustrated by his failure to restore what never had been, namely a perfect world of "peaceable kingdoms" across New England.

Increase Mather strode through the middle of this first century of the Puritan experiment. With one eye on what might have been and the other on the awful world around him, Mather had little choice but to look to the future—and little reason to be optimistic about it. Aware of the commercial contentiousness around him, he created further division in the name of restoring peace and harmony to the Puritan world. His efforts to succeed should tell us a good deal about the Puritan mind and spirit. His failure should tell us something about the state of the Puritan experiment.

The Crossroads of Puritanism

Increase Mather, John Leverett, and William Hubbard all stood at the crossroads of Puritanism in its New England manifestation. Mather and his more worldly opponents also offer a glimpse of a society at war with itself. Those wars had reached a fever pitch by the 1670s and remained close to that that level through the remainder of the century, as New England Puritans battled old English efforts to reassert political control and suffered over charges and countercharges of witchcraft at Salem.

In both instances Increase Mather watched for more evidence of Puritan backsliding and new signals from an angry God. Much to his chagrin, he did not have to look far to continue finding much evidence of both. But such confirmation brought little solace to Increase Mather. The world his father had set out to create was passing before his very eyes.

But did a Puritan world of harmony and peace ever truly exist? Probably not. Such an answer would no doubt have disappointed the Reverend Mather, even as it enlivens our understanding of his world. What follows in these selections suggests to the modern reader that Puritan lives and disputes were much more complicated—and much more a part of everyday Puritan reality—than Increase Mather ever wanted them to be.

John C. Chalberg
Consulting Editor

CHAPTER 1

The Vision and the Voyage

Chapter Preface

Puritanism was a movement within English Protestantism established to reform the church and society. Most of the fundamental beliefs of the Puritans who migrated to America in the 1630s were developed and tempered over the previous decades of religious turmoil in England.

Henry VIII had officially broken ties with the Roman Catholic church in 1534 and established himself, instead of the pope, as head of the Church of England. However, many of the offices and practices of the church that led to the Protestant Reformation in Europe remained, including the preponderance of elaborate rituals, the clergy's sparse education, and an authoritarian and hierarchical church structure.

After Henry's death in 1547 religion continued to divide England. Under Edward VI some modest Protestant reforms were accomplished. However, his successor, Mary I, attempted to return England to the Roman Catholic church; consequently many Protestant leaders fled to other European countries, where they were further influenced by the work of John Calvin and his theocratic government in Geneva, Switzerland. When Queen Elizabeth I ascended to the English throne in 1558, many exiled leaders returned. In her quest for social stability, Elizabeth steered a middle course between those who wanted to return to Roman Catholicism and those who wished to reform and "purify" the church further. This second group became known as Puritans.

During Elizabeth's long reign (1558-1603) some Puritans despaired of ever reforming the Church of England. A few Puritans, led by Robert Browne in 1579, separated from the Church of England entirely and clandestinely formed their own congregations. The majority of Puritans, led by people such as Thomas Cartwright and William Perkins, attempted to work within the Church of England to enact gradual reforms to remove remaining vestiges of Roman Catholicism. However, their efforts met with limited success. Elizabeth's successors, James I and Charles I, were even less sympathetic to Puritanism, and the Puritans increasingly found themselves subject to government persecution under the new archbishop of Canterbury, William Laud. The failure to reform the church combined with economic and social dislocation in England led a growing number of Puritans to believe that both England and its church were hopelessly corrupt and subject to God's punishment.

It was against this backdrop that some Puritan leaders decided to establish a new church and a new society in America. The prospect was daunting; in Virginia, then the only established English colony in America, over two-thirds of the 6,500 English colonists had perished of starvation, disease, and Indian attacks between 1619 and 1625. Yet between 1620 and 1640 thousands of men, women, and children made the long voyage and settled in what is now New England.

The Puritans who formed the Massachusetts Bay Company, under the leadership of the wealthy Puritan lawyer John Winthrop, wanted more than religious freedom, according to most historians. They sought to establish a model society—and an uncorrupted Christian church. Historian Robert Kelley writes in *The Shaping of the American Past:*

> When John Winthrop's fleet arrived in Massachusetts Bay in 1630, . . . it was in pursuit of a utopian goal: to found in the New World a pure and undefiled Zion that would serve as an example to the Old World. They were not escaping from England, they were on an "errand into the wilderness." "For wee must consider," as Governor Winthrop said, "that wee shall be as a Citty upon a Hill, the eies of all people are uppon us."

The incomplete Protestant Reformation in England had as one of its unintended fruits a new settlement in America with utopian goals. The viewpoints in this chapter examine the vision that propelled the Puritans to leave for America.

VIEWPOINT 1

"New-England is a fit Country for the seating of an English Colonie, for the propagation of Religion."

An American Colony Would Have Many Practical Benefits

John White (1575-1648)

The Reverend John White was an English clergyman from Dorchester who was active in the Puritan movement. In 1623 he became a stockholder in the Dorchester Company, which hoped to establish settlements in New England to serve as bases for English fishermen. Such settlements, he argued, would benefit the native Indians by teaching them Christianity and would help the poor of England by providing them land and new opportunity. White emphasizes these two points in a tract published in 1630 called *The Planters' Plea*.

After the collapse of the Dorchester Company in 1626, White was one of the early leaders of what was to become the Massachusetts Bay Company. From 1630 to 1684 it established and presided over the Massachusetts Bay Colony, consisting of Boston and its surroundings. White maintained an active interest in the colony, shipping provisions and corresponding with its leaders. Unlike several of his minister colleagues, however, White never made the voyage to America himself.

From John White, *The Planters' Plea*. Reprinted in *Tracts and Other Papers Relating Principally to the Origin, Settlement, and Progress of the Colonies of North America from the Discovery of the Country to the Year 1776*. Volume 2, Section 3. Peter Force, editor. Washington, DC, 1836-1846.

That New-England is a fit Country for the seating of an English Colonie, for the propagation of Religion.

1. *Argument or occasion, trade into the countrey.* Not onely our acquaintance with the soil and Natives there, but more especially our opportunity of trading thither for Furres and fish, perswade this truth, if other things be answerable. It is well knowne, before our breach with Spaine, we usually sent out to New-England, yearely forty or fifty saile of ships of reasonable good burthen for fishing onely. And howsoever it fals out that our New-found-land voyages prove more beneficiall to the Merchants; yet it is as true, these to New-England are found farre more profitable to poore Fishermen; so that by that time all reckonings are cast up, these voyages come not farre behind the other in advantage to the State.

2. *The fitnesse of the countrey for our health and maintenance.* No Countrey yeelds a more propitious ayre for our temper, then New-England, as experience hath made manifest, by all relations: manie of our people that have found themselves alway weake and sickly at home, have become strong, and healthy there: perhaps by the drynesse of the ayre and constant temper of it, which seldome varies suddenly from cold to heate, as it doth with us: So that Rheumes are very rare among our English there; Neyther are the Natives at any time troubled with paine of teeth, sorenesse of eyes, or ache in their limbes. It may bee the nature of the water conduceth somewhat this way; which all affirme to keepe the body alwaies temperately soluble, and consequently helps much to the preventing, and curing of the Gout, and Stone, as some have found by experience. As for provisions for life: The Corne of the Country (which it produceth in good proportion with reasonable labour) is apt for nourishment, and agrees, although not so well with our taste at first; yet very well with our health; nay, is held by some Physitians, to be restorative. If wee like not that, wee may make use of our owne Graines, which agree well with that soil, and so doe our Cattle: nay, they grow unto a greater bulke of body there, then with us in England. Unto which if wee adde the fish, fowle, and Venison, which that Country yeelds in great abundance, it cannot be questioned but that soil may assure sufficient provision for food. And being naturally apt for Hempe and Flax especially, may promise us Linnen sufficient with our labour, and woollen too if it may be thought fit to store it with sheepe.

The Empty Land

3. *Argument from the emptinesse of the Land.* The Land affords void ground enough to receive more people then this State can spare, and that not only wood grounds, and others, which are

unfit for present use: but, in many places, much cleared ground for tillage, and large marshes for hay and feeding of Cattle, which comes to passe by the desolation hapning through a three yeeres Plague, about twelve or sixteene yeeres past, which swept away most of the Inhabitants all along the Sea coast, and in some places utterly consumed man, woman and childe, so that there is no person left to lay claime to the soil which they possessed; In most of the rest, the Contagion hath scarce left alive one person of an hundred. And which is remarkable, such a Plague hath not been knowne, or remembred in any age past; nor then raged above twenty or thirty miles up into the Land, nor seized upon any other but the Natives, the English in the heate of the Sicknesse commercing with them without hurt or danger. Besides, the Natives invite us to sit downe by them, and offer us what ground wee will: so that eyther want of possession by others, or the possessors gift, and sale, may assure our right: we neede not feare a cleare title to the soil.

An Opportunity to Do Good

Robert Cushman was the business agent of the 1620 Mayflower *settlers, negotiating with both the English government and the English merchant-investors. After visiting the Plymouth settlement in November and December 1621, he wrote a tract called* Reasons and Considerations Touching the Lawfulness of Removing Out of England into the Parts of America. *It aimed in part to convince other English separatists to join the Pilgrims in America.*

So here falleth in our question, how a man that is born and bred, and hath lived some years, may remove himself into another country.

I answer, a man must not respect only to live, and do good to himself, but he should see where he can live to do most good to others; for, as one saith, "He whose living is but for himself, it is time he were dead." Some men there are who of necessity must here live, as being tied to duties, either to church, commonwealth, household, kindred, etc. But others, and that many, who do no good in none of those, nor can do none, as being not able, or not in favor, or as wanting opportunity, and live as outcasts, nobodies, eye-sores, eating but for themselves, teaching but themselves, and doing good to none, either in soul or body, and so pass over days, years, and months, yea, so live and so die. Now such should lift up their eyes and see whether there be not some other place and country to which they may go to do good.

---

4. *Argument from the usefulness of that Colonie to this State.* In all Colonies it is to bee desired that the daughter may answer something backe by way of retribution to the mother that gave her be-

ing. Nature hath as much force, and founds as strong a relation be-tweene people and people, as betweene person and person: So that a Colonie denying due respect to the State from whose bowels it is-sued, is as great a monster, as an unnaturall childe. Now, a Colonie planted in New-England may be many wayes usefull to this State.

As first, in furthering our Fishing-voyages (one of the most honest, and every way profitable imployment that the Nation un-dertakes) It must needs be a great advantage unto our men after so long a voyage to be furnished with fresh Victuall there; and that supplyed out of that Land, without spending the provisions of our owne countrey. But there is hope besides, that the Colonie shall not onely furnish our Fisher-men with Victuall, but with Salt too, unlesse mens expectation and conjectures much deceive them: and so quit unto them a great part of the charge of their voyage, beside the hazard of adventure.

Next, how serviceable this Country must needs be for provi-sions for shipping, is sufficiently knowne already: At present it may yeeld Planks, Masts, Oares, Pitch, Tarre, and Iron; and here-after (by the aptnesse of the Soil for Hempe) if the Colonie in-crease, Sailes and Cordage. What other commodities it may af-ford besides for trade, time will discover. Of Wines among the rest, there can be no doubt; the ground yeelding naturall Vines in great abundance and varietie; and of these, some as good as any are found in France by humane culture. But in the possibilitie of the serviceablenesse of the Colonie to this State, the judgement of the Dutch may somewhat confirme us, who have planted in the same soil, and make great account of their Colonie there.

5. *Argument from the benefit of such a Colony to the Natives.* But the greatest advantage must needes come unto the Natives them-selves, whom wee shall teach providence and industry, for want whereof they perish oftentimes, while they make short provisions for the present, by reason of their idlenesse, and that they have, they spend and wast unnecessarily, without having respect to times to come. Withall, commerce and example of our course of living, cannot but in time breed civility among them, and that by Gods blessing may make way for religion consequently, and for the saving of their soules. Unto all which may bee added, the safety and protection of the persons of the Natives, which are se-cured by our Colonies. In times past the Tarentines (who dwell from those of Mattachusets bay, neere which our men are seated; about fifty or sixty leagues to the North-East) inhabiting a soil un-fit to produce that Countrey graine, being the more hardy people, were accustomed yearely at harvest to come down in their Ca-noes, and reape their fields, and carry away their Corne, and de-stroy their people, which wonderfully weakened, and kept them low in times past: from this evill our neighbourhood hath wholy

freed them, and consequently secured their persons and estates; which makes the Natives there so glad of our company.

Possible Objections

Objection 1. But if we have any spare people, Ireland is a fitter place to receive them then New-England. Being 1, Nearer. 2, Our owne. 3, Void in some parts. 4, Fruitfull. 5, Of importance for the securing of our owne Land. 6, Needing our helpe for their recovery out of blindnesse and superstition.

Answer. Ireland is well-nigh sufficiently peopled already, or will be in the next age. Besides, this worke needs not hinder that, no more then the plantation in Virginia, Bermudas, S. Christophers, Barbados, which are all of them approved, and incouraged as this is. As for religion, it hath reasonable footing in Ireland already, and may easily be propagated further, if wee bee not wanting to our selves. This Countrey of New-England is destitute of all helpes, and meanes, by which the people might come out of the snare of Satan. Now although it be true, that I should regard my sonne more then my servant; yet I must rather provide a Coate for my servant that goes naked, then give my sonne another, who hath reasonable clothing already.

Objection 2. But New-England hath divers discommodities, the Snow and coldnesse of the winter, which our English bodies can hardly brooke: and the annoyance of men by Muskitoes, and Serpents: and of Cattle, and Corne, by wild beasts.

Answer. The cold of Winter is tolerable, as experience hath, and doth manifest, and is remedied by the abundance of fuell. The Snow lyes indeed about a foot thicke for ten weekes or there about; but where it lies thicker, and a month longer as in many parts of Germany, men finde a very comfortable dwelling. As for the Serpents, it is true, there are some, and these larger then our Adders; but in ten yeares experience no man was ever indangered by them; and as the Countrey is better stored with people, they will be found fewer, and as rare as among us here. As for the wilde beasts, they are no more, nor so much dangerous or hurtfull here, as in Germany and other parts of the world. The Muskitoes indeed infest the planters, about foure moneths in the heat of Summer; but after one yeares acquaintance, men make light account of them; some sleight defence for the hands and face, smoake, and a close house may keepe them off. Neither are they much more noysome then in Spaine, Germany, and other parts; nay, then the fennish parts of Essex, and Lincolne-shire. Besides, it is credibly reported, that twenty miles inward into the Countrey they are not found: but this is certaine, and tried by experience, after foure or five yeares habitation they waxe very thinne: It may be the hollownesse of the ground breeds them, which the treading of the earth by men and Cattle doth remedy in time.

Objection 3. But if the propagation of religion bee the scope of the plantation, New-England which is so naked of inhabitants, is the unfittest of any place for a Colony; it would more further that worke to set downe in some well-peopled countrey, that might afford many subjects to worke upon, and win to the knowledge of the truth.

Answer. But how shall we get footing there? the Virginian Colony may bee our precedent; where our men have beene entertained with continuall broyles by the Natives, and by that meanes shut out from all hope of working any reformation upon them, from which, their hearts must needes be utterly averse by reason of the hatred which they beare unto our persons: whereas, New-England yeelds this advantage, that it affords us a cleare title to our possessions there; and good correspondence with the Natives; whether out of their peaceable disposition, or out of their inability to make resistance, or out of the safety which they finde by our neighbourhood, it skills not much; this is certaine, it yeelds a faire way to work them to that tractablenesse which will never bee found in the Virginians: Neither have wee any cause to complaine for want of men to worke upon; the in-land parts are indifferently populous, and Naragansetbay and river, which borders upon us, is full of Inhabitants, who are quiet with us, and Trade with us willingly, while wee are their neighbours, but are very jealous of receiving either us or the Dutch into the bowells of their Country, for feare wee should become their Lords.

Besides, in probabilitie, it will be more advantagious to this worke to beginne with a place not so populous: For as the resistance will be lesse, so by them having once received the Gospell, it may be more easily and successefully spread to the places better peopled, who will more easily receive it from the commendation of their owne Countriemen, then from strangers, and flocke to it as Doves to the windowes.

Though in the place where they plant, there are not many Natives, yet they have an opportunitie, by way of trafficke and commerce (which at least is generally once a yeare) with the Natives in a large compasse, though farre distant from them, by which meanes they grow into acquaintance with them, and may take many advantages of convaying to them the knowledge of Christ, though they live not with them.

Labor and Wealth

Objection 4. But the Countrey wants meanes of wealth that might invite men to desire it; for there is nothing to bee expected in New-England but competency to live on at the best, and that must bee purchased with hard labour, whereas divers other parts of the

33

West-Indies offer a richer soil, which easily allures Inhabitants, by the tender of a better condition then they live in at present.

Answer. As unanswerable argument, to such as make the advancement of their estates, the scope of their undertaking; but no way a discouragement to such as aime at the propagation of the Gospell, which can never bee advanced but by the preservation of Piety in those that carry it to strangers; Now wee know nothing sorts better with Piety than Competency; a truth which Agur hath determined long agoe, Proverbs 30:8. Nay, Heathen men by the light of Nature were directed so farre as to discover the overflowing of riches to be enemie to labour, sobriety, justice, love and magnanimity: and the nurse of pride, wantonnesse, and contention; and therefore laboured by all meanes to keepe out the love and desire of them from their well-ordered States, and observed and professed the comming in and admiration of them to have beene the foundation of their ruine. If men desire to have a people degenerate speedily, and to corrupt their mindes and bodies too, and besides to toll in theeves and spoilers from abroad; let them seeke a rich soil, that brings in much with little labour; but if they desire that Piety and godlinesse should prosper; accompanied with sobriety, justice and love, let them choose a Countrey such as this is; even like France, or England, which may yeeld sufficiency with hard labour and industry: the truth is, there is more cause to feare wealth then poverty in that soil.

VIEWPOINT 2

"It will be a service to the church of great consequence to carry the gospel into those parts of the world . . . and to raise a bulwark against the kingdom of anti-Christ which the Jesuits labor to rear up in those parts."

An American Colony Would Serve the True Christian Church

John Winthrop (1588-1649)

John Winthrop was one of the most important leaders of the Puritan settlement of New England. He served as governor of the Massachusetts Bay Colony for thirteen of the nineteen years he resided in America following his migration in 1630. A prosperous landholder and lawyer, Winthrop was one of the wealthiest and most distinguished of the Puritans who concluded that the true Christian church was hopelessly corrupted in England and that the faith could be preserved only by migration. In a tract written in 1629 Winthrop summarizes his reasons for his decision to migrate to America. In part he repeats the practical reasons stated by John White and others. In addition, Winthrop counters the argument made by many Puritans that renewed efforts should be made to reform the church in England rather than desert it. Winthrop sought to justify the migration to America as a way to rescue the Christian church from corruption in England.

From John Winthrop, *Reasons to Be Considered for . . . the Intended Plantation in New England,* reprinted in the Massachusetts Historical Society's *Proceedings* 8 (1864-1865): 420-425. Courtesy of the Massachusetts Historical Society.

Reasons to be considered for justifying the undertakers of the intended plantation in New England and for encouraging such whose hearts God shall move to join with them in it.

First, it will be a service to the church of great consequence to carry the gospel into those parts of the world, to help on the coming in of fullness of the Gentiles, and to raise a bulwark against the kingdom of anti-Christ which the Jesuits labor to rear up in those parts.

Rescuing the Church

2. All other churches of Europe are brought to desolation, and our sins, for which the Lord begins already to frown upon us, do threaten us fearfully, and who knows but that God hath provided this place to be a refuge for many whom he means to save out of the general calamity. And seeing the church hath no place left to fly into but the wilderness, what better work can there be than to go before and provide tabernacles and food for her, against she cometh thither?

3. This land grows weary of her inhabitants, so as man who is the most precious of all creatures is here more vile and base than the earth we tread upon, and of less price among us than a horse or a sheep; masters are forced by authority to entertain servants, parents to maintain their own children. All towns complain of the burthen of their poor, though we have taken up many unnecessary, yea unlawful, trades to maintain them. And we use the authority of the law to hinder the increase of people, as urging the execution of the state against cottages and inmates, and thus it is come to pass that children, servants, and neighbors (especially if the[y] be poor) are counted the greatest burthen, which if things were right it would be the chiefest earthly blessing.

4. The whole earth is the Lord's garden, and He hath given it to the sons of men with a general condition, Gen. 1:28, "Increase and multiply, replenish the earth and subdue it," which was again renewed to Noah. The end is double moral and natural: that man might enjoy the fruits of the earth, and God might have his due glory from the creature. Why then should we stand here striving for places of habitation (many men spending as much labor and cost to recover or keep sometimes an acre or two of land as would procure them many hundred as good or better in an other country) and in the meantime suffer a whole continent as fruitful and convenient for the use of man to lie waste without any improvement?

5. We are grown to that height of intemperance in all excess of riot, as no man's estate almost will suffice to keep sail with his

Many Reasons

Thomas Sheperd was one of many Puritan clergymen who were harassed and persecuted by the Church of England and decided to move to America. In his autobiography Sheperd summarizes his reasons for the voyage.

The reasons which swayed me to come to New England were many: (1) I saw no call to any other place in old England, nor way of subsistence in peace and comfort to me and my family; (2) Divers people in old England of my dear friends desired me to go to New England, there to live together, and some went before and wrote to me of providing a place for a company of us, one of which was John Bridge. And I saw divers families of my Christian friends who were resolved thither to go with me; (3) I saw the Lord departing from England when Mr. Hooker and Mr. Cotton were gone, and I saw the hearts of most of the godly set and bent that way, and I did think I should feel many miseries if I stayed behind; (4) My judgment was then convinced not only of the evil of ceremonies, but of mixed communion and joining with such in sacraments, though I ever judged it lawful to join with them in preaching; (5) I saw it my duty to desire the fruition of all God's ordinances, which I could not enjoy in old England; (6) My dear wife did much long to see me settled there in peace and so put me on to it; (7) Although it was true, I should stay and suffer for Christ, yet I saw no rule for it now the Lord had opened a door of escape. Otherwise I did incline much to stay and suffer, especially after our sea storms; (8) Though my ends were mixed and I looked much to my own quiet, yet the Lord let me see the glory of those liberties in New England and made me purpose if ever I should come over to live among God's people as one come out from the dead, to His praise, though since I have seen as the Lord's goodness so my own exceeding weakness to be as good as I thought to have been. And although they did desire me to stay in the North and preach privately, yet (1) I saw that this time could not be long without trouble from King Charles; (2) I saw no reason to spend my time privately, when I might possibly exercise my talent publicly in New England; (3) I did hope my going over might make them follow me; (4) I considered how sad a thing it would be for me to leave my wife and child (if I should die) in that rude place of the North where was nothing but barbarous wickedness generally, and how sweet it would be to leave them among God's people, though poor; (5) my liberty in private was daily threatened, and I thought it wisdom to depart before the pursuivants came out, for so I might depart with more peace and less trouble and danger to me and my friends; and I knew not whether God would have me to hazard my person and comfort of me and all mine for a disorderly manner of preaching privately in those parts. So after I had preached my farewell sermon at Newcastle, I departed.

equals, and he who fails herein must live in scorn and contempt. Hence it comes that all arts and trades are carried in that deceitful and unrighteous course, as it is almost impossible for a good and upright man to maintain his charge and live comfortably in any of them.

6. The fountains of learning and religion are so corrupted (as beside the unsupportable charge of the education) most children (even the best wits and fairest hopes) are perverted, corrupted, and utterly overthrown by the multitude of evil examples and the licentious government of those seminaries, where men strain at gnats and swallow camels, use all severity for maintenance of capes and other complements, but suffer all ruffian-like fashion and disorder in manners to pass uncontrolled.

7. What can be a better work and more honorable and worthy a Christian than to help raise and support a particular church while it is in the infancy, and to join his forces with such a company of faithful people as by a timely assistance may grow strong and prosper, and for want of it may be put to great hazard, if not wholly ruined.

8. If any such who are known to be godly, and live in wealth and prosperity here, shall forsake all this to join themselves to this church, and to run a hazard with them of a hard and mean condition, it will be an example of great use both for removing the scandal of worldly and sinister respects which is cast upon the adventurers, to give more life to the faith of God's people in their prayers for the plantation, and to encourage others to join the more willingly in it.

9. It appears to be a work of God for the good of His church, in that He hath disposed the hearts of so many of His wise and faithful servants (both ministers and others) not only to approve of the enterprise but to interest themselves in it, some in their persons and estates, others by their serious advice and help otherwise. And all by their prayers for the welfare of it, Amos 3. The Lord revealeth His secrets to His servants the prophets; it is likely He hath some great work in hand which He hath revealed to His prophets among us, whom He hath stirred up to encourage His servants to this plantation, for He doth not use to seduce His people by His own prophets but commits that office to the ministry of false prophets and lying spirits.

Answering Objections

Divers objections which have been made against this plantation with their answers and resolutions.

Objection 1: We have no warrant to enter upon that land which hath been so long possessed by others.

Answer 1: That which lies common and hath never been replenished or subdued is free to any that will possess and improve it, for God hath given to the sons of men a double right to the earth: there is a natural right and a civil right. The first right was natural when men held the earth in common, every man sowing and feeding where he pleased, and then as men and the cattle increased they appropriated certain parcels of ground by enclosing, and peculiar manurance, and this in time gave them a civil right. Such was the right which Ephron the Hittite had in the field of Machpelah, wherein Abraham could not bury a dead corpse without leave, though for the out parts of the country which lay common he dwelt upon them and took the fruit of them at his pleasure. The like did Jacob, which fed his cattle as bold in Hamor's land (for he is said to be the lord of the country) and other places where he came as the native inhabitants themselves. And that in those times and places men accounted nothing their own but that which they had appropriated by their own industry appears plainly by this: that Abimelech's servants in their own country, when they oft contended with Isaac's servants about wells which they had digged, yet never strove for the land wherein they were. So likewise between Jacob and Laban: he would not take a kid of Laban's without his special contract, but he makes no bargain with him for the land where they feed, and it is very probable if the country had not been as free for Jacob as for Laban, that covetous wretch would have made his advantage of it and have upbraided Jacob with it, as he did with his cattle. And for the natives in New England, they enclose no land, neither have any settled habitation, nor any tame cattle to improve the land by, and so have no other but a natural right to those countries. So as if we leave them sufficient for their use, we may lawfully take the rest, there being more than enough for them and us.

Secondly, we shall come in with the good leave of the Natives, who find benefit already by our neighborhood and learn of us to improve part to more use than before they could do the whole. And by this means we come in by valuable purchase, for they have of us that which will yield them more benefit than all the land which we have from them.

Thirdly, God hath consumed the Natives with a great plague in those parts so as there be few inhabitants left.

Objection 2: It will be a great wrong to our church to take away the good people, and we shall lay it the more open to the judgment feared.

Answer 1: The departing of good people from a country doth not cause a judgment but foreshew it, which may occasion such as remain to turn from their evil ways that they may prevent it, or to take some other course that they may escape it.

Secondly, such as go away are of no observation in respects of those who remain, and they are likely to do more good there than here. And since Christ's time, the church is to be considered as universal without distinction of countries, so as he who doeth good in any one place serves the church in all places in regard of the unity.

Thirdly, it is the revealed will of God that the gospel should be preached to all nations, and though we know not whether those barbarians will receive it at first or not, yet it is a good work to serve God's providence in offering it to them; and this is fittest to be done by God's own servants, for God shall have glory by it though they refuse it, and there is good hope that the posterity *shall by this means be gathered into Christ's sheepfold.*

Service to God

John Winthrop recorded additional personal reasons for moving to America, possibly in response to friends who wrote urging him not to move to a "remote plantation."

In my youth I did seriously consecrate my life to the service of the church, intending the ministry, but was diverted from that course by the counsel of some whose judgment I did much reverence. But it hath often troubled me since, so as I think I am the rather bounded to take the opportunity for spending the small remainder of my time to the best service of the church which I may.

Which way the stream of God's providence leads a man to the greatest good, he may, nay, he must go.

Objection 3: We have feared a judgment a great while, but yet we are safe. It were better therefore to stay till it come, and either we may fly then, or if we be overtaken in it, we may well content ourselves to suffer with such a church as ours is.

Answer: It is likely this consideration made the churches beyond the seas, as the Palatinate, Rochelle, etc., to sit still at home and not to look out for shelter while they might have found it. But the woeful spectacle of their ruin may teach us more wisdom, to avoid the plague when it is foreseen, and not to tarry as they did till it overtake us. If they were now at their former liberty, we might be sure they would take other courses for their safety, and though half of them had miscarried in their escape, yet had it not been so miserable to themselves nor scandalous to religion as this desperate backsliding, and abjuring the truth, which many of the ancient professors among them, and the whole posterity which remain, are now plagued into.

Objection 4: The ill success of other plantations may tell us what will become of this.

Answer 1: None of the former sustained any great damage but Virginia; which happened through their own sloth and security.

2. The argument is not good, for thus it stands: some plantations have miscarried, therefore we should not make any. It consists in particulars and so concludes nothing. We might as well reason thus: many houses have been burnt by kilns, therefore we should use none; many ships have been cast away, therefore we should content ourselves with our home commodities and not adventure men's lives at sea for those things which we might live without; some men have been undone by being advanced to great places, therefore we should refuse our preferment, etc.

3. The fruit of any public design is not to be discerned by the immediate success; it may appear in time that former plantations were all to good use.

4. There were great and fundamental errors in the former which are like to be avoided in this, for first their main end was carnal and not religious; secondly, they used unfit instruments—a multitude of rude and misgoverned persons, the very scum of the people; thirdly, they did not establish a right form of government.

The Way of God Is Difficult

Objection 5: It is attended with many and great difficulties.

Answer: So is every good action. The heathen could say *ardua virtutis via*. And the way of God's kingdom (the best way in the world) is accompanied with most difficulties. Straight is the gate and narrow is the way that leadeth to life. Again, the difficulties are no other than such as many daily meet with and such as God hath brought others well through them.

Objection 6: It is a work above the power of the undertakers.

Answer 1: The welfare of any body consists not so much in quantity as in due portion and disposition of parts, and we see other plantations have subsisted divers years and prospered from weak means.

2. It is no wonder, for great things may arise from weak, contemptible beginnings; it hath been oft seen in kingdoms and states and may as well hold in towns and plantations. The Waldenses were scattered into the Alps and mountains of Piedmont by small companies, but they became famous churches whereof some remain to this day; and it is certain that the Turks, Venetians, and other states were very weak in their beginnings.

Objection 7: The country affords no natural fortifications.

Answer: No more did Holland and many other places which had greater enemies and nearer at hand, and God doth use to place His people in the midst of perils that they may trust in Him

41

and not in outward means and safety; so when He would choose a place to plant His beloved people in, He seateth them not in an island or other place fortified by nature, but in a plain country beset with potent and bitter enemies round about, yet so long as they served Him and trusted in His help they were safe. So the Apostle Paul saith of himself and his fellow laborers, that they were compassed with dangers on every side and were daily under the sentence of death that they might learn to trust in the living God.

Objection 8: The place affordeth no comfortable means to the first planters, and our breeding here at home have made us unfit for the hardship we are like to endure.

Answer 1: No place of itself hath afforded sufficient to the first inhabitants; such things as we stand in need of are usually supplied by God's blessing upon the wisdom and industry of man, and whatsoever we stand in need of is treasured in the earth by the Creator and is to be fetched thence by the sweat of our brows.

2. We must learn with Paul to want as well as to abound; if we have food and raiment (which are there to be had), we ought to be contented. The difference in quality may a little displease us, but it cannot hurt us.

3. It may be by this means God will bring us to repent of our former intemperance, and so cure us of that disease which sends many amongst us untimely to their graves and others to hell; so He carried the Israelites into the wilderness and made them forget the flesh pots of Egypt, which was sorry pinch to them at first, but he disposed to their good in the end. Deut. 30: 3, 16.

Tempting God

Objection 9: We must look to be preserved by miracle if we subsist, and so we shall tempt God.

Answer 1: They who walk under ordinary means of safety and supply do not tempt God, but such will be our condition in this plantation therefore, etc. The proposition cannot be denied; the assumption we prove thus: that place is as much secured from ordinary dangers as many hundred places in the civil parts of the world, and we shall have as much provision beforehand as such towns do use to provide against a siege or dearth, and sufficient means for raising a succeeding store against that is spent. If it be denied that we shall be as secure as other places, we answer that many of our sea towns, and such as are upon the confines of enemies' countries in the continent, lie more upon and nearest to danger than we shall. And though such towns have sometimes been burnt or spoiled, yet men tempt not God to dwell still in them, and though many houses in the country amongst us lie open to thieves and robbers (as many have found by sad experience), yet no man will say that those which dwell in such places must be preserved by miracle.

2. Though miracles be now ceased, yet men may expect more than ordinary blessing from God upon all lawful means, where the work is the Lord's and He is sought in it according to His will, for it is usual with Him to increase or weaken the strength of the means as He is pleased or displeased with the instruments and the action, else we must conclude that God hath left the government of the world and committed all power to the creature, that the success of all things should wholly depend upon the second causes.

VIEWPOINT 3

"For we must consider that we shall be like a City upon a Hill; the eyes of all people are on us."

A Puritan Vision of the New Colony

John Winthrop (1588-1649)

John Winthrop, a prosperous landowner and lawyer, was made governor of the new Massachusetts Bay Company in 1629. He was the acknowledged leader of approximately four hundred colonists who left England on four ships on April 7, 1630, and arrived in Massachusetts Bay on June 12. Additional settlers soon followed and by year-end a thousand colonists were establishing homes in what was to become Boston.

During the voyage in the fleet's flagship *Arbella*, Winthrop delivered a sermon describing his vision for the new community to be established in America. Entitled "A Modell of Christian Charity," it is one of the most famous documents of Puritanism and of early American history. Winthrop describes how Christian ideals would shape the colony, and he concludes by stating that the new settlement will be a "City upon a Hill," setting a godly example for others, including the corrupt England being left behind. Winthrop and others had before their voyage formally disavowed any intent of separating from the Church of England, as the 1620 Plymouth settlers had. Rather, they sought to reform it. Historian Francis J. Bremer writes in *The Puritan Experiment:*

> Settlement of New England came to be seen as an errand into the wilderness; the creation of a model Puritan community would convert England—and through England the world—both by its example and by the prayers of its inhabitants.

From John Winthrop, *The Winthrop Papers*. Volume 2. Edited by Allyn B. Forbes. Boston: Massachusetts Historical Society, 1931. Courtesy of the Massachusetts Historical Society.

God Almighty, in His most holy and wise providence, has so disposed of the condition of mankind, as in all times some must be rich; some poor; some high and eminent in power and dignity; others mean and in subjection.

The Reason Hereof: first, to hold conformity with the rest of His works, being delighted to show forth the glory of His wisdom in the variety and difference of the creatures and the glory of His power, in ordering all these differences for the preservation and good of the whole; and the glory of His greatness in that, as it is the glory of princes to have many officers, so this Great King will have many stewards, counting Himself more honored in dispensing His gifts to man by man than if He did it by His own immediate hand.

Second, that He might have the more occasion to manifest the work of His spirit; first, upon the wicked in moderating and restraining them, so that the rich and mighty should not eat up the poor, nor the poor and despised rise up against their superiors and shake off their yoke; second, in the regenerate in exercising His graces in them, as in the great ones their love, mercy, gentleness, temperance, etc.; in the poor and inferior sort, their faith, patience, obedience, etc.

Third, that every man might have need of others, and from hence they might be all knit more nearly together in the bond of brotherly affection. From hence it appears plainly that no man is made more honorable than another or more wealthy, etc., out of any particular or singular respect to himself, but for the glory of his Creator and the common good of the creature, man. Therefore, God still reserves the property of these gifts to Himself, as [in] Ezek. 16:17; He there calls wealth His gold and His silver, etc.; [in] Prov. 3:9 He claims their service as His due "Honor the Lord with thy riches," etc. All men are thus (by Divine Providence) ranked into two sorts, rich and poor; under the first are included all men such as are able to live comfortably by their own means duly improved; and all others are poor according to the former distribution.

Two Rules

There are two rules whereby we are to walk one toward another: *justice and mercy*. These are always distinguished in their act and in their object, yet may they both concur in the same subject in each respect, as sometimes there may be an occasion of showing mercy to a rich man in some sudden danger of distress; and also doing of mere justice to a poor man in regard of some particular contract, etc. There is likewise a double law by which we are regulated in our conversation one toward another: in both the former respects, the law of nature and the law of grace, or the moral law or the law of the gospel (we may omit the law of justice as not properly belonging to this purpose otherwise than it may fall into consideration in some particular case). By the first of these laws, man . . . is commanded to love his neighbor as himself. Upon this ground stands all the precepts of the moral law which concerns our dealings with men. To apply this to the works of mercy, this law requires two things: first, that every man afford his help to another in every want or distress; second, that he perform this out of the same affection which makes him careful of his own good, according to that of our Savior, (Matt. 7: 12) "Whatsoever ye would that men should do to you. . . ."

John Winthrop, perhaps the preeminent non-clergy leader of the Massachusetts Bay Colony from 1630 to 1649, was one of the wealthiest of the Puritans that moved to America.

The law of grace or the gospel has some difference from the former as in these respects: First, the law of nature was given to man in the estate of innocence; the law of the gospel in the estate of regeneracy. Second, the law of nature propounds one man to another, as the same flesh and image of God, the law of gospel as a brother in Christ also, and in the communion of the same spirit, and so teaches us to put a difference between Christians and others. . . . The law of nature could give no rules for dealing with enemies, for all are considered as friends in the state of innocence, but the gospel commands love to an enemy. . . . "If thine enemy hunger, feed him; love your enemies; do good to them that hate you" (Matt. 5:44).

This law of the gospel propounds, likewise, a difference of seasons and occasions. There is a time when a Christian must sell all and give to the poor as they did in the apostles' times. There is a time also when Christians (though they give not all yet) must give beyond their ability. . . . Likewise, community of perils calls for extraordinary liberality and so does community in some special service for the Church. Lastly, when there is no other means whereby our Christian brother may be relieved in this distress, we must help him beyond our ability, rather than tempt God in putting him upon help by miraculous or extraordinary means. . . .

Having already set forth the practice of mercy according to the rule of God's law, it will be useful to lay open the grounds of it; also being the other part of the Commandment, and that is the affection from which this exercise of mercy must arise. The apostle tells us that this love is the fulfilling of the law (Rom. 13:10). Not that it is enough to love our brother and no more. . . . Just as, when we bid a man to make the clock strike, he does not lay his hand on the hammer, which is the immediate instrument of the sound, but sets to work the first manner or main wheel, knowing that it will certainly produce the sound which he intends, so the way to draw men to the works of mercy is not by force of argument on the goodness or necessity of the work, for though this course may persuade a rational mind to some present act of mercy (as is frequent in experience), yet it cannot work the habit of mercy into a soul so that it will be prompt on all occasions to produce the same effect except by framing the affections of love in the heart, which will as natively bring forth mercy as any cause produces an effect.

Love

The definition which the Scripture gives us of love is this: love is the bond of perfection (Col. 3:14). First, it is a bond, or ligament. Second, it makes the work perfect. There is no body that does not consist of parts, and that which knits these parts together gives the body its perfection, because it makes each part so contiguous to the others that they mutually participate with each other, both in strength and infirmity, in pleasure and in pain. To instance the most perfect of all bodies: Christ and His church make one body. The several parts of this body considered apart before they were united were as disproportionate and as much disordered as so many contrary qualities or elements, but when Christ came and by His spirit and love knit all these parts to Himself and to each other, it became the most perfect and best proportioned body in the world. . . .

The next consideration is how this love comes to be wrought. Adam in his first estate was a perfect model of mankind in all their generations, and in him this love was perfected. . . . But Adam rent himself from his Creator, rent all his posterity also one from another; whence it comes that every man is born with this principle in him, to love and seek himself only. And thus a man continues till Christ comes and takes possession of his soul, and infuses another principle—love to God and our brother. . . .

The third consideration concerns the exercise of this love, which is twofold—inward or outward. The outward has been handled in the former preface of this discourse; for unfolding the other we must take . . . that maxim of philosophy, *simile simili gaudet*, or, like will to like. . . . The ground of love is a recognition of some resemblance in the things loved to that which affects it. This is the reason why the Lord loves the creature to the extent that it has any of His image in it; He loves His elect because they are like Himself; He beholds them in His Beloved Son. So a mother loves her child, because she thoroughly conceives a resemblance of herself in it. Thus it is between the members of Christ. Each discerns by the work of the spirit his own image and resemblance in another, and therefore cannot but love him as he loves himself.

We Do Not Go as Separatists

Many, if not all, Puritans sought to differentiate themselves from Separatists who wished to break away from the Church of England. Francis Higginson was the leading minister of a group of Puritans who sailed to Massachusetts in 1628, to be joined two years later by John Winthrop and his group. Cotton Mather, in his 1702 history of New England titled Magnalia Christi Americana, *quotes Higginson's remarks to his followers as they saw England for the last time.*

We will not say as the Separatists were wont to say at their leaving of England, Farewell Babylon, farewell Rome! but we will say, farewell dear England! farewell the Church of God in England, and all the Christian friends there! We do not go to New England as Separatists from the Church of England, though we cannot but separate from the corruptions in it, but we go to practice the positive part of church reformation, and propagate the gospel in America.

If any shall object that it is not possible that love should be bred or upheld without hope of requital, it is granted. But that is not our cause, for this love is always under reward; it never gives but always receives with advantage. . . . Among members of the same body, love and affection are reciprocal in a most equal and sweet kind of commerce. . . . In regard to the pleasure and content that the exercise of love carries with it, we may see in the natural body that the mouth receives and minces the food which serves to nourish all the other parts of the body, yet it has no cause to complain. For first, the other parts send back by secret passages a due proportion of the same nourishment in a better form for the strengthening and comforting of the mouth. Second, the labor of the mouth is accompanied by pleasure and content which far exceed the pains it takes, so it is all a labor of love.

Among Christians, the party loving reaps love again, as was shown before, which the soul covets more than all the wealth in the world. Nothing yields more pleasure and content to the soul than when it finds that which it may love fervently, for to love and be loved is the soul's paradise, both here and in heaven. In the state of wedlock there are many comforts to bear out the troubles of that condition, but let those who have tried the most say whether there is any sweetness . . . comparable to the exercise of mutual love. . . .

Applying Our Principles

Now to make some application of this discourse to the situation which gave the occasion of writing it. Herein are four things to be propounded: the persons, the work, the end, the means.

First, for the persons, we are a company professing ourselves fellow members of Christ. . . . Though we are absent from each other by many miles, and have our employments at far distance, we ought to account ourselves knitted together by this bond of love, and live in the exercise of it, if we would have the comfort of our being in Christ. This was common in the practice of Christians in former times; they used to love any of their own religion even before they were acquainted with them.

Second, the work we have in hand is by mutual consent with a special overruling Providence, with a more than ordinary mandate from the churches of Christ to seek out a place to live and associate under a due form of government both civil and ecclesiastical. In such cases as this the care of the public must hold sway over all private interests. To this not only conscience but mere civil policy binds us, for it is a true rule that private estates cannot exist to the detriment of the public.

Third, the end is to improve our lives to do more service to the Lord and to comfort and increase the body of Christ of which we are members, so that ourselves and our posterity may be better preserved from the common corruptions of this evil world in order to serve the Lord and work out our salvation under the power and purity of His holy ordinances.

Fourth, the means whereby this must be effected are twofold.

First, since the work and end we aim at are extraordinary, we must not content ourselves with usual ordinary means. Whatsoever we did or ought to have done when we lived in England, we must do that and more also wherever we go. That which most people in their churches only profess as a truth, we must bring into familiar and constant practice. We must love our brothers without pretense; we must love one another with a pure heart and fervently; we must bear one another's burdens; we must not look only on our own things but also on the things of our brethren. Nor must we think that the Lord will bear with such failings at our hands as He does from those among whom we have lived, for three reasons: (1) Because of the closer bonds of marriage between the Lord and us, wherein He has taken us to be His own in a most strict manner, which makes Him more jealous of our love and obedience, just as He told the people of Israel, "You only have I known of all the families of the Earth; therefore will I punish you for your transgressions" (Amos 3:2); (2) Because the Lord will be sanctified in those who come near Him. We know that there were many who corrupted the service of the Lord, some setting up altars to other gods before Him, others offering both strange fires and sacrifices; yet no fire came from heaven, or other sudden judgment upon them . . . ; (3) When God gives a special commission He wants it strictly observed in every article. . . .

Thus stands the case between God and us. We are entered into covenant with Him for this work. We have taken out a commission. The Lord has given us leave to draw our own articles; we have promised to base our actions on these ends, and we have asked Him for favor and blessing. Now if the Lord shall please to hear us, and bring us in peace to the place we desire, then He has ratified this covenant and sealed our commission, and will expect strict performance of the articles contained in it. But if we neglect to observe these articles, which are the ends we have propounded, and—dissembling with our God—shall embrace this present world and prosecute our carnal intentions, seeking great things for ourselves and our posterity, the Lord will surely break out in wrath against us and be revenged of such a perjured people, and He will make us know the price of the breach of such a covenant.

Now the only way to avoid this shipwreck and to provide for our posterity is to follow the counsel of Micah: to do justly, to love mercy, to walk humbly with our God. For this end, we must be knit together in this work as one man; we must hold each other in brotherly affection; we must be willing to rid ourselves of our excesses to supply others' necessities; we must uphold a familiar commerce together in all meekness, gentleness, patience, and liberality. We must delight in each other, make others' conditions our own and rejoice together, mourn together, labor and suffer together, always having before our eyes our commission and common work, our community as members of the same body.

So shall we keep the unity of the spirit in the bond of peace. The Lord will be our God and delight to dwell among us as His own people. He will command a blessing on us in all our ways, so that we shall see much more of His wisdom, power, goodness, and truth than we have formerly known. We shall find that the God of Israel is among us, and ten of us shall be able to resist a thousand of our enemies. The Lord will make our name a praise and glory, so that men shall say of succeeding plantations: "The Lord make it like that of New England." For we must consider that we shall be like a City upon a Hill; the eyes of all people are on us.

If we deal falsely with our God in this work we have undertaken and so cause Him to withdraw His present help from us, we shall be made a story and a byword throughout the world; we shall open the mouths of enemies to speak evil of the ways of God and all believers in God; we shall shame the faces of many of God's worthy servants and cause their prayers to be turned into curses upon us, till we are forced out of the new land where we are going.

VIEWPOINT 4

"You are to become a body politic, using among yourselves civil government, and are not furnished with any persons of special eminence above the rest."

A Separatist Vision of the New Colony

John Robinson (1575-1625)

Ten years before John Winthrop and his group arrived in Massachusetts Bay, a group of English people seeking religious freedom had founded Plymouth Colony some miles south. They are known today as the Pilgrims, although that term was not used at the time. Unlike the Winthrop-led Puritans, the Plymouth settlers were Separatists—they believed that the Church of England was no longer the true church, and they formally renounced all ties with it rather than attempt to reform it from within. Forming new churches was illegal in England, and in 1606 a group of Separatists moved to the Netherlands. Finding conditions unsatisfactory there, some of the Separatists in Leyden in the Netherlands obtained a colonial charter from England and subsequently made the voyage to America on the *Mayflower*.

The religious leader of the Separatists was John Robinson, an early member of the group that had moved to the Netherlands. He led the Leyden congregation during most of its existence. He did not join the group on the *Mayflower*, staying instead in Leyden with other members of the Congregation who did not make the voyage. Plans to eventually join the settlement were thwarted

From John Robinson, *The Journal of the Pilgrims at Plymouth in New England in 1620, etc., etc.* 2d ed. George B. Cheever, editor. New York, 1849.

by his death in 1625. However, prior to the *Mayflower*'s departure in August 1620 he wrote a letter of instruction and encouragement to the colonists. The last paragraphs, on choosing leaders, are thought to have inspired the Mayflower Compact, the first written framework of government in the United States, formulated in November 1620 aboard the *Mayflower*.

Loving and Christian Friends:

I do heartily and in the Lord salute you all, as being they with whom I am present in my best affection, and most earnest longings after you, though I be constrained for a while to be bodily absent from you. I say constrained, God knowing how willingly and much rather than otherwise I would have borne my part with you in this first brunt, were I not by strong necessity held back for the present. Make account of me in the meanwhile, as of a man divided in myself with great pain, and as (natural bonds set aside) having my better part with you. And though I doubt not but in your godly wisdoms you both foresee and resolve upon that which concerns your present state and condition, both severally and jointly, yet have I thought but my duty to add some further spur of provocation unto them who run already, if not because you need it, yet because I owe it in love and duty.

And first, as we are daily to renew our repentance with our God, especially for our sins known, and generally for our unknown trespasses, so does the Lord call us in a singular manner upon occasions of such difficulty and danger as lie upon you, to a both more narrow search and careful reformation of our ways in his sight, lest He, calling to remembrance our sins forgotten by us or unrepented of, take advantage against us, and in judgment leave us for the same to be swallowed up in one danger or other; whereas on the contrary, sin being taken away by earnest repentance and the pardon thereof from the Lord, sealed up into a man's conscience by his spirit, great shall be his security and peace in all dangers, sweet his comforts in all distresses, with happy deliverance from all evil, whether in life or in death.

A Call for Watchfulness

Now next after this heavenly peace with God and our own consciences, we are carefully to provide for peace with all men what in us lies, especially with our associates, and for that end watchfulness must be had, that we neither at all in ourselves do give, no, nor easily take offense being given by others. Woe be unto the world for offenses, for though it be necessary (considering the malice of Satan and man's corruption) that offenses come, yet woe unto the man or woman either by whom the offense comes, says Christ (Matt. 18:7). And if offenses in the unseasonable use of things in themselves indifferent be more to be feared than death itself, as the Apostle teaches (I Cor. 9:15), how much more in things simply evil, in which neither honor of God nor love of man is thought worthy to be regarded.

The Mayflower Compact

The Mayflower Compact was drafted on November 11, 1620, shortly after the Mayflower *landed on Cape Cod in New England, an area north of the land granted to the Pilgrims by their colonial charter. The Pilgrims constituted only one-third of the people on the* Mayflower. *The Compact was meant to stem any rebellious tendencies of the others and serve as a governing document defining a "Civil Body Politick" until a new charter from London could be arranged.*

In the Name of God, Amen. We, whose names are underwritten, the Loyal Subjects of our dread Sovereign Lord King James, by the Grace of God, of Great Britain, France, and Ireland, King, Defender of the Faith, etc. Having undertaken for the Glory of God, and Advancement of the Christian Faith, and the Honour of our King and Country, a Voyage to plant the first Colony in the northern Parts of Virginia; Do by these Presents, solemnly and mutually, in the Presence of God and one another, covenant and combine ourselves together into a civil Body Politick, for our better Ordering and Preservation, and Furtherance of the Ends aforesaid: And by Virtue hereof do enact, constitute, and frame, such just and equal Laws, Ordinances, Acts, Constitutions, and Officers, from time to time, as shall be thought most meet and convenient for the general Good of the Colony; unto which we promise all due Submission and Obedience.

Neither yet is it sufficient that we keep ourselves by the grace of God from giving offense, except withal we be armed against the taking of it when given by others. For how imperfect and lame is the work of grace in that person, who wants charity to cover a multitude of offenses, as the Scriptures speak. Neither are you to be exhorted to this grace only upon the common grounds of Christianity, which are, that persons ready to take offense, either want charity to cover offenses, or wisdom duly to weigh human frailty; or lastly are gross, though close hypocrites, as Christ our Lord teaches (Matt. 7:1-3), as indeed in mine own experience, few or none have been found who sooner give offense, than such as easily take it; neither have they ever proved sound and profitable members in societies, who have nourished in themselves that touchy humor. But besides these, there are diverse special motives provoking you above others to great care and conscience this way. As first, you are many of you strangers, as to the persons, so to the infirmities one of another, and so stand in need of more watchfulness this way, lest when such things fall out in men and women as you suspected not, you be inordinately affected with them; which does require at your hands much wisdom and charity for the covering and preventing of incident offenses that way. And lastly, your intended course of civil community will minister continual occasion of offense, and will be as fuel for that fire, except you diligently quench it with brotherly forbearance. And if taking of offense causelessly or easily at men's doings be so carefully to be avoided, how much more heed is to be taken that we take not offense at God himself, which yet we certainly do so oft as we do murmur at His providence in our crosses, or bear impatiently such afflictions as wherewith He pleases to visit us. Store we up, therefore, patience against the evil day, without which we take offense at the Lord himself in His holy and just works.

A fourth thing there is carefully to be provided for, to wit, that with your common employments you join common affections truly bent upon the general good, avoiding as a deadly plague of your both common and special comfort all retiredness of mind for proper advantage, and all singularly affected any manner of way; let every man repress in himself and the whole body in each person, as so many rebels against the common good, all private respects of men's selves, not sorting with the general convenience. And as men are careful not to have a new house shaken with any violence before it be well settled and the parts firmly knit, so be you, I beseech you, brethren, much more careful, that the house of God which you are and are to be, be not shaken with unnecessary novelties or other oppositions at the first settling thereof.

Choosing Rulers

Lastly, whereas you are to become a body politic, using among yourselves civil government, and are not furnished with any persons of special eminence above the rest, to be chosen by you into office of government, let your wisdom and godliness appear, not only in choosing such persons as do entirely love, and will diligently promote the common good, but also in yielding unto them all due honor and obedience in their lawful administrations, not beholding in them the ordinariness of their persons, but God's ordinance for your good; nor being like unto the foolish multitude, who more honor the gay coat than either the virtuous mind of the man or glorious ordinance of the Lord. But you know better things: that the image of the Lord's power and authority which the magistrate bears is honorable in all persons, be they ever so mean. And this duty you both may the more willingly, and ought the more conscionably, to perform because you are, at least for the present, to have only them for your ordinary governors, which yourselves shall choose for that work.

Sundry other things of importance I could put you in mind of and of those before mentioned in more words, but I will not so far wrong your godly minds as to think you heedless of these things, there being also diverse among you so well able to admonish both themselves and others of what concerns them. These few things, therefore, and the same in few words I do earnestly commend unto your care and conscience, joining therewith my daily incessant prayers unto the Lord, that He who has made the heavens and the earth, the sea and all rivers of waters, and whose providence is over all His works, especially over all His dear children for good, would so guide and guard you in your ways, as inwardly by His Spirit, so outwardly by the hand of His power, as that both you and we also, for and with you, may have after matter of praising His name all the days of your and our lives.

Fare you well in Him in whom you trust, and in whom I rest.

VIEWPOINT 5

"If any people in the world have been lifted up to heaven as to Advantages and Priviledges, we are the people."

God Has Blessed New England

William Stoughton (1631-1701)

William Stoughton was a Puritan minister who turned from theology to politics and became one of the leading New England political figures in the latter part of the seventeenth century. Among his posts were deputy governor, acting governor, and chief justice of the special court that tried and condemned the witches at Salem in 1692.

The following viewpoint is taken from an election sermon Stoughton preached April 29, 1668, and printed two years later. It is a good example of a sermon common to the time. In it, Stoughton restates to the Puritans that they have a special covenant with God, and he describes the many blessings God has showered on the colony. Stoughton exhorts his congregation to look back to their parents' actions in living their lives and fulfilling their side of the covenant.

From William Stoughton's sermon *New-England's True Interest; Not to Lie*, 1668.

And here I shall consider that the words Of the Text are spoken concerning a People, even the Body of a Nation; and so my endeavour shall be to apply the Truths delivered, unto this present Assembly standing before the Lord this day as the *Body of this People:* Such in several respects is the Capacity of this solemn Congregation, and unto you *as such*, my desire is to speak in the Name of the Lord. For many a day and year, even from our first beginnings hath this word of the Lord been verified concerning us in this Wilderness; *The Lord hath said of* New-England, *Surely they are my People, Children that will not lie, so hath he been our Saviour.* Upon this Basis have all the *Saviourly Undertakings* of the Lord been founded in the midst of us, and upon this bottom do we unto this day abide.

The solemn work of this day is *Foundation-work;* not to lay a new Foundation, but to continue and strengthen, and beautifie, and build upon that which hath been laid. Give me leave therefore, Honoured and Beloved, to awaken, and call upon you, in the Name of him who sends me, with reference unto those *Foundations* that are held forth to us in the Text, for if these should be *out of course*, what could the Righteous do? If we should so frustrate and deceive the Lords Expectations, that his Covenant-interest in us, and the Workings of his Salvation be made to cease, then All were lost indeed; Ruine upon Ruine, Destruction upon Destruction would come, until one stone were not left upon another. . . .

Divine Probation

Use 1. *Of Information;* to let New-England know what that gracious infinitely wise, holy and awful dispensation of divine Providence is, under which the Lord hath set us and continued us unto this day. We must look upon our selves as under a *solemn divine Probation;* It hath been and it is a Probation-time, even to this whole People. Under great hopes, and singular eminent Expectations hath the Lord our God been trying of us, and is yet trying us in the wayes of his Salvation. There is this *one* voice of all his Providences towards us; they call aloud unto us in this language of a Probation-time, *To day if this my people will hear my voice;* To day if they will come up to the Lords Expectations, and answer his promises; To day, that is, whilest it is a day of Salvation, whilest the Lord is yet so wonderfully preserving of us, displaying his Banner over us, holding underneath the Everlasting Arms, and making us to taste so much of his loving kindness and tender mercies every way. Divine Expectations frustrated will issue dreadfully, when the Lord shall make us know his *breach of promise*, Numb. 14. 34. This we must know, that the Lords promises, and expectations of great things, have singled out *New-England*, and all sorts and ranks of men amongst us, above any Nation or people in the world; and this hath been and is a time and season of eminent trial to us. If I should say that the very world, or common ordinary Professors expect great things from us at this day, there is a great deal of weight in it; If I say that the faithful precious suffering Saints of God in all other places, that have heard of the Lords Providences towards us, do expect and promise great things from us, this is farre more; But to mention the Lords own Expectations, this is most of all, these are certainly most solemn and awfull. Every Expectation of God is most just and righteous. *Are not my wayes equal?* saith God, *Ezek.* 18. 29. Yes, most equal, blessed God; Bountiful and Rich hast thou been in all thy free Bestowings; equal and just art thou in all thy greatest Expectations. If we do but run over the forementioned grounds of divine Expectation, it will be sufficient to commit the judgement of this case even to *our selves*, as *Isa.* 5. 3.

A People in Covenant with God

> *In his famous 1651 sermon* The Gospel-Covenant, *Peter Bulkeley, a leading Puritan clergyman, echoed John Winthrop's phrase comparing New England to a city on a hill.*

And for ourselves here, the people of New England, we should in a special manner labor to shine forth in holiness above other people. We have that plenty and abundance of ordinances and means of grace, as few people enjoy the like; we are as a city set upon a hill, in the open view of all the earth, the eyes of the world are upon us, because we profess ourselves to be a people in covenant with God, and therefore not only the Lord our God, with whom we have made covenant, but heaven and earth, angels and men, that are witnesses of our profession, will cry shame upon us if we walk contrary to the covenant which we have professed and promised to walk in. If we open the mouths of men against our profession, by reason of the scandalousness of our lives, we (of all men) shall have the greater sin. . . .

Let us study so to walk that this may be our excellency and dignity among the nations of the world among which we live; that they may be constrained to say of us, only this people is wise, a holy and blessed people; that all that see us may see and know that the name of the Lord is called upon us; and that we are the seed which the Lord hath blessed.

As for special Relation unto God; whom hath the Lord more signally exalted then his people in this Wilderness? The Name and

Interest of God, and Covenant-relation to him, it hath been written upon us in Capital Letters from the beginning. God had his *Creatures* in this Wilderness before we came, and his *Rational Creatures* too, a multitude of them; but as to *Sons* and *Children* that are Covenant-born unto God, Are not we the *first* in such a Relation? in this respect we are surely the Lords *first-born* in this Wilderness. Of the poor Natives before we came we may say as *Isa.* 63. 19. *They were not called by the Lords Name, he bear not Rule over them:* But we have been from the beginning, and we are the *Lords*.

As for Extraction and Descent, if we be considered as a *Posterity,* O what Parents and Predecessors may we the most of us look back unto, through whose Loins the Lord hath stretched forth the line of his Covenant, measuring of us out, and taking us in to be a peculiar Portion to himself?

As for Restipulations, and Engagements back again to God; what awfull publick Transactions of this kinde have there been amongst us? Hath not the eye of the Lord beheld us laying *Covenant-Engagements* upon our selves? hath not his ear heard us solemnly *Avouching* him, and him alone, to be our God and Saviour? Hath not a great part of the world been a witness of these things, even of our explicite ownings of, and Covenantings with the Lord as our God, laying this as a foundation-stone in our Building; and of this we may say, It hath been a special Exasperation unto Adversaries and Ill-willers, that despised *New-England* hath laid claim to, and publickly avouched and challenged a special Interest in God above others.

Divine Advantages

As for our Advantages and Priviledges in a Covenant-state, here time and strength would fail to reckon up what we have enjoyed of this kinde; if any people in the world have been lifted up to heaven as to Advantages and Priviledges, we are the people. Name what you will under this Head, and we have had it. We have had *Moses* and *Aaron* to lead us; we have had Teachings and Instructions, *line upon line, and precept upon precept;* we have had Ordinances and Gospel-dispensations the choicest of them; we have had Peace and Plenty; we have had Afflictions and Chastisements in measure; we have had the Hearts, and Prayers, and Blessing of the Lords people every where; we have had the Eye and Hand of God, watching and working every way for our good; our Adversaries have had their Rebukes, we have had our Encouragement, and a wall of fire round about us. What could have been done more for us then hath been done?

And then in the last place, as to *New-Englands first wayes;* what glorious things might here be spoken, unto the praise of free-grace, and to justifie the Lords Expectations upon this ground?

Surely God hath often spoke concerning His Churches here, as in *Jer. 2. 2. I remember the kindness of thy youth, etc.* O what were the open Professions of the Lords people that first entred this Wilderness? How did our fathers entertain the Gospel, and all the pure Institutions thereof, and those Liberties which they brought over? What was their Communion and Fellowship in the Administrations of the Kingdome of Jesus Christ? What was the pitch of their Brotherly love, of their Zeal for God and his Wayes, and against wayes destructive of Truth and Holiness? What was their Humility, their Mortification, their Exemplariness? How much of Holiness to the Lord was written upon all their wayes and transactions? God sifted a whole Nation that he might send choice Grain over into this Wilderness.

Thus it hath been with us as to grounds of Divine Expectation: And therefore let us in the fear of God learn this great truth to day, and receive the instruction thereof sealed up unto all our souls; *That the great God hath taken up great Expectations of us, and made great Promises to himself concerning us, and this hath been, and is* New-Englands *day and season of Probation.*

VIEWPOINT 6

"The Glory of the Lord seems to be on the wing. Oh! Tremble for it is going."

God Has Withdrawn His Blessing from New England

Increase Mather (1639-1723)

Increase Mather was one of the most prominent Puritan ministers and writers. Son of Richard Mather and father of Cotton Mather, both notable Puritan clergymen, Increase Mather was born in Dorchester, Massachusetts, and educated at Harvard and at Trinity College in Dublin, Ireland. In addition to serving as pastor of the Dorchester Church (where his father and son also preached), Mather served as president of Harvard and was the author of more than one hundred published works, including sermons, political tracts, and histories.

The following viewpoint is taken from a pamphlet published in 1702, more than seventy years after John Winthrop had proclaimed the new colony to be a "city upon a hill." In the intervening time much had happened, including Indian wars, a Puritan revolution in England (and subsequent restoration of the monarchy), the loss of Winthrop's original charter, and the growth of religious dissent within the colonies. Mather decries many of the new developments, comparing them unfavorably with what he views as the supreme achievements of an earlier generation. He argues that the colony should return to the religious ideals of its founders.

From Increase Mather, *Ichabod; or, A Discourse, Shewing What Cause There Is to Fear That the Glory of the Lord Is Departing from New England.* Boston, 1702.

God has not seemed to take pleasure in the American world, so as to fix and settle His Glory therein. The Scripture sayes, The Kingdom of God is like Leaven hid in *Three measures* of Meal until *the whole* was Leavened. *Luk.* 23. 22. Which some take to be a Prediction, that the Gospel should spread through *Asia, Europe* and *Africa,* then the only known parts of the world. What God will do for the future with *America,* is not for us to determine. Act. 1. 7. *It is not for you to know the Times, and the Seasons which the Father has put in His own power.* But it is our Duty humbly to observe his Providence. Now the Lord has not hitherto seen meet to shine upon this so as on the other *Hemisphere.* The greatest part of its Inhabitants are Pagans. Most of those that have any thing of the *Christian* Name are really *Anti-Christian.* And the generality of them that pretend unto the Protestant Religion, are a lose sort of men, and a Scandal to any Religion. There was an attempt (about an Hundred and Fifty Years since) to settle the Protestant Religion in the *Southern America,* and some Eminent Christians and Ministers, from *Geneva* were ingaged in it; but it soon come to nothing. And the late miscarriage of the *Caledonia* design is an awful Providence, and looks uncomfortably on *America.* There is more of the Divine Glory in *New-England* then in all *America* besides. We have the greater Cause not to be high-minded, but to fear.

Especially if we consider . . . *That the Glory is in some measure, & in an awful degree removed from us already.* The Glory of the Lord seems to be on the wing. Oh! Tremble for it is going, it is gradually departing. Although there is that of the Divine Glory still remaining among us, which we ought to be very Thankful for; Nevertheless, much of it is gone, which thought should humble and abase us in the dust before the Lord. . . . You that are Aged persons, and can remember what *New-England* was Fifty Years ago, that saw these Churches in *their first Glory;* Is there not a sad decay and diminution of the Glory? We may weep to think of it. . . . Ancient men, though they bless God for what they *Do* see of His Glory remaining in these Churches, they cannot but mourn when they remember what they *Have* seen, far surpassing what is at present. . . . Time was, when these Churches were *Beautiful as* Tirzah, *Comely as* Jerusalem, *Terrible as an Army with Banners.* What a glorious Presence of Christ was there in all His Ordinances? Many were Converted, and willingly Declared what God had done for their Souls: and there were added to the Churches daily such as should be Saved. But are not Sound Conversions become rare at this day, and this in many Congregations? *Discipline* in the Churches was upheld in the power of it; and a special Presence of the Lord Jesus Christ went along with it. . . . We may fall into Tears, considering how the power of Discipline is fallen in our Churches. Some Scandalous practices which not only the *Waldenses*, but the Reformed Churches in *France*, and in *Holland*, have in their Discipline declared to be Censurable Evils, are now indulged in some Churches in *New-England*. Look into Pulpits, and see if there is such a Glory there, as once there was? *New-England* has had Teachers very Eminent for Learning, & no less Eminent for Holiness, & all Ministerial accomplishments. When will *Boston* see a COTTON, & a NORTON, again? When will *New-England* see a HOOKER, a SHEPARD, a MITCHEL, not to mention others? No little part of the Glory was laid in the Dust, when those Eminent Servants of Christ were laid in their Graves. Look into our Civil State: Does Christ reign there as once He did? Is there that Glory in Courts as once there was? Is not our House in diverse parts of this Land, in some danger of falling for want of Pillars to support it? Look into *Towns*: How few do we find that are a Glory to the places where they live? When *Vacancies* are made, it is a difficult thing to find persons fit to make up those Breaches. And almost every where 'tis so, whether in our Ecclesiastical, Military, or Civil State. So that what our Great *Hooker* long since predicted, that the *People of* New-England *would be punished with the want of Eminent Men to manage Publick affairs, both in Church and State*, is in part sadly verified already. How many Churches, how many Towns are there in *New-England*, that we may Sigh over them, and say, *The Glory is gone!* Look into *Families:* Are there not those which once were *Glorious* ones because of the *Religion* which flourished in them, which now are not so. How many Children or Grand-Children are there in *New-England*, of whom it may be said, as in Judg. 2.17. *They turned quickly out of the way, which their Fathers walked in, Obeying the Commandments of the Lord, but they did not so. . . .*

New England Under Probation

But, *Is there no way to prevent the Removal of the Glory from us?* Yes there is. I have not spoken these things that we should Despair, but that we might be *Awakened* to do what we may to prevent further and greater Removals of our Glory. As yet, our Day is not expired: *As yet we have a Gracious Time of Visitation: As yet*, we are under a *Probationary* dispensation. How long or how short that shall be, is with God. Only it does not use to last very long in a Land of such Light and means of Grace as *New-England* has been. *The brightest dayes are commonly short ones.*

But, *What then is to be done? . . .*

1. *Let the Life and Power of Godliness be revived.* That has been the singular Glory of *New-England*: The generality of the *First Planters* were men Eminent for Godliness. We are the Posterity of the

Increase Mather was one of the leading second-generation Puritan leaders in America.

Good, Old Puritan Nonconformists in *England*, who were a Strict and Holy people. Such were our Fathers who followed the Lord into this wilderness, when it was a Land not sown. Oh! That the present and succeeding Generations in *New-England* might be like the *First Generation* of Christians, who transplanted and settled themselves in this part of the world. Then might we with Confidence pray and believe that God would accomplish for us, that which *Solomon* pray'd for in the behalf of his People, I King. 8. 57. *The Lord our God be with us as He was with our Fathers, Let Him not leave us nor forsake us.* Yea, Let us be as our Fathers were, as to Holiness in all manner of Conversation, and the Lord our God *will be with us* as He was with them. We shall have the same Glory remaining with us which they had.

2. *Let us abide in those Truths respecting the Order of the Gospel, which our Fathers have left with us as a Legacy.* Herein is the difference between *New-England* and all other Plantations. As for other Plantations, they were settled with respect to *Trade*, or some other worldly interest: But it was not so with *New-England*. Our Fathers in coming into this part of the world, did not propose to themselves worldly advantages, but the contrary. It was purely on a Religious account that they ventured themselves and Little ones over the vast Ocean into this which was then a wast and *howling Wilderness*. Although of later Times we have too much changed that which was our Glory, not *Seeking the Kingdom of God in the First*

place, not making Religion, but Trade and Land, and Earthly accommodations our *Interest:* And God has remarkably smitten us in that which has been our *Idol.* In this we are degenerated from the Piety of our Ancestors. But what in Religion was it that induced them to come into this Land? Not the main *Articles of Faith,* for in those they differed not from other *Protestant Churches.* But it was regard to the *Order of the Gospel* that brought them hither. That so they might Erect a Spiritual Kingdom for the Lord Jesus Christ to Reign over. That they might Build Churches which should be *Ordered* in all Respects according to the mind of Christ declared in the *Gospel.* On which account a *Defection* from those Truths will in *New-England* be a greater Sin and Provocation to God, then in any other part of the world. Considering the Glorious Light which has been shining here, there are practices which in other parts of the world would be a great *Reformation,* but in *New-England* a *Degeneracy.* No one needs to Enquire *What is the Order of the Gospel!* You have it declared in *the Platform of Church Discipline,* agreed unto by the *Elders and Messengers of these Churches,* above Fifty Years ago. A *Platform* which is drawn out of the Scriptures of Truth, by men Eminent for Learning and Holiness, and such as were *Confessors* and great Sufferers for the Testimony which they had born to the Kingdom of Christ; and in those respects as likely to have the Truth revealed to them as any men in the world. And that Book was the result of many prayers and Extraordinary seekings to God for the sending forth of his Light and Truth in the matters which were to be debated, and are therein determined. Blessed Mr. *Norton* went to Heaven Exhorting these Churches to continue in the Profession and Practice of that *Discipline;* withal declaring that their safety and the presence of Christ with them depended thereon. Some of his words were these; *"Let our Polity be a Gospel Polity.* This is the very work of our Generation, and the very work we ingaged for into this wilderness; this is the scope and end of it: that which is written on the Forehead of NEW-ENGLAND, viz. *The compleat walking in the Faith of the Gospel according to the Order of the Gospel,*—You have the *Platform of Church Discipline* given to you in way of Counsel as the Confession of our Faith in this way of Church-Government—If any be departed from it, let them look to it—*Our Fidelity in this Cause is our Crown: See that it be not taken from us."* Thus did that Great man express himself, in the *last Sermon* that ever he Preached, which was but Three dayes before his translation to Glory. And if I, (who am not worthy to be compared with him) knew that this would be *the last Sermon* that ever I should Preach, (as I know not but it may be so) my *Dying Farewel* to these Churches should be the very same. For I know and am perswaded by the Lord Jesus, that if ever these Churches shall *Depart* from that *Holy Platform,* the *Glory* of the Lord will *Depart* from them.

CHAPTER 2

Dealing with
Religious Dissent

Chapter Preface

Religion was a central component of the Puritan vision. The Puritans left England to establish a pure church. Yet within a few short years the Puritans who founded the Massachusetts Bay Colony found themselves sharply divided over matters of religion. This chapter focuses on two of the early religious crises of the period: the expulsion of Roger Williams and the Antinomian crisis that resulted in the expulsion of Anne Hutchinson and her followers.

In examining the religious dissent that so divided the Massachusetts Bay Colony it is important to examine several features of Puritan life and thought concerning religion and the church. Most professing Puritans in the early decades of American settlement, including those who disagreed with the Massachusetts leadership, shared a fundamental set of doctrines. Historian Andrew Delbanco writes in *The Reader's Companion to American History*:

> Doctrinally, Puritans adhered to the Five Points of Calvinism as codified at the Synod of Dort in 1619: (1) unconditional election (the idea that God had decreed who was damned and who was saved from before the beginning of the world); (2) limited atonement (the idea that Christ died for the elect only); (3) total depravity (humanity's utter corruption since the Fall); (4) irresistible grace (regeneration as entirely the work of God, which cannot be resisted and to which the sinner contributes nothing); and (5) the perseverance of the saints (the elect, despite their backsliding and faintness of heart, cannot fall away from grace).

As one might imagine, a central question facing every Puritan was who were among the elect. Were oneself, one's family and neighbors, and one's ministers and political leaders among God's chosen? Such considerations gave the disputes surrounding Roger Williams, Anne Hutchinson, and other religious dissenters a deep sense of urgency. When Anne Hutchinson and her followers accused the Puritan leaders of teaching untrue doctrine, the implication was that the Puritan ministers and leaders were not among the elect. The logical next step for dissenters was to accuse them of being "enemies of the Lord," as John Wheelwright, brother-in-law and supporter of Anne Hutchinson, stated in a controversial sermon that brought the crisis to its head.

Anxious members of the Puritan community knew that if the leaders of the Puritans, such as John Winthrop and Thomas Dudley, were not among God's elect, the whole Puritan experiment was doomed. If, however, they *were* among God's elect, then reason suggested that the accusations of Hutchinson and her followers must stem from Satan's attempts to destroy the community.

Desiring to restore peace and unity to the community (as well as preserve their own standing as leaders), the authorities of Massachusetts Bay Colony responded to dissent by banishing the dissenters. This strategy was made possible in part by the Puritan's location. Many historians, including Daniel Boorstin, have commented on the striking differences between Puritanism in America and in England, especially in the area of religious toleration. The vast and unexplored New World made the option of purifying the community via banishment a possibility in New England that was impossible in England. Boorstin writes in *The Americans: the Colonial Experience:*

> In New England the critics, doubters, and dissenters were expelled from the community; in England the Puritans had to find ways of living with them. It was in England, therefore, that a modern theory of toleration began to develop. . . . The leaders of Massachusetts Bay Colony enjoyed the luxury, no longer feasible in 17th century England, of a pure and simple orthodoxy.

Boorstin concludes that the actions the Puritan leaders took towards Williams, Hutchinson, and other dissenters may seem harsh today, but they did have a certain benefit:

> The failure of New England Puritans to develop a theory of toleration . . . was not in all ways a weakness. . . . Theirs was not a philosophic enterprise; they were, first and foremost, community-builders. . . . Had they spent as much of their energy in debating with each other as did their English contemporaries, they might have lacked the singlemindedness needed to overcome the dark, unpredictable perils of a wilderness. They might have merited praise as precursors of modern liberalism, but they might never have helped found a nation.

VIEWPOINT 1

"It is no wonder that so many having been demanded the cause of my sufferings have answered, that they could not tell for what, since Mr. Cotton himself knows not distinctly."

Roger Williams's Banishment Was Not Justified

Roger Williams (c. 1603-1683)

The banishment of Roger Williams, who was forced to flee from the Massachusetts Bay Colony in January 1636, was one of the first instances in which Puritan efforts to create a uniform Christian community foundered against dissent and division. Williams, historian Alan Heimert writes, "was perhaps the purest of American Puritans."

The son of a London shopkeeper, Williams was educated at Cambridge University and left England for America in 1630. Highly regarded for his intellect and piety by many, including Massachusetts governor John Winthrop, Williams was offered a pastoral position by several churches. He refused them all on the grounds that they had not officially repudiated the Church of England. Williams moved to the Pilgrim colony of Plymouth, where he lived for several years. Eventually he returned to Massachusetts to become the minister of the Salem church. His sermons became in-

From Roger Williams, "Mr. Cotton's Letter Lately Printed, Examined, and Answered." In *Publications of the Narragansett Club*. Volume 1. Providence, 1866.

creasingly critical of Puritan leadership in several respects: He maintained that the New England churches should fully separate themselves from the Church of England; he questioned the legitimacy of the Massachusetts colonial charter, arguing that the king of England had no legal authority to grant land owned by the American Indians; and he interpreted Scripture in such a way as to directly challenge the authority of the civil government. Historian Francis J. Bremer writes in *The Puritan Experiment:*

> Like other Puritan clergy, Williams used typology—the demonstration of New Testament occurrences as fulfillments of Old Testament premonitions—as a tool of scriptural analysis. But whereas most Puritans who employed this device emphasized the analogous relationship between ancient and modern events—seeing, for instance, Israel as a model for New England—Williams emphasized the radical difference the incarnation had effected. He specifically came to deny that Israel was a "type" for anything thereafter and denied that the civil magistrate in modern times had any right or obligation to become involved in spiritual affairs. Fearing the contamination of God's ordinances by the secular state, he denied the magistrates' authority to punish breaches of the first table of the ten commandments (which effectively denied the Puritan state's right to protect the true faith) and argued that a magistrate ought not tender oaths to unregenerated men (which would have abolished all civil oaths).

After several attempts at private and public consultation with Williams by religious and political leaders had failed to get him to moderate or back away from his views, the General Court of Massachusetts on October 9, 1635, convicted Williams of promulgating "newe & dangerous opinions against the aucthoritie of magistrates." Williams left Salem in January 1636. In April 1636 he purchased land from the Narragansett Indians and founded the new colony of Rhode Island, a colony disdained by its New England counterparts because of its laws granting "liberty of conscience."

The debates between Williams and the Massachusetts authorities did not stop with his banishment. In 1642 Williams went back to England for two years to secure a charter for Rhode Island. While there he engaged in an interesting debate via pamphlet with John Cotton, one of the leading American Puritan leaders. The following viewpoint is taken from a pamphlet first published in England in 1644. It is a reply to a letter Cotton wrote Williams in 1636, which "providentially" appeared in published form in London while Williams was there. In his public reply to Cotton's letter Williams defends his actions and beliefs and attacks Cotton and his Puritan cohorts for his trial and banishment. He argues that the authorities had no right to banish him from the community because of his beliefs.

71

But because the Reader may ask both Mr. Cotton and me, what were the grounds of such a sentence of Banishment against me, which are here called sandy, I shall relate in brief what those grounds were, some whereof he is pleased to discuss in this Letter, and others of them not to mention.

After my public trial and answers at the general Court, one of the most eminent Magistrates (whose name and speech may by others be remembered) stood up and spake:

Mr. Williams (said he) holds forth these 4 particulars; First, that we have not our land by patent from the King, but that the natives are the true owners of it, and that we ought to repent of such a receiving it by patent. Secondly, that it is not lawful to call a wicked person to swear, to pray, as being actions of Gods Worship. Thirdly, that it is not lawful to hear any of the ministers of the parish assemblies in England. Fourthly, that the civil magistrates power extends only to the bodies and goods, and outward state of men, etc.

I acknowledge the particulars were rightly summed up, and I also hope, that, as I then maintained the rocky strength of them to my own and other consciences satisfaction so (through the Lords assistance) I shall be ready for the same grounds, not only to be bound and banished, but to die also, in New England, as for most holy truths of God in Christ Jesus.

Self-Banishment

Yes but (said he) upon those grounds you banished your self from the society of the churches in these countries.

I answer, if Mr. Cotton means my own voluntary withdrawing from those churches resolved to continue in those evils, and persecuting the witnesses of the Lord presenting light unto them, I confess it was my own voluntary act; yea, I hope the act of the Lord Jesus sounding forth in me (a poor despised rams horn) the blast which shall in his own holy season cast down the strength and confidence of those inventions of men in the worshipping of the true and living God. And lastly, his act in enabling me to be faithful in any measure to suffer such great and mighty trials for his names sake. But if by banishing my self he intend the act of civil banishment from their common earth and aire, I then observe with grief the language of the dragon in a lambs lip. Among other expressions of the dragon are not these common to the witnesses of the Lord Jesus rent and torn by his persecutions? Go now, say you are persecuted, you are persecuted for Christ, suffer for your conscience: no, it is your schisme, heresy, obstinacy, the devil hath deceived thee, thou hast justly brought this upon thee, thou hast banished thy self, etc. Instances are abundant in so many books of Martyrs, and the experience of all men, and therefore I spare to recite in so short a treatise.

Christian vs. Secular Authority

Roger Williams's debate with John Cotton resulted in perhaps his most famous work, the pamphlet entitled The Bloody Tenent of Persecution, *published in England in 1644. In the tract Williams makes a clear distinction between the authority of a minister or priest, and the authority of a magistrate or governor. He argues that those in civil authority should not wield additional authority because they are Christians.*

Now what kind of magistrate soever the people shall agree to set up, whether he receive Christianity before he be set in office, or whether he receive Christianity after, he receives no more power of magistracy than a magistrate that hath received no Christianity. For neither of them both can receive more than the commonweal, the body of people and civil state, as men, communicate unto them and betrust with them.

All lawful magistrates in the world, both before the coming of Christ Jesus and since (excepting those unparalleled typical magistrates of the church of Israel), are but derivatives and agents immediately derived and employed as eyes and hands, serving for the good of the whole: hence they have and can have no more power than fundamentally lies in the bodies or fountains themselves, which power, might, or authority is not religious, Christian, &c., but natural, humane and civil.

And hence it is true, that a Christian captain, Christian merchant, physician, lawyer, pilot, father, master, and (so consequently) magistrate, &c., is no more a captain, merchant, physician, lawyer, pilot, father, master, magistrate, &c., than a captain, merchant, &c. of any other conscience or religion.

Secondly, if he mean this civil act of banishing, why should he call a civil sentence from the civil State, within a few weeks execution in so sharp a time of New Englands cold. Why should he call this a banishment from the churches, except he silently confess, that the frame or constitution of their churches is but implicitly national (which yet they profess against) for otherwise why was I not yet permitted to live in the world, or commonwealth, except for this reason, that the commonwealth and church is yet but one, and he that is banished from the one, must necessarily be banished from the other also. . . .

Mr. Cotton. And yet it may be they passed that sentence against you, not upon that ground: but for ought I know, for your other corrupt Doctrines, which tend to the disturbance both of civil and holy peace, as may appear by that answer which was sent to the brethren of the Church of Salem and your self.

I answer, it is no wonder that so many having been demanded the cause of my sufferings have answered, that they could not tell for what, since Mr. Cotton himself knows not distinctly what cause to assign: but said, it may be they passed not that sentence on that ground, etc. Oh, where was the waking care of so excellent and worthy a man, to see his brother and beloved in Christ so afflicted, he knows not distinctly for what.

He alleged a scripture, to prove the sentence righteous, and yet concluded it may be it was not for that, but for other corrupt Doctrines which he named not, nor any Scripture to prove them corrupt, or the sentence righteous for that cause. O that it may please the Father of lights to awaken both himself and other of my honored countrymen, to see how though their hearts wake (in respect of personal grace and life of Jesus) yet they sleep insensible of much concerning the purity of the Lords worship, or the sorrows of such whom they call brethren, and beloved in Christ, afflicted by them.

Corrupt Doctrines

But though he name not these corrupt doctrines, a little before I have, as they were publicly summed up and charged upon me, and yet none of them tending to the breach of holy or civil peace, of which I have ever desired to be unfainedly tender, acknowledging the Ordinance of Magistracie to be properly and adequately fitted by God, to preserve the civil state in civil peace and order: as he had also appointed a spiritual government and governors in matters pertaining to his worship and the consciences of men, both which governments, governors, laws, offences, punishments, are essentially distinct, and the confounding of them brings all the world into combustion. . . .

Ans. However Mr. Cotton believes and writes of this point, yet has he not duly considered these following particulars:

First the faithful labors of many witnesses of Jesus Christ, extant to the world, abundantly proving, that the Church of the Jews under the Old Testament in the type, and the Church of the Christians under the New Testament in the Antitype, were both separate from the world; and that when they have opened a gap in the hedge or wall of separation between the garden of the church and the wilderness of the world, God hath ever broke down the wall it self, removed the candlestick, etc. and made his garden a wilderness, as at this day. And that therefore if he will ever please to restore his garden and paradise again, it must of necessity be walled in peculiarly unto himself from the world, and that all that shall be saved out of the world are to be transplanted out of the wilderness of world, and added unto his church or garden.

"His banishment proceeded not against him, or his, for his own refusal of any worship, but for seditious opposition against the patent, and against the oath of fidelity offered to the people."

Roger Williams's Banishment Was Justified

John Cotton (1584-1652)

From 1633 to 1652 John Cotton was the teaching pastor of First Church in Boston. He was considered one of the main spiritual leaders of the American Puritan community. Many of his writings were originally published in England, where Cotton sought through a variety of pamphlets and tracts to defend the Puritan experiment in America to English Puritans and others.

Among the pamphlets Cotton wrote were several in response to tracts written by Roger Williams, a Puritan pastor who had been expelled from Massachusetts because of certain opinions. In 1644 Cotton found that a letter he had privately written to Williams in 1636 had been published in England and that Williams had published a reply attacking Cotton's arguments. In response Cotton wrote a pamphlet in which he defended Massachusetts' action against Williams in the 1630s. Cotton argues that Williams essentially banished himself because of his repeated attacks on the Puritan community and his refusal to cooperate with the authorities.

From John Cotton, "A Reply to Mr. Williams His Examination" In *Publications of the Narragansett Club.* Volume 2. Providence, 1867.

The grounds of the sentence of [Roger Williams's] banishment, some whereof he says I am pleased to discuss in the Letter, and others not to mention; He said were rightly summed up by one of the magistrates after his public trial, and answers.

Mr. Williams (said that public person) held forth these four particulars.

1. That we have not our land by patent from the King, but that the natives are the true owners of it; and that we ought to repent of such a receiving it by patent.

2. That it is not lawful to call a wicked person to swear, to pray, as being actions of Gods worship.

3. That it is not lawful to hear any of the ministers of the Parish Assemblies in England.

4. That the civil magistrates power extends only to the bodies, and goods, and outward state of men, etc. . . .

Whom that eminent magistrate was, that so summed up the grounds of Mr. Williams his banishment in those four particulars above mentioned, Mr. Williams does wisely conceal his name, lest if he were named, he should be occasioned to bear witness against such fraudulent expression of the particulars: whereof some were no causes of his banishment at all, and such as were causes, were not delivered in such general terms. . . . It is evident the two latter causes which he gives of his banishment, were no causes at all, as he expressed them. There are many known to hold both these opinions, that it is not lawful to hear any of the ministers of the parish assemblies in England, and that the civil magistrates power extended only to the bodies, and goods, and outward estates of men: and yet they are tolerated not only to live in the commonwealth, but also in the fellowship of the churches.

The two former, though they be not so much noised, yet there be many, if not most, that hold, that we have not our land, meerly by right of patent from the King, but that the natives are true owners of all that they possess, or improve. Neither do I know any among us, that either then were, or now are of another mind.

And as for the other point; that it is not lawful to call a wicked person to swear, or pray.

Though that be not commonly held, yet it is known to be held of some, who yet are tolerated to enjoy both civil, and church-liberties among us.

To come therefore to particulars: Two things there were, which (to my best observation, and remembrance) caused the sentence of his banishment: and two other fell in, that hastened it.

1. His violent and tumultuous carriage against the patent. By

the patent it is, that we received allowance from the King to depart his kingdom, and to carry our goods with us, without offence to his officers, and without paying custom to himself....

WILLIAMS GOING INTO EXILE.

John Cotton argued that the banishment of Roger Williams from Massachusetts in the winter of 1636 was legitimate and justified.

2. The second offence, which procured his banishment, was occasioned as I touched before. The magistrates, and other members of the general court upon intelligence of some Episcopal, and malignant practises against the country, they made an order of court to take trial of the fidelity of the people, (not by imposing upon them, but) by offering to them an oath of fidelity: that in case any should refuse to take it, they might not betrust them with place of public charge, and command. This oath when it came abroad, he vehemently withstood it, and dissuaded sundry from it, partly because it was, as he said, Christ's prerogative, to have his office established by oath: partly because an oath was a part of God's worship, and God's worship was not to be put upon carnal persons, as he conceived many of the people to be. So by his tenent neither might church-members, nor other godly

77

men, take the oath, because it was the establishment not of Christ, but of mortal men in their office; nor might men out of the church take it, because in his eye they were but carnal. So the court was forced to desist from that proceeding: which practise of his was held to be the more dangerous, because it tended to unsettle all the kingdoms, and commonwealths in Europe.

These were (as I took it) the causes of his banishment: two other things fell in upon these that hastened the sentence. The former fell out thus: the magistrates discerning by the former passages, the heady and turbulent spirit of Mr. Williams, both they, and others advised the Church of Salem not to call him to office in their church; nevertheless, the major part of the church made choice of him. Soon after, when the church made suit to the court for a parcel of land adjoining to them, the court delayed to grant their request (as hath been mentioned before) because the church had refused to hearken to the magistrates, and others in forbearing the choice of Mr. Williams. Whereupon Mr. Williams took occasion to stir up the church to join with him in writing Letters of Admonition unto all the churches, whereof those magistrates were members, to admonish them of their open transgression of the rule of justice. Which letters coming to the several churches, provoked the magistrates to take the more speedy course with so heady, and violent a spirit.

But to prevent his sufferings, (if it might be) it was moved by some of the elders, that themselves might have liberty (according to the Rule of Christ) to deal with him, and with the church also in a church-way. It might be, the church might hear us, and he the church; which being consented to, some of our churches wrote to the church of Salem, to present before them the offensive spirit, and way of their officer, (Mr. Williams) both in judgement, and practise. The church finally began to hearken to us, and accordingly began to address themselves to the healing of his spirit. Which he discerning, renounced communion with the church of Salem, pretending they held communion with the churches in the bay, and the churches in the bay held communion with the parish-churches in England, because they suffered their members to hear the word amongst them in England, as they came over into their native country. He then refusing to resort to the public assembly of the church. Soon after sundry began to resort to his family, where he preached to them on the Lords day. But this carriage of his in renouncing the church upon such an occasion, and with them all the churches in the country, and the spreading of his leaven to sundry that resorted to him; this gave the magistrates the more cause to observe the heady unruliness of his spirit, and the incorrigibleness thereof by any church-way, all the churches in the country being then renounced by him. And this was the other occasion which hastened the sentence of his banishment, upon the former grounds.

If upon these grounds Mr. Williams be ready, (as he professeth)

Bodies and Souls

In response to Roger Williams's famous 1644 tract The Bloody Tenent of Persecution, *John Cotton wrote* The Bloody Tenent, Washed, and Made White in the Bloud of the Lambe *in 1647 to again defend the practices of Puritan Massachusetts. In this excerpt he responds to Williams's argument that the government should not concern itself with matters of the soul.*

Discusser [Roger Williams]
But the civil magistrate has his charge of the bodies and good of the subject; as the spiritual officers of Christ's city or kingdom have the charge of their souls and soul-safety.
Defender [John Cotton]
Reply 1. If it were true, that the magistrate has charge only of the bodies and goods of the subject, yet that might justly excite to watchfulness against such pollutions of religion as tend to apostasy. For if the church and people of God fall away from God, God will visit the city and country with public calamity, if not captivity, for the church's sake. . . .

Reply 2. It is a carnal and wordly and, indeed, an ungodly imagination to confine the magistrate's charge to the bodies and goods of the subject, and to exclude them from the care of their souls. Did ever God commit the charge of the body to any governors to whom he did not commit (in His way) the care of souls also? Has God committed to parents the charge of the children's bodies, and not the care of their souls? to masters the charge of their servants' bodies, and not of their souls? To captains the charge of their soldiers' bodies, and not of their souls? Shall the captains suffer false worship, yea idolatry, publicly professed and practiced in the camp, and yet look to prosper in battle? The magistrates, to whom God has committed the charges of bodies and outward man of the subject, are they not also to take care to procure faithful teachers to be sent among them? . . . The truth is, church governors and civil governors do herein stand parallel one to another. The church governors, though to them be chiefly committed the charge of souls as their adequate objects, yet, in order to the good of the souls of their people, to exhort from idleness, negligence, from intemperancy in meats and drinks, from oppression, and deceit, and theirin provide both for the health of their bodies and the safety of their estates. So civil governors, though to them be chiefly committed the bodies and goods of the people (as their adequate object), yet, in order to [accomplish] this, they may, and ought to, procure spiritual helps to their souls and to prevent such spiritual evils as that the prosperity of religion among them might advance the prosperity of the civil state.

not only to be bound, and banished, but also to die in New England; let him remember, (what he knows) *Non poena, sed causa facit Martyrem;* No Martyr of Christ did ever suffer for such a cause. . . .

The Wiliness of the Spirit

Again, he recoileth to his civil banishment, and observeth, That if by banishing himself I meant his civil banishment, then 1. He discerneth the language of the dragon in a lambs lip; to put the sufferings of the Saints upon themselves, and the devil. 2. That I silently confess, that the frame and constitution of our churches is implicitly national. Else if the commonwealth, and church were not one, how could he that is banished from the one, be necessarily banished from the other also?

Reply. It was far from my meaning, and words, when I spake of his banishing of himself from the fellowship of all the churches in the country, to intend his civil banishment. I knew his civil banishment was not merely his own act. I knew also that he might have been banished from the commonwealth, and yet have retained (as some others have done) fellowship with some churches, if not with all the churches in the country. And therefore both his observations are but empty flourishes, and vanish like bubbles. It is the wiliness of the spirit of the serpent, to hide his head under figleaved evasions. . . .

But, saith he, if it be butchery to separate conscientiously and peaceably from the spiritual communion of a church, or Saints, what shall it be called by the Lord Jesus, to cut off persons, them, and theirs, branch, and root, from any civil being in their territories, etc. Because their consciences dare not bow down to any worship, but what the Lord Jesus hath appointed, and being also otherwise subject to the civil estate, and laws thereof?

Here be many extenuations, and mincings of his own carriage, and as many false aggravations of guilt upon his sentence of banishment, and the authors of it.

As, 1. In that he was cut off, he and his, branch and root, from any civil being in these territories, because their consciences durst not bow down to any worship, but what they believe the Lord had appointed: Whereas the truth is, his banishment proceeded not against him, or his, for his own refusal of any worship, but for seditious opposition against the patent, and against the oath of fidelity offered to the people.

2. That he was subject to the civil estate, and laws thereof, when yet he vehemently opposed the civil foundation of the civil estate, which was the patent: and earnestly also opposed the law of the general court, by which the tender of that oath was enjoined: and also wrote letters of admonition to all the churches, whereof the magistrates were members, for deferring to give present answer

to a petition of Salem, who had refused to hearken to a lawful motion of theirs.

3. That he did but separate from the spiritual society of a church, or Saints: whereas he both drew away many others also, and as much as in him lay, separated all the churches from Christ.

4. In that he maketh the cutting off of persons, them and theirs, branch and rush, from civil territories, a far more heinous and odious offence in the eyes of the Lord Jesus, than himself to cut off, not only himself and his, branch and rush, but many of his neighbors (by sedition) from spiritual communion with the churches, and all the churches from communion with Christ. As if the cutting of persons, them and theirs, branch and rush, from the covenant, and spiritual ordinances in the church, were a matter of no account in respect of cutting off from civil liberties in the territories of the commonwealth.

5. In that, what himself did, he predicated as done conscientiously and peaceably, as if what the court had done against him, they had not done conscientiously also, and with regard to public peace, which they saw he disturbed, and stood stiffly in his own course, though he was openly convinced in open court (as I showed before) that he could not maintain his way, but by sinning against the light of his own conscience.

VIEWPOINT 3

"But ... worst of all ... was Mistress Hutchinson's double weekly lecture.... Where ... she would ... vent her mischievous opinions as she pleased."

The Antinomians Are Destroying the Community

Thomas Welde (1595-1661)

Banishing Roger Williams did not end religious dissent and controversy in the Massachusetts Bay Colony. From 1636 to 1638 the Puritan community was sharply divided in what became known as the Antinomian crisis. A key figure in the debate was Anne Hutchinson, the wife of an English merchant who with her husband had followed her English clergyman, John Cotton, to the New World in 1634. She made it a practice following Sunday services to hold meetings at which the Scriptures and Cotton's sermons were discussed. These meetings grew in popularity and resulted in divisions within the Puritan community over who was truly part of God's elect. Hutchinson and her brother-in-law, John Wheelwright, were ultimately excommunicated from their church because of their beliefs. They were forced to leave the colony.

The following summary of events surrounding Anne Hutchinson's banishment was written in 1644 by Thomas Welde, a minister who had taken an active role in the campaign against Hutchinson. Welde had returned to England in 1641 to represent the colony in its dealings with the English government. In 1644

From Thomas Welde's preface to John Winthrop's *A Short Story of the Rise, Reign, and Ruine of the Antinomians, Familists, and Libertines,* 1644.

82

he wrote a preface to a work by John Winthrop directed primarily at English readers, giving the authorities' view of the Antinomian crisis. This viewpoint is excerpted from Welde's preface.

After we had escaped the cruel hands of persecuting prelates, and the dangers at sea, and had prettily well outgrown our wilderness troubles in our first plantings in New England; and when our commonwealth began to be founded, and our churches sweetly settled in peace (God abounding to us in more happy enjoyments than we could have expected), lest we should now grow secure, our wise God (who seldom suffers His own in this their wearisome pilgrimage to be long without trouble) sent a new storm after us, which proved the sorest trial that ever befell us since we left our native soil.

Which was this, that some going thither from hence, full fraught with many unsound and loose opinions, after a time began to open their packs and freely vend their wares to any that would be their customers. Multitudes of men and women, church members and others, having tasted of their commodities were eager after them and were straight infected before they were aware, and some being tainted conveyed the infection to others and thus that plague first began amongst us. . . .

But the last and worst of all, which most suddenly diffused the venom of these opinions into the very veins and vitals of the people in the country, was Mistress Hutchinson's double weekly lecture, which she kept under a pretense of repeating sermons, to which resorted sundry of Boston and other towns about, to the number of fifty, sixty, or eighty at once. Where, after she had repeated the sermon, she would make her comment upon it, vent her mischievous opinions as she pleased, and wreathed the scriptures to her own purpose; where the custom was for her scholars to propound questions and she (gravely sitting in the chair) did make answers thereunto. The great respect she had at first in the hearts of all, and her profitable and sober carriage of matters, for a time made this her practice less suspected by the godly magistrates and elders of the church there, so that it was winked at for a time (though afterward reproved by the Assembly and called into Court), but it held so long, until she had spread her leaven so far that had not providence prevented, it had proved the canker of our peace and ruin of our comforts.

By all these means and cunning slights they used, it came about that those errors were so soon conveyed before we were aware, not only into the church of Boston, where most of these seducers lived, but also into all the parts of the country round about.

These opinions being thus spread and grown to their full ripeness and latitude through the nimbleness and activity of their fomenters, began now to lift up their heads full high, to stare us in the face and to confront all that opposed them.

The Hand of God

John Winthrop's account of the Antinomian crisis, A Short Story of the Rise, Reign, and Ruine of the Antinomians, *first published in 1644, concludes with the assertion that God's justice triumphed at the end.*

Here is to bee seen the presence of God in his Ordinances, when they are faithfully attended according to his holy will, although not free from human infirmities: This *American Jesabel* kept her strength and reputation, even among the people of God, till the hand of Civill Justice laid hold on her, and then shee began evidently to decline, and the faithfull to bee freed from her forgeries; and now in this last act, when shee might have expected (as most likely shee did) by her seeming repentance of her errors, and confessing her undervaluing of the Ordinances of Magistracy and Ministracy, to have redeemed her reputation in point of sincerity, and yet have made good all her former work, and kept open a back doore to have returned to her vomit again, by her paraphrasticall retractions, and denying any change in her judgement, yet such was the presence and blessing of God in his own Ordinance, that this subtilty of Satan was discovered to her utter shame and confusion, and to the setting at liberty of many godly hearts, that had been captivated by her to that day; and that Church which by her means was brought under much infamy, and neere to dissolution, was hereby sweetly repaired, and a hopefull way of establishment, and her dissembled repentance cleerly detected, God giving her up since the sentence of excommunication, to that hardnesse of heart, as shee is not affected with any remorse, but glories in it, and feares not the vengeance of God, which she lyes under, as if God did work contrary to his own word, and loosed from heaven, while his Church had bound upon earth.

And that which added vigor and boldness to them was this, that now by this time they had some of all sorts and quality in all places to defend and patronize them: some of the magistrates, some gentlemen, some scholars and men of learning, some burgesses of our General Court, some of our captains and soldiers, some chief men in towns, and some men eminent for religion, parts, and wit. So that wheresoever the case of the opinions came in agitation, there wanted not patrons to stand up to plead for them; and if any of the opinionists were complained of in the courts for their misdemeanors, or brought before the churches for conviction or censure, still some or other of that party would not only suspend giving their vote against them, but would labor to justify them, side with them, and protest against any sentence that should pass upon them, and so be ready not only to harden the delinquent against all means of conviction, but to raise a mutiny if the major part should carry it against them. So in town meetings, military trainings, and all other societies, yea almost in every family, it was hard if that some or other were not ready to rise up in defense of them, even as of the apple of their own eye.

Now, oh their boldness, pride, insolency, alienations from their old and dearest friends, the disturbances, divisions, contentions they raised amongst us, both in church and state and in families, setting division betwixt husband and wife! Oh the sore censures against all sorts that opposed them, and the contempt they cast upon our godly magistrates, churches, ministers, and all that were set over them when they stood in their way!

Now the faithful ministers of Christ must have dung cast on their faces, and be no better than legal preachers, Baal's priests, Popish factors, scribes, Pharisees, and opposers of Christ himself. Now they must be pointed at, as it were with the finger, and reproached by name—such a church officer is an ignorant man and knows not Christ; such an one is under a covenant of works; such a pastor is a proud man and would make a good persecutor; such a teacher is grossly Popish—so that through these reproaches occasion was given to men to abhor the offerings of the Lord.

Now, one of them in a solemn convention of ministers dared to say to their faces that they did not preach the covenant of free grace and that they themselves had not the seal of the spirit, etc. Now, after our sermons were ended at our public lectures, you might have seen half a dozen pistols discharged at the face of the preacher, I mean so many objections made by the opinionists in the open assembly against our doctrine delivered, if it suited not their new fancies, to the marvelous weakening of holy truths delivered (what in them lay) in the hearts of all the weaker sort; and this done not once and away but from day to day after our sermons. Yea, they would come when they heard a minister was upon such a point as was like to strike at their opinions, with a purpose to oppose him to his face.

Now, you might have seen many of the opinionists rising up and contemptuously turning their backs upon the faithful pastor of that church and going forth from the assembly when he began to pray or preach. . . .

Now, might you have seen open contempt cast upon the face of the whole General Court in subtle words to this very effect: that the magistrates were Ahabs, Amaziahs, scribes, and Pharisees, enemies to Christ, led by Satan, that old enemy of free grace, and that it were better that a millstone were hung about their necks, and they were drowned in the sea, than they should censure one of their judgment, which they were now about to do.

Another of them you might have seen so audaciously insolent, and high flown in spirit and speech, that she bade the Court of Magistrates (when they were about to censure her for her pernicious carriages) take heed what they did to her, for she knew by an infallible revelation that for this act which they were about to pass against her, God would ruin them, their posterity, and that whole commonwealth.

By a little taste of a few passages instead of multitudes here presented, you may see what an height they were grown unto in a short time, and what a spirit of pride, insolency, contempt of authority, division, sedition they were acted by. It was a wonder of mercy that they had not set our commonwealth and churches on a fire, and consumed us all therein.

They being mounted to this height and carried with such a strong hand (as you have heard) and seeing a spirit of pride, subtlety, malice, and contempt of all men that were not of their minds breathing in them (our hearts sadded and our spirits tired), we sighed and groaned to Heaven, we humbled our souls by prayer and fasting that the Lord would find out and bless some means and ways for the cure of this sore and deliver his truth and ourselves from this heavy bondage. Which (when His own time was come) He hearkened unto and in infinite mercy looked upon our sorrows and did, in a wonderful manner, beyond all expectation, free us by these means following.

The Authorities' Response

1. He stirred up all the ministers' spirits in the country to preach against those errors and practices that so much pestered the country to inform, to confute, to rebuke, etc., thereby to cure those that were diseased already and to give antidotes to the rest to preserve them from infection. And though this ordinance went not without its appointed effect in the latter respect, yet we found it not so effectual for the driving away of this infection as we desired for they (most of them) hardened their faces and bent their wits how to oppose and confirm themselves in their way.

2. We spent much time and strength in conference with them, sometimes in private before the elders only, sometimes in our public congregation for all comers. Many, very many hours and half days together we spent therein to see if any means might prevail. We gave them free leave, with all lenity and patience, to lay down what they could say for their opinions, and answered

them, from point to point, and then brought clear arguments from evident scriptures against them and put them to answer us even until they were oftentimes brought to be either silent, or driven to deny common principles, or shuffle off plain scripture. And yet such was their pride and hardness of heart that they would not yield to the truth, but did tell us they would take time to consider our arguments, and in mean space meeting with some of their abetters, strengthened themselves again in their old way, that when we dealt with them next time we found them further off than before, so that our hopes began to languish of reducing them by private means.

The Excommunication of Anne Hutchinson

In March 1638, four months after Anne Hutchinson was sentenced by the General Court to banishment from the colony, she was brought to trial again by the Boston Church in a separate procedure that resulted in her being excommunicated from the congregation. The trial transcript, which has been reprinted in the Proceedings of the Massachusetts Historical Society, *concludes with her notice of excommunication.*

Forasmuch as you, Mrs. Hutchinson, have highly transgressed and offended and forasmuch as you have soe many ways *troubled the Church with your Erors* and have drawen away many a poor soule and have *upheld your Revelations:* and forasmuch as *you have made a Lye*, etc. Therefor in the name of our Lord Jesus Christ and in the name of the Church I doe not only pronounce you worthy to be cast out, but *I doe cast you out* and in the name of Christ *I doe deliver you up to Sathan* that you may learne no more to blaspheme to seduce and to lye. And I doe account you from this time forth to be a Hethen and a Publican and soe to be held of all the Bretheren and Sisters of this Congregation, and of others. Therfor *I command you* in the name of Christ Jesus and of this Church *as a Leper to withdraw your selfe out of the Congregation;* that as formerly you have dispised and contemned the Holy Ordinances of God and turned your Backe one them, soe you may now have no part in them nor benefit by them.

3. Then we had an assembly of all the ministers and learned men in the whole country which held for three weeks together at Cambridge (then called New Town), Mr. Hooker and Mr. Bulkeley (alias Buckley) being chosen moderators, or prolocutors, the magistrates sitting present all that time, as hearers and speakers also when they saw fit. A liberty was also given to any of the country to come in and hear (it being appointed, in great part for the satisfaction of the people), and a place was appointed for all the opinionists to come in and take liberty of speech (only due order observed) as much as any of ourselves had, and as freely.

The first week we spent in confuting the loose opinions that we gathered up in the country. . . . The other fortnight we spent in a plain syllogistical dispute (*ad vulgus* as much as might be), gathering up nine of the chiefest points (on which the rest depended), and disputed of them all in order, pro and con. In the forenoons we framed our arguments and in the afternoons produced them in public, and the next day the adversary gave in their answers and produced also their arguments on the same questions; then we answered them and replied also upon them the next day. . . .

4. Then after this mean was tried, the magistrates saw that neither our preaching, conference, nor yet our assembly meeting did effect the cure, but that still after conference had together the leaders put such life into the rest that they all went on in their former course, not only to disturb the churches but miserably interrupt the civil peace, and that they threw contempt both upon courts and churches, and began now to raise sedition amongst us to the endangering [of] the commonwealth. Hereupon, for these grounds named (and not for their opinions, as themselves falsely reported, and as our godly magistrates have been much traduced here in England), for these reasons (I say) being civil disturbances, the magistrate convents them . . . and censures them. Some were disfranchised, others fined, the incurable amongst them banished.

This was another mean of their subduing, some of the leaders being down and others gone, the rest were weakened, but yet they (for all this) strongly held up their heads many a day after.

God's Displeasure

5. Then God Himself was pleased to step in with His casting voice and bring in His own vote and suffrage from Heaven, by testifying His displeasure against their opinions and practices, as clearly as if He had pointed with His finger, in causing the two fomenting women in the time of the height of the opinions to produce out of their wombs, as before they had out of their brains, such monstrous births as no chronicle (I think) hardly ever recorded the like. Mistress Dyer brought forth her birth of a woman child, a fish, a beast, and a fowl, all woven together in one, and without an head. . . . Mistress Hutchinson being big with child, and growing towards the time of her labor as other women do, she brought forth not one (as Mistress Dyer did) but (which was more strange to amazement) thirty monstrous births or thereabouts at once, some of them bigger, some lesser, some of one shape, some of another, few of any perfect shape, none at all of them (as far as I could ever learn) of human shape. . . .

Now I am upon Mistress Hutchinson's story, I will digress a little to give you a further taste of her spirit. . . . The Church of

Boston sent unto her four of their members, (men of a lovely and winning spirit, as most likely to prevail) to see if they could convince and reduce her, according to 2 Thes. 3. 13. When they came first unto her, she asked from whom they came, and what was their business; They answered, We are come in the name of the Lord Jesus, from the Church of Christ at Boston, to labour to convince you of &c.—At that word she (being filled with as much disdain in her countenance, as bitterness in her spirit) replied, what, from the Church at Boston? I know no such Church, neither will I own it, call it the Whore and Strumpet of Boston, no Church of Christ; so they said no more, seeing her so desperate, but returned. Behold the spirit of error, to what a pass it drives a man!

Providence from Heaven

This loud-speaking providence from Heaven in the monsters, did much awaken many of her followers (especially the tenderer sort) to attend God's meaning therein; and made them at such a stand, that they dared not sleight so manifest a sign from Heaven, that from that time we found many of their ears boared (as they had good cause) to attend to counsel, but others yet followed them.

6. The last stroke that slew the opinions, was the falling away of their leaders.

1. Into more hideous and soul-destroying delusions, which ruin (indeed) all Religion; as, that the souls of men are mortal like the beasts.

That there is no such thing as inherent righteousness.

That these bodies of ours shall not rise again.

That their own revelations of particular events were as infallible as the Scripture, &c.

2. They also grew (many of them) very loose and degenerate in their practices (for these opinions will certainly produce a filthy life by degrees). As no prayer in their families, no Sabbath, insufferable pride, frequent and hideous lying; divers of them being proved guilty, some of five, other of ten gross lies; another falling into a lie, God smote him in the very act, that he sunk down into a deepe swoon, and being by hot waters recovered, and coming to himself, said, Oh God, thou mightst have struck me dead, as Ananias and Saphira, for I have maintained a lie. Mistress Hutchinson and others cast out of the Church for lying, and some guilty of fouler sins than all these, which I here name not.

These things exceedingly amazed their followers, (especially such as were led after them in the simplicity of their hearts, as many were) and now they began to see that they were deluded by them. . . .

Now they would freely discover the sleights the Adversaries had used to undermine them by, and steal away their eyes from the truth and their brethren, which before (whiles their hearts were sealed) they could not see. And the fruit of this was, great praise to the Lord, who had thus wonderfully wrought matters about; gladness in all our hearts and faces, and expressions of our renewed affections by receiving them again into our bosoms, and from that time until now have walked (according to their renewed Covenants) humbly and lovingly amongst us, holding forth Truth and Peace with power.

But for the rest, which (notwithstanding all these means of conviction from heaven and earth, and the example of their seduced brethrens return) yet stood obdurate, yea more hardened (as we had cause to fear) than before; we convented those of them that were members before the Churches, and yet, labored once and again to convince them, not only of their errors, but also of sundry exorbitant practices which they had fallen into; as manifest Pride, contempt of authority, neglecting to fear the Church, and lying, &c. but after no means prevailed, we were driven with sad hearts to give them up to Satan: Yet not simply for their opinions (for which I find we have been slanderously traduced) but the chiefest cause of their censure was their miscarriages (as have been said) persisted in with great obstinacy.

The persons cast out of the churches were about nine or ten, as far as I can remember, who for a space continued very hard and impenitent, but afterward some of them were received into fellowship again, upon their repentance.

These persons cast out, and the rest of the ringleaders that had received sentence of banishment, with many others infected by them, that were neither censured in court nor in churches, went all together out of our jurisdiction and precinct into an island, called Rhode Island (surnamed by some the island of errors), and there they live to this day, most of them, but in great strife and contention in the civil estate and otherwise, hatching and multiplying new opinions, and cannot agree, but are miserably divided into sundry sects and factions.

The Fate of Anne Hutchinson

But Mistress Hutchinson being weary of the island, or rather the island weary of her, departed from thence with all her family, her daughter and her children, to live under the Dutch, near a place called by seamen, and in the map, Hellgate. (And now I am come to the last act of her tragedy, a most heavy stroke upon herself and hers, as I received it very lately from a godly hand in New England.) There the Indians set upon them and slew her and all her family, her daughter, and her daughter's husband, and all their children, save one that escaped (her own husband being dead before), a dreadful blow. Some write that the Indians did burn her to death with fire, her house and all the rest named

90

that belonged to her; but I am not able to affirm by what kind of death they slew her, but slain it seems she is, according to all reports. I never heard that the Indians in those parts did ever before this commit the like outrage upon any one family, or families, and therefore God's hand is the more apparently seen herein, to pick out this woeful woman, to make her and those belonging to her an unheard of heavy example of their cruelty above all others.

VIEWPOINT 4

"Now if you do condemn me for speaking what in my conscience I know to be truth I must commit myself unto the Lord."

The Antinomians Are Following the Spirit of God

Anne Hutchinson (1591-1643) et al.

Anne Hutchinson was one of the key figures of the Antinomian crisis of 1636-1638. Daughter of a dissenting English clergyman, wife of a relatively prosperous English merchant, and mother of fourteen children, she quickly gained standing as a religious lay leader in the Puritan community of Boston, Massachusetts, after moving there from England in 1634. The biweekly meetings held at her home to discuss the sermons of her minister, John Cotton, drew as many as sixty people.

What she and her followers said during those meetings disturbed the leaders of the Massachusetts Bay Colony, including governor John Winthrop and deputy governor Thomas Dudley. They were especially disturbed by suggestions that ministers other than Cotton were in error. Historian Barbara Ritter Dailey writes in *The Reader's Companion to American History:*

> She [Hutchinson] brought attention to Cotton's spirit-centered theology, championing him and her brother-in-law John Wheel-

From the court records of the examination of Anne Hutchinson at the court of Newtown, Massachusetts, November 1637.

wright as true Christian ministers against the "legal" preachers who taught that a moral life was sufficient grounds for salvation. With Cotton and Wheelwright, Hutchinson believed that redemption was God's gift to his elect and could not be earned by human effort.

Hutchinson's activities resulted in a division within the colony between her supporters and opponents. Many of the leaders of the colony viewed her as a threat to the social order of the colony, undoubtedly in part because she was a woman making judgments and statements in areas traditionally the realm of the all-male clergy.

A gathering of ministers questioned and examined Cotton, who was able to moderate his views enough to be cleared of heresy. Hutchinson and Wheelwright were not as accommodating, and both were found guilty of sedition and heresy and were banished from the colony. Testimony from Hutchinson's trial before the General Court of Massachusetts, held in November 1637, is reprinted here; in the absence of written tracts or materials by Hutchinson, it provides one of the few records of her words.

At first Hutchinson was largely able to parry the questions about her views and to confound her questioners when they attempted to pin down heretical ideas. During the second day of her trial, whether from fatigue from the constant questioning or some other cause is not clear, she launched into a long explanation of why she came to New England, claiming that she received direct revelation from the Holy Spirit. For her questioners this was enough evidence to find her guilty of heresy and to banish her from the colony.

Hutchinson moved to Roger Williams's new colony of Rhode Island. She later moved to what is now Long Island, New York, where she and her family were killed by Indians in 1643.

The Examination of Mrs. Ann Hutchinson at the court at Newtown.

Mr. Winthrop, governor. Mrs. Hutchinson, you are called here as one of those that have troubled the peace of the commonwealth and the churches here; you are known to be a woman that hath had a great share in the promoting and divulging of those opinions that are causes of this trouble, and to be nearly joined not only in affinity and affection with some of those the court had taken notice of and passed censure upon, but you have spoken divers things as we have been informed very prejudicial to the honour of the churches and ministers thereof, and you have maintained a meeting and an assembly in your house that hath been condemned by the general assembly as a thing not tolerable nor comely in the sight of God nor fitting for your sex, and notwithstanding that was cried down you have continued the same, therefore we have thought good to send for you to understand how things are, that if you be in an erroneous way we may reduce you that so you may become a profitable member here among us, otherwise if you be obstinate in your course that then the court may take such course that you may trouble us no further, therefore I would intreat you to express whether you do not hold and assent in practice to those opinions and factions that have been handled in court already, that is to say, whether you do not justify Mr. Wheelwright's sermon and the petition.

The 1637 trial of Anne Hutchinson before the General Court of Massachusetts led to her being banished from the colony.

Mrs. Hutchinson. I am called here to answer before you but I hear no things laid to my charge.

Gov. I have told you some already and more I can tell you. (*Mrs. H.*) Name one Sir.

Gov. Have I not named some already?

Mrs. H. What have I said or done?

Gov. Why for your doings, this you did harbour and countenance those that are parties in this faction that you have heard of. (*Mrs H.*) That's matter of conscience, Sir.

Gov. Your conscience you must keep or it must be kept for you.

Mrs. H. Must not I then entertain the saints because I must keep my conscience.

Gov. Say that one brother should commit felony or treason and come to his other brother's house, if he knows him guilty and conceals him he is guilty of the same. It is his conscience to entertain him, but if his conscience comes into act in giving countenance and entertainment to him that hath broken the law he is guilty too. So if you do countenance those that are transgressors of the law you are in the same fact.

Mrs. H. What law do they transgress?

Gov. The law of God and of the state.

Mrs. H. In what particular?

Gov. Why in this among the rest, whereas the Lord doth say honour thy father and thy mother.

Mrs. H. Ey Sir in the Lord. (*Gov.*) This honour you have broke in giving countenance to them.

Mrs. H. In entertaining those did I entertain them against any act (for there is the thing) or what God hath appointed?

Gov. You knew that Mr. Wheelwright did preach this sermon and those that countenance him in this do break a law.

Mrs. H. What law have I broken?

Gov. Why the fifth commandment.

Mrs. H. I deny that for he saith in the Lord.

Gov. You have joined with them in the faction.

Mrs. H. In what faction have I joined with them?

Gov. In presenting the petition.

Mrs. H. Suppose I had set my hand to the petition what then? (*Gov.*) You saw that case tried before.

Mrs. H. But I had not my hand to the petition.

Gov. You have councelled them. (*Mrs. H.*) Wherein?

Gov. Why in entertaining them.

Mrs. H. What breach of law is that Sir?

Gov. Why dishonouring of parents.

Mrs. H. But put the case Sir that I do fear the Lord and my parents, may not I entertain them that fear the Lord because my parents will not give me leave?

Gov. If they be the fathers of the commonwealth, and they of another religion, if you entertain them then you dishonour your parents and are justly punishable.

Mrs. H. If I entertain them, as they have dishonoured their parents I do.

Gov. No but you by countenancing them above others put honor upon them.

Mrs. H. I may put honor upon them as the children of God and as they do honor the Lord.

Gov. We do not mean to discourse with those of your sex but only this; you do adhere unto them and do endeavour to set forward this faction and so you do dishonour us.

Mrs. H. I do acknowledge no such thing neither do I think that I ever put any dishonour upon you.

Gov. Why do you keep such a meeting at your house as you do every week upon a set day?

Mrs. H. It is lawful for me so to do, as it is all your practices and can you find a warrant for yourself and condemn me for the same thing? The ground of my taking it up was, when I first came to this land because I did not go to such meetings as those were, it was presently reported that I did not allow of such meetings but held them unlawful and therefore in that regard they said I was proud and did despise all ordinances, upon that a friend came unto me and told me of it and I to prevent such aspersions took it up, but it was in practice before I came therefore I was not the first.

Gov. For this, that you appeal to our practice you need no confutation. If your meeting had answered to the former it had not been offensive, but I will say that there was no meeting of women alone, but your meeting is of another sort for there are sometimes men among you.

Mrs. H. There was never any man with us.

Gov. Well, admit there was no man at your meeting and that you was sorry for it, there is no warrant for your doings, and by what warrant do you continue such a course?

Biblical Justification

Mrs. H. I conceive there Lyes a clear rule in Titus, that the elder women should instruct the younger and then I must have a time wherein I must do it.

Gov. All this I grant you, I grant you a time for it, but what is this to the purpose that you Mrs. Hutchinson must call a company together from their callings to come to be taught of you?

Mrs. H. Will it please you to answer me this and to give me a rule for then I will willingly submit to any truth. If any come to my house to be instructed in the ways of God what rule have I to put them away?

Gov. But suppose that a hundred men come unto you to be instructed will you forbear to instruct them?

Mrs. H. As far as I conceive I cross a rule in it.

Gov. Very well and do you not so here?

Mrs. H. No Sir for my ground is they are men.

Gov. Men and women all is one for that, but suppose that a man should come and say Mrs. Hutchinson I hear that you are a woman that God hath given his grace unto and you have knowledge in the word of God I pray instruct me a little, ought you not to instruct this man?

Mrs. H. I think I may.—Do you think it not lawful for me to teach women and why do you call me to teach the court?

Gov. We do not call you to teach the court but to lay open yourself.

Mrs. H. I desire you that you would then set me down a rule by which I may put them away that come unto me and so have peace in so doing.

Gov. You must shew your rule to receive them.

Mrs. H. I have done it.

Gov. I deny it because I have brought more arguments than you have.

Mrs. H. I say, to me it is a rule.

[John] Endicot. You say there are some rules unto you. I think there is a contradiction in your own words. What rule for your practice do you bring, only a custom in Boston.

Mrs. H. No Sir that was no rule to me but if you look upon the rule in Titus it is a rule to me. If you convince me that it is no rule I shall yield.

Gov. You know that there is no rule that crosses another, but this rule crosses that in the Corinthians. But you must take it in this sense that elder women must instruct the younger about their business, and to love their husbands and not to make them to clash.

Mrs. H. I do not conceive but that it is meant for some publick times.

Gov. Well, have you no more to say but this?

Mrs. H. I have said sufficient for my practice.

Gov. Your course is not to be suffered for, besides that we find such a course as this to be greatly prejudicial to the state, besides the occasion that it is to seduce many honest persons that are called to those meetings and your opinions being known to be different from the word of God may seduce many simple souls that resort unto you, besides that the occasion which hath come of late hath come from none but such as have frequented your meetings, so that now they are flown off from magistrates and ministers and this since they have come to you, and besides that it will not well stand with the commonwealth that families should be neglected for so many neighbours and dames and so much time spent, we see no rule of God for this, we see not that any should have authority to set up any other exercises besides what authority hath already set up and so what hurt comes of this you will be guilty of and we for suffering you.

Mrs. H. Sir I do not believe that to be so.

Gov. Well, we see how it is we must therefore put it away from you, or restrain you from maintaining this course.

Mrs. H. If you have a rule for it from God's word you may.

Gov. We are your judges, and not you ours and we must compel you to it.

Ms. H. If it please you by authority to put it down I will freely let you for I am subject to your authority.

[Simon] Bradstreet. I would ask this question of Mrs. Hutchinson, whether you do think this is lawful? for then this will follow that all other women that do not are in a sin.

Mrs. H. I conceive this is a free will offering.

Bradst. If it be a free will offering you ought to forbear it because it gives offence.

Mrs. H. Sir, in regard of myself I could, but for others I do not yet see light but shall further consider of it.

Bradst. I am not against all women's meetings but do think them to be lawful.

The Meetings

[Thomas] Dudley, dep. gov. Here hath been much spoken concerning Mrs. Hutchinson's meetings and among other answers she saith that men come not there, I would ask you this one question then, whether never any man was at your meeting?

Gov. There are two meetings kept at their house.

Dep. Gov. How; is there two meetings?

Mrs. H. Ey Sir, I shall not equivocate, there is a meeting of men and women and there is a meeting only for women.

Dep. Gov. Are they both constant?

Mrs. H. No, but upon occasions they are deferred.

Mr. Endicot. Who teaches in the men's meetings none but men, do not women sometimes?

Mrs. H. Never as I heard, not one.

Dep. Gov. I would go a little higher with Mrs. Hutchinson. About three years ago we were all in peace. Mrs. Hutchinson from that time she came hath made a disturbance, and some that came over with her in the ship did inform me what she was as soon as she was landed. I being then in place dealt with the pastor and teacher of Boston and desired them to enquire of her, and then I was satisfied that she held nothing different from us, but within half a year after, she had vented divers of her strange opinions and had made parties in the country, and at length it comes that Mr. Cotton and Mr. Vane were of her judgment, but Mr. Cotton hath cleared himself that he was not of that mind, but now it appears by this woman's meeting that Mrs. Hutchinson hath so forestalled the minds of many by their resort to her meeting that now she hath a potent party in the country. Now if all these things have endangered us as from that foundation and if she in particular hath disparaged all our ministers in the land that they have preached a covenant of works, and only Mr. Cotton a covenant of grace, why this is not to be suffered, and therefore being driven to the foundation and it being found that Mrs. Hutchinson is she that hath depraved all the ministers and hath been the cause of what is fallen out, why we must take away the foundation and the building will fall.

Mrs. H. I pray Sir prove it that I said they preached nothing but a covenant of works.

Dep. Gov. Nothing but a covenant of works, why a Jesuit may

A Petition Supporting John Wheelwright

The petition that John Winthrop refers to in cross-examining Anne Hutchinson was presented to the General Court in March 1637 in support of John Wheelwright, a minister and brother-in-law of Hutchinson who was also ultimately banished for his religious views. Although the signers of the petition were supporters of both Wheelwright and Hutchinson, she did not sign the document herself.

Whereas our deare Brother is censured of sedition; wee beseech your Worships to consider, that either the person condemned must bee culpable of some seditious fact, or his doctrine must bee seditious, or must breed sedition in the hearts of his hearers or else wee know not upon what grounds hee should bee censured. Now to the first, wee have not heard any that have witnessed against our brother for any seditious fact. Secondly, neither was the doctrine it selfe, being no other but the very expressions of the Holy Ghost himselfe, and therefore cannot justly be branded with sedition. Thirdly, if you look at the effects of his Doctrine upon the hearers, it hath not stirred up sedition in us, not so much as by accident; wee have not drawn the sword, as sometimes *Peter* did, rashly, neither have wee rescued our innocent Brother, as sometimes the *Israelites* did *Jonathan*, and yet they did not seditiously. The Covenant of free Grace held forth by our Brother, hath taught us rather to become humble suppliants to your Worships, and if wee should not prevaile, wee would rather with patience give our cheekes to the smiters. Since therefore the Teacher, the Doctrine, and the hearers bee most free from sedition (as wee conceive) wee humbly beseech you in the name of the Lord Jesus Christ, your Judge and ours, and for the honour of this Court, and the proceedings thereof, that you will bee pleased either to make it appeare to us, and to all the world, to whom the knowledge of all these things will come, wherein the sedition lies, or else acquit our Brother of such a censure.

---

preach truth sometimes.

Mrs. H. Did I ever say they preached a covenant of works then?

Dep. Gov. If they do not preach a covenant of grace clearly, then they preach a covenant of works.

Mrs. H. No Sir, one may preach a covenant of grace more clearly than another, so I said.

Dep. Gov. We are not upon that now but upon position.

Mrs. H. Prove this then Sir that you say I said.

Accusations and Denials

Dep. Gov. When they do preach a covenant of works do they preach truth?

Mrs. H. Yes Sir, but when they preach a covenant of works for salvation, that is not truth.

Dep. Gov. I do but ask you this, when the ministers do preach a covenant of works do they preach a way of salvation?

Mrs. H. I did not come hither to answer to questions of that sort.

Dep. Gov. Because you will deny the thing.

Mrs. H. Ey, but that is to be proved first.

Dep. Gov. I will make it plain that you did say that the ministers did preach a covenant of works.

Mrs. H. I deny that.

Dep. Gov. And that you said they were not able ministers of the new testament, but Mr. Cotton only.

Mrs. H. If ever I spake that I proved it by God's word.

Court. Very well, very well.

Mrs. H. If one shall come unto me in private, and desire me seriously to tell them what I thought of such an one. I must either speak false or true in my answer.

Dep. Gov. Likewise I will prove this that you said the gospel in the letter and words holds forth nothing but a covenant of works and that all that do not hold as you do are in a covenant of works.

Mrs. H. I deny this for if I should so say I should speak against my own judgment.

Mr. Endicot. I desire to speak seeing Mrs. Hutchinson seems to lay something against them that are to witness against her.

Gov. Only I would add this. It is well discerned to the court that Mrs. Hutchinson can tell when to speak and when to hold her tongue. Upon the answering of a question which we desire her to tell her thoughts of she desires to be pardoned.

Mrs. H. It is one thing for me to come before a public magistracy and there to speak what they would have me to speak and another when a man comes to me in a way of friendship privately there is difference in that. . . .

Gov. Here are six undeniable ministers who say it is true and yet you deny that you did say that they did preach a covenant of works and that they were not able ministers of the gospel, and it appears plainly that you have spoken it, and whereas you say that it was drawn from you in a way of friendship, you did profess then that it was out of conscience that you spake and said The fear of man is a snare wherefore should I be afraid, I will speak plainly and freely.

Mrs. H. That I absolutely deny, for the first question was thus answered by me to them. They thought that I did conceive there was a difference between them and Mr. Cotton. At the first I was somewhat reserved, then said Mr. Peters I pray answer the question directly as fully and as plainly as you desire we should tell you our minds. Mrs. Hutchinson we come for plain dealing and telling you our hearts. Then I said I would deal as plainly as I could, and whereas they say I said they were under a covenant of works and in the state of the apostles why these two speeches cross one another. I might say they might preach a covenant of works as did the apostles, but to preach a covenant of works and to be under a covenant of works is another business.

Dep. Gov. There have been six witnesses to prove this and yet you deny it.

Mrs. H. I deny that these were the first words that were spoken.

Gov. You make the case worse, for you clearly shew that the ground of your opening your mind was not to satisfy them but to satisfy your own conscience. . . .

Mrs. H. I acknowledge using the words of the apostle to the Corinthians unto him, that they that were ministers of the letter and not the spirit did preach a covenant of works. Upon his saying there was no such scripture, then I fetched the Bible and shewed him this place 2 Cor. iii. 6. He said that was the letter of the law. No said I it is the letter of the gospel.

Gov. You have spoken this more than once then.

Mrs. H. Then upon further discourse about proving a good estate and holding it out by the manifestation of the spirit he did acknowledge that to be the nearest way, but yet said he, will you not acknowledge that which we hold forth to be a way too wherein we may have hope; no truly if that be a way it is a way to hell.

Gov. Mrs. Hutchinson, the court you see hath laboured to bring you to acknowledge the error of your way that so you might be reduced, the time now grows late, we shall therefore give you a little more time to consider of it and therefore desire that you attend the court again in the morning.

The next morning.

Gov. We proceeded the last night as far as we could in hearing of this cause of Mrs. Hutchinson. There were divers things laid to her charge, her ordinary meetings about religious exercises, her speeches in derogation of the ministers among us, and the weaking of the hands and hearts of the people towards them. Here was sufficient proof made of that which she was accused of in that point concerning the ministers and their ministry, as that they did preach a covenant of works when others did preach a covenant of grace, and that they were not able ministers of the new testament, and that they had not the seal of the spirit, and this was spoken not as was pretended out of private conference, but out of conscience and warrant from scripture alledged the fear of man is a snare and seeing God had given her a calling to it she would freely speak. Some other speeches she used, as that the letter of the scripture held forth a covenant of works, and this is offered to be proved by probable grounds. If there be anything else that the court hath to say they may speak. . . .

The Spirit of God

Mrs. H. If you please to give me leave I shall give you the ground of what I know to be true. Being much troubled to see the falseness of the constitution of the church of England, I had like to have turned separatist; whereupon I kept a day of solemn humiliation and pondering of the thing; this scripture was brought unto me—he that denies Jesus Christ to be come in the flesh is antichrist—This I considered of and in considering found that the papists did not deny him to be come in the flesh, nor we did not deny him—who then was antichrist? Was the Turk antichrist only? The Lord knows that I could not open scripture; he must by his prophetical office open it unto me. So after that being unsatisfied in the thing, the Lord was pleased to bring this scripture out of the Hebrews. He that denies the testament denies the testator, and in this did open unto me and give me to see that those which did not teach the new covenant had the spirit of antichrist, and upon this he did discover the ministry unto me and ever since. I bless the Lord, he hath let me see which was the clear ministry and which the wrong. Since that time I confess I have been more choice and he hath let me to distinguish between the voice of my beloved and the voice of Moses, the voice of John Baptist and the voice of antichrist, for all those voices are spoken of in scripture. Now if you do condemn me for speaking what in my conscience I know to be truth I must commit myself unto the Lord.

Mr. Nowell. How do you know that that was the spirit?

Mrs. H. How did Abraham know that it was God that bid him offer his son, being a breach of the sixth commandment?

Dep. Gov. By an immediate voice.

Mrs. H. So to me by an immediate revelation.

Dep. Gov. How! an immediate revelation.

Mrs. H. By the voice of his own spirit to my soul. I will give you another scripture, Jer. 46 27, 28—out of which the Lord shewed me what he would do for me and the rest of his servants—But after he was pleased to reveal himself to me I did presently like Abraham run to Hagar. And after that he did let me see the atheism of my own heart, for which I begged of the Lord that it might not remain in my heart, and being thus, he did shew me this (a twelvemonth after) which I told you of before. Ever since that time I have been confident of what he hath revealed unto me.

[*Text obliterated*] another place out of Daniel chap. 7. and he and for us all, wherein he shewed me the sitting of the judgment and the standing of all high and low before the Lord and how thrones and kingdoms were cast down before him. When our teacher came to New-England it was a great trouble unto me, my brother Wheelwright being put by also. I was then much troubled concerning the ministry under which I lived, and then that place in the 30th of Isaiah was brought to my mind. Though the Lord give thee bread of adversity and water of affliction yet shall not thy teachers be removed into corners any more, but thine eyes shall see thy teachers. The Lord giving me this promise and they being gone there was none then left that I was able to hear, and I could not be at rest but I must come hither. Yet that place of Isaiah did much follow me, though the Lord give thee the bread of adversity and water of affliction. This place lying I say upon me then this place in Daniel was brought unto me and did shew me that though I should meet with affliction yet I am the same God that delivered Daniel out of the lion's den, I will also deliver thee. —Therefore I desire you to look to it, for you see this scripture fulfilled this day and therefore I desire you that as you tender the Lord and the church and commonwealth to consider and look what you do. You have power over my body but the Lord Jesus hath power over my body and soul, and assure yourselves thus much, you do as much as in you lies to put the Lord Jesus Christ from you, and if you go on in this course you begin you will bring a curse upon you and your posterity, and the mouth of the Lord hath spoken it. . . .

The Verdict

Gov. The court hath already declared themselves satisfied concerning the things you hear, and concerning the troublesomeness of her spirit and the danger of her course amongst us, which is not to be suffered. Therefore if it be the mind of the court that Mrs. Hutchinson for these things that appear before us is unfit for our society, and if it be the mind of the court that she shall be banished out of our liberties and imprisoned till she be sent away, let them hold up their hands.

All but three. . . .

Mrs Hutchinson, the sentence of the court you hear is that you are banished from out of our jurisdiction as being a woman not fit for our society, and are to be imprisoned till the court shall send you away.

Mrs. H. I desire to know wherefore I am banished?

Gov. Say no more, the court knows wherefore and is satisfied.

VIEWPOINT 5

"The intent of the law is to preserve the body; and for this end to have none received into any fellowship . . . who are likely to disturb the same."

Immigration to Massachusetts Should Be Restricted

John Winthrop (1588-1649)

In May 1637 the Massachusetts General Court, the governing body of the colony, issued an order that stipulated that "none should be received to inhabit within this jurisdiction but such as should be allowed by some of the magistrates." At the time the colony was rife with division between supporters (called Antinomians) and opponents of Anne Hutchinson, a religious lay leader who had charged that the colony was straying from its spiritual roots. Governor John Winthrop wrote in his journal that "it was very probable that [the Antinomians] expected many of their opinion to come out of England." The new rules, making immigration contingent on approval by Winthrop and his followers in power, were designed to prevent such an occurrence.

The new immigration rules caused an outcry by such people as former governor Henry Vane, a supporter of Anne Hutchinson, who called the order tyranny. Winthrop, responding to criticism, wrote "A Defense of an Order of Court Made in the Year 1637," in which he argued that the law was necessary to preserve the Puritan community they were all attempting to create.

From John Winthrop, *The Winthrop Papers*. Volume 3. Edited by Allyn B. Forbes. Boston: Massachusetts Historical Society, 1943. Courtesy of the Massachusetts Historical Society.

A *Declaration of the Intent and Equity of the Order Made at the Last Court, to This Effect, That None Should Be Received to Inhabit Within This Jurisdiction but Such as Should Be Allowed by Some of the Magistrates*

For clearing of such scruples as have arisen about this order, it is to be considered, first, what is the essential form of a commonweal or body politic such as this is, which I conceive to be this: The consent of a certain company of people, to cohabit together, under one government, for their mutual safety and welfare.

In this description all these things do concur to the well-being of such a body: (1) persons; (2) place; (3) consent; (4) government or order; (5) welfare.

It is clearly agreed, by all, that the care of safety and welfare was the original cause or occasion of commonweal and of many families subjecting themselves to rulers and laws; for no man has lawful power over another, but by birth or consent, so likewise, by the law of propriety, no man can have just interest in that which belongs to another, without his consent.

Fundamental Conclusions

From the premises will arise these conclusions.

1. No commonweal can be founded but by free consent.

2. The persons so incorporating have a public and relative interest each in other, and in the place of their cohabitation and goods, and laws, etc., and in all the means of their welfare so as none other can claim privilege with them but by free consent.

3. The nature of such an incorporation ties every member thereof to seek out and entertain all means that may conduce to the welfare of the body, and to keep off whatsoever does appear to tend to their damage.

4. The welfare of the whole is to be put to apparent hazard for the advantage of any particular members.

From these conclusions I thus reason.

1. If we here be a corporation established by free consent, if the place of our cohabitation be our own, then no man has right to come into us, etc., without our consent.

2. If no man has right to our lands, our government privileges, etc., but by our consent, then it is reason we should take notice of before we confer any such upon them.

3. If we are bound to keep off whatsoever appears to tend to our ruin or damage, then we may lawfully refuse to receive such whose dispositions suit not with ours and whose society (we know) will be hurtful to us, and therefore it is lawful to take knowledge of all men before we receive them.

4. The churches take liberty (as lawfully they may) to receive or reject at their discretion; yea, particular towns make orders to the like effect; why then should the commonweal be denied the like liberty, and the whole more restrained than any part?

In addition to immigration restrictions, Puritan leaders sought to enforce social conformity by means of such devices as the pillory.

5. If it be sin in us to deny some men place, etc., among us, then it is because of some right they have to this place, etc., for to deny a man that which he has no right unto is neither sin nor injury.

6. If strangers have right to our houses or lands, etc., then it is either of justice or of mercy; if of justice, let them plead it, and we shall know what to answer; but if it be only in way of mercy, or by the rule of hospitality, etc., then I answer: (1) A man is not a fit object of mercy except he be in misery. (2) We are not bound to exercise mercy to others to the ruin of ourselves. (3) There are few that stand in need of mercy at their first coming hither. As for hospitality, that rule does not bind further than for some present occasion, not for continual residence.

Family Matters

7. A family is a little commonwealth, and a commonwealth is a great family. Now as a family is not bound to entertain all comers, no not every good man (otherwise than by way of hospitality) no more is a commonwealth.

8. It is a general received rule, *turpius ejicitur quam non admittitur hospes, [i.e.]* it is worse to receive a man whom we must cast

107

out again than to deny him admittance.

9. The rule of the apostle (John 2:10) is that such as come and bring not the true doctrine with them should not be received to house, and by the same reason not into the commonweal.

10. . . . The intent of the law is to preserve the welfare of the body; and for this end to have none received into any fellowship with it who are likely to disturb the same, and this intent (I am sure) is lawful and good. Now, then, if such to whom the keeping of this law is committed be persuaded in their judgments that such a man is likely to disturb and hinder the public weal, but some others who are not in the same trust judge otherwise, yet they are to follow their own judgments rather than the judgments of others who are not alike interested; as in trial of an offender by jury, the twelve men are satisfied in their consciences, upon the evidence given, that the party deserves death; but there are twenty or forty standersby who conceive otherwise, yet is the jury bound to condemn him according to their own consciences, and not to acquit him upon the different opinion of other men, except their reasons can convince them of the error of their consciences, and this is according to the rule of the apostle (Rom. 14:5). Let every man be fully persuaded in his own mind.

If it be objected that some profane persons are received and others who are religious are rejected, I answer: (1) It is not known that any such thing has as yet fallen out. (2) Such a practice may be justifiable as the case may be, for younger persons (even profane ones) may be of less danger to the commonweal (and to the churches also) than some older persons, though professors of religion; for our Savior Christ, when he conversed with publicans, etc., says that such were nearer the Kingdom of Heaven than the religious Pharisees, and one that is of large parts and confirmed in some erroneous way is likely to do more harm to church and commonweal, and is of less hope to be reclaimed, than persons who have not yet become hardened, in the contempt of the means of grace.

Rejecting Good Christians

Lastly, whereas it is objected that by this law we reject good Christians and, so consequently, Christ himself; I answer: (1) It is not known that any Christian man has been rejected. (2) A man that is a true Christian may be denied residence among us, in some cases, without rejecting Christ, as admit a true Christian should come over and should maintain community of goods, or that magistrates ought not to punish the breakers of the first table, or the members of churches for criminal offenses; or that no man were bound to be subject to those laws or magistrates to which they should not give an explicit consent, etc. I hope no man will say that not to receive such an one were to reject Christ; for such opinions (though being maintained in simple ignorance, they might stand with a state of grace yet) they may be so dangerous to the public weal, in many respects, as it would be our sin and unfaithfulness to receive such among us, except it were for trial of their reformation. I would demand then in the case in question (for it is bootless curiosity to refrain openness in things public), whereas it is said that this law was made of purpose to keep away such as are of Mr. [John] Wheelwright his judgment (admit it were so which yet I cannot confess), where is the evil of it? If we conceive and find by sad experience that his opinions are such, as by his own profession cannot stand with external peace, may we not provide for our peace by keeping of such as would strengthen him and infect others with such dangerous tenets? And if we find his opinions such as will cause divisions and make people look at their magistrates, ministers, and brethren as enemies to Christ and antichrists, etc., were it not sin and unfaithfulness in us to receive more of those opinions, which we already find the evil fruit of? Nay, why do not those who now complain join with us in keeping out of such, as well as formerly they did in expelling Mr. [Roger] Williams for the like, though less dangerous? Where this change of their judgments should arise, I leave them to themselves to examine, and I earnestly entreat them so to do; and for this law let the equally minded judge what evil they find in it, or in the practice of those who are betrusted with the execution of it.

VIEWPOINT 6

"This law we judge to be most wicked and sinful."

Immigration Restrictions Are Unfair

Henry Vane (1613-1662)

Henry Vane, the son of an adviser to King Charles I in England, converted to Puritanism while young and emigrated to Massachusetts in 1635. The following year he was elected to the governorship at the age of twenty-two, in part because of his powerful connections in England. His American political career was cut short when he sided with Anne Hutchinson against John Winthrop in the Antinomian controversy, and he returned to England in 1637. Shortly before his return he wrote a tract attacking the immigration restrictions established by Winthrop and other Puritan leaders, questioning the concepts of community and liberty promulgated by them.

Vane went on to become one of the leading parliamentary and political figures of the English revolution during which Charles I was beheaded and the monarchy was replaced by a Protectorate under English Puritan leader Oliver Cromwell. Following Cromwell's death and the restoration of the monarchy under Charles II, Vane himself was executed for treason.

Henry Vane, "A Brief Answer to a Certain Declaration, Made of the Intent and Equity of the Order of the Court, That None Should Be Received to Inhabit Within This Jurisdiction but Such as Should Be Allowed by Some of the Magistrates." In Thomas Hutchinson, *A Collection of Papers Relating to the History of Massachusetts Bay*. Boston, 1769.

A Brief Answer to a Certain Declaration, Made of the Intent and Equity of the Order of the Court, That None Should Be Received to Inhabit within This Jurisdiction but Such As Should Be Allowed by Some of the Magistrates . . .

. . . The description which is set down in effect [in Winthrop's *Defense of an Order of Court*] is this: A commonwealth is a certain company of people consenting to cohabit together under one government, for their mutual safety and welfare. In which description this main fault is found. At the best it is but a description of a commonwealth at large, and not of such a commonwealth as this (as is said), which is not only Christian, but dependent upon the grant also of our sovereign; for so are the express words of that order of court to which the whole country was required to subscribe. . .

The commonwealth here described may be a company of Turkish pirates as well as Christian professors, unless the consent and government be better limited than it is in this definition; for sure it is, all pagans and infidels, even the Indians here amongst us, may come within this compass. And is this such a body politic as ours, as you say? God forbid. Our commonwealth we fear would be twice miserable, if Christ and the king should be shut out so. Reasons taken from the nature of a commonwealth not founded upon Christ, nor by his majesty's charters, must needs fall to the ground, and fail those that rely upon them . . .

This law we judge to be most wicked and sinful, and that for these reasons.

1. Because this law doth leave these weighty matters of the commonwealth, of receiving or rejecting such as come over, to the approbation of magistrates, and suspends these things upon the judgment of man, whereas the judgment is God's (Deuteronomy 1:17) . . .

2. Because here is liberty given by this law to expel and reject those which are most eminent Christians, if they suit not with the disposition of the magistrates, whereby it will come to pass, that Christ and his members will find worse entertainment amongst us than the Israelites did amongst the Egyptians and Babylonians . . .

3. This law doth cross many laws of Christ. Christ would have us render unto Caesar the things that are Caesar's (Matthew 22:21). But this law will not give unto the king's majesty his right of planting some of his subjects amongst us, except they please them. Christ bids us not to forget to entertain strangers (Hebrews 13:2.). But here by this law we must not entertain, for any continuance of time, such strangers as the magistrates like not, though they be never so gracious, allowed of both by God and good men.

VIEWPOINT 7

"It doth not a little grieve my spirit to hear what sad things are reported daily of your tyranny and persecutions in New England."

The Puritans Should Be More Tolerant

Richard Saltonstall

The question of how to deal with challenges to orthodox Puritan theology and ideas was a continuing concern of many leaders of the New England Puritans. Ironically, during this same period the Puritans in England were moving toward increasing toleration of differing beliefs. This was partly a result of circumstances: The English Puritans, embroiled in a civil war and the problems of governing a nation, learned to compromise with each other and with other religious groups in order to survive. They did not have the option the American Puritans had of simply banishing dissenters from the community.

Some of the differences between English and American Puritan views can be seen in the following viewpoint by Richard Saltonstall, a former resident of New England who in 1650 composed a letter to his "much esteemed friends Mr. [John] Cotton and Mr. [John] Wilson, preachers to the church which is at Boston in New-England." Saltonstall criticizes what he views as unwarranted punishments of religious differences.

Richard Saltonstall's letter to John Cotton and John Wilson in 1650. In *Hutchinson Papers.* Volume 2. Albany, NY: Prince Society, 1865.

Reverend and dear friends, whom I unfeignedly love and respect:

It doth not a little grieve my spirit to hear what sad things are reported daily of your tyranny and persecutions in New England, as that you fine, whip, and imprison men for their consciences. First, you compel such to come into your assemblies as you know will not join with you in your worship, and when they shew their dislike thereof or witness against it, then you stir up your magistrates to punish them for such (as you conceive) their public affronts. Truly, friends, this your practice of compelling any in matters of worship to do that whereof they are not fully persuaded is to make them sin, for so the Apostle (Rom. 14 and 23) tells us, and many are made hypocrites thereby, conforming in their outward man for fear of punishment. We pray for you and wish you prosperity every way, hoped the Lord would have given you so much light and love there that you might have been eyes to God's people here, and not to practice those courses in a wilderness which you went so far to prevent. These rigid ways have laid you very low in the hearts of the saints. I do assure you I have heard them pray in the public assemblies that the Lord would give you meek and humble spirits, not to strive so much for uniformity as to keep the unity of the spirit in the bond of peace.

Some Foundations of Religion

When I was in Holland about the beginning of our wars, I remember some Christians there that then had serious thoughts of planting in New England desired me to write to the governor thereof to know if those that differ from you in opinion, yet holding the same foundation in religion, as Anabaptists, Seekers, Antinomians, and the like, might be permitted to live among you, to which I received this short answer from your then governor, Mr. Dudley: God forbid (said he) our love for the truth should be grown so cold that we should tolerate errors. And when (for satisfaction of myself and others) I desired to know your grounds, he referred me to the books written here between the Presbyterians and Independents, which if that had been sufficient, I needed not have sent so far to understand the reasons of your practice. I hope you do not assume to yourselves infallibility of judgment when the most learned of the Apostles confesseth he knew but in part and saw but darkly as through a glass. For God is light, and no further than he doth illuminate us can we see, be our parts and learning never so great. Oh that all those who are brethren, though yet they cannot think and speak the

A Story of Persecution

Many targets of Puritan prosecution were Baptists (or Anabaptists)—people who denied the validity of infant baptism and argued that that sacrament was meant only for converted adult believers. Preaching Baptist doctrine was made a criminal offense by the Massachusetts General Court in 1644. In 1651 three Baptists, John Clarke, Obadiah Holmes, and John Crandall, arrived in the town of Lynn, Massachusetts, at the invitation of William Witter, where they led services at Witter's house. They were arrested and sentenced to be fined or whipped. Clarke wrote of their experiences in a 1652 pamphlet, Ill-Newes from New England. *Clarke hoped in vain that the tract published in England would persuade the English authorities to force Massachusetts to end such intolerance.*

After my sentence [a fine of twenty pounds] was read, the sentences of the other two were likewise pronounced; the sentence of Obadiah Holmes was to pay by the aforesaid time thirty pounds, or be well whipped; and the sentence of John Crandall was to pay five pounds, or be well whipped. This being done, I desired to know whether I might not speak a few things to the court. . . . I said . . . we are strangers and strangers to your laws, and may be transgressors of them before we are aware; we would, therefore, desire this courtesy of you as strangers, that you would show us the law by which we are transgressors. . . . At length the governor [John Endecott] stepped up, and told us we had denied Infant Baptism, and being somewhat transported, broke forth and told me I had deserved death, and said, he "would not have such trash brought into their jurisdiction." Moreover, he said, "you go up and down and secretly insinuate into those that are weak, but you cannot maintain it before our ministers, you may try, and discourse or dispute with them, etc." To this I had much to reply, but that he commanded the jailor to take us away. . . .

This tragedy being thus enacted in the face of the country, must needs awaken and rouse up the minds and spirits of many, cause said thoughts to arise in their hearts, and to flow forth at their mouths as men offended to see strangers professing godliness so discourteously used, for no civil transgression, but merely for conscience.

same things, might be of one accord in the Lord. Now the God of patience and consolation grant you to be thus minded towards one another, after the example of Jesus Christ our blessed Saviour, in whose everlasting arms of protection he leaves you who will never leave to be

Your truly and much affectionate friend in the nearest union,

Richard Saltonstall

VIEWPOINT 8

"We are loath to be blown up and down (like chaff) by every wind of new notions."

The Puritans Are Not Too Intolerant

John Cotton (1584-1652)

John Cotton preached the farewell sermon to John Winthrop's fleet in 1630. Two years later he joined Winthrop in Boston, Massachusetts. From 1633 to 1652 he was the teaching pastor of First Church in Boston and was widely regarded as one of the spiritual leaders of the Puritan community. He wrote pamphlets, theological works, and children's catechisms, and he participated in drawing up the Cambridge Platform of 1648, which became the basic organizational plan for American Congregational churches.

The following viewpoint is taken from a letter he wrote around 1650 in response to a letter by Richard Saltonstall, an English Puritan minister, which had criticized religious intolerance. Cotton defends laws of compulsory worship attendance and other practices as a necessary part of creating and maintaining a righteous community.

John Cotton's reply to Saltonstall's letter. In *Hutchinson Papers*. Volume 2. Albany, NY: Prince Society, 1865.

Honored and dear Sir:

My brother Wilson and self do both of us acknowledge your love . . . in the late lines we received from you. . . . [As to] the complaints you hear . . . against our tyranny and persecutions in fining, whipping, and imprisoning men for their consciences, be pleased to understand we look at such complaints as altogether injurious in respect of ourselves, who had no hand or tongue at all to promote either the coming of the persons you aim at into our assemblies, or their punishment for their carriage there. Righteous judgment will not take up reports, much less reproaches, against the innocent. The cry of the sins of Sodom was great and loud and reached up to heaven, yet the righteous God (giving us an example what to do in the like case), He would first go down to see whether their crime were altogether according to the cry before He would proceed to judgment (Gen. 18:20, 21), and when He did find the truth of the cry, He did not wrap up all alike promiscuously in the judgment, but spared such as He found innocent. We are amongst those whom (if you knew us better) you would account of (as the matron of Abel spake of herself) peaceable in Israel, 2 Sam. 20:19.

People Treated Justly

Yet neither are we so vast in our indulgence or toleration as to think the men you speak of suffered an unjust censure. For one of them (Obadiah Holmes) being an excommunicate person himself, out of a church in Plymouth patent, came into this jurisdiction and took upon him to baptize, which I think himself will not say he was compelled here to perform. And he was not ignorant that the rebaptizing of an elder person, and that by a private person out of [church] office and under excommunication, are all of them manifest contestations against the order and government of our churches established (we know) by God's law, and (he knoweth) by the laws of the country. And we conceive we may safely appeal to the ingenuity of your own judgment whether it would be tolerated in any civil state for a stranger to come and practice contrary to the known principles of their church-estate? As for his whipping, it was more voluntarily chosen by him than inflicted on him. His censure by the court was to have paid (as I know) thirty pounds or else to be whipped. His fine was offered to be paid by friends for him freely, but he chose rather to be whipped; in which case, if his suffering of stripes was any worship of God at all, surely it could be accounted no better than will-worship. The other (Mr. Clarke) was wiser in that point, and his offense was less, so was his fine less, and himself (as I hear) was contented to have it paid for him, whereupon he was released. The imprisonment of either of them was no detriment. I believe they fared neither of them better at home, and I am sure Holmes had not been so well clad of many years before.

But be pleased to consider this point a little further. You think to compel men in matter of worship is to make men sin, according to Rom. 14:23. If the worship be lawful in itself, the magistrate compelling him to come to it compelleth him not to sin, but the sin is in his will that needs to be compelled to a Christian duty. Josiah compelled all Israel, or (which is all one) made to serve the Lord their God, 2 Chron. 34:33, yet his act herein was not blamed but recorded amongst his virtuous actions. For a governor to suffer any within his gates to profane the Sabbath is a sin against the fourth commandment, both in the private householder and in the magistrate; and if he requires them to present themselves before the Lord, the magistrate sinneth not, nor doth the subject sin so

The Evils of Toleration

Nathaniel Ward, a member of the clergy in Massachusetts, was disturbed by the growth of religious tolerance in England. In 1645 he wrote The Simple Cobler of Aggawam in America, *a tract that in blunt and colorful language decried religious toleration and defended Massachusetts's practice of punishing religious dissent.*

My heart has naturally detested four things: The standing of the Apocrypha in the Bible; foreigners dwelling in my country, to crowd our native subjects into the corners of the earth; alchemized coins; tolerations of diverse religions, or of one religion in segregant shapes. He that willingly assents to the last, if he examines his heart by daylight, his conscience will tell him he is either an atheist, or a heretic, or a hypocrite, or at best a captive to some lust. Poly-piety is the greatest impiety in the world. True religion is *ignis probationis,* which does *congregare homogenea segregare heterogenea* [ordeal by fire, which draws together the like and separates the unlike]. . . .

He that is willing to tolerate any religion, or discrepant way of religion, besides his own, unless it be in matters merely indifferent, either doubts of his own or is not sincere in it.

He that is willing to tolerate any unsound opinion, that his own may also be tolerated, though never so sound, will for a need hang God's Bible at the devil's girdle.

Every toleration of false religions or opinions has as many errors and sins in it as all the false religions and opinions it tolerates, and one sound one more.

That state that will give liberty of conscience in matters of religion must give liberty of conscience and conversation in their moral laws, or else the fiddle will be out of tune and some of the strings crack.

great a sin as if he did refrain to come. If the magistrate connive at his absenting himself from Sabbath duties, the sin will be greater in the magistrate than can be in the other's passive coming. Naaman's passive going into the house of Rimmon did not violate the peace of his conscience, 2 Kings 5:18, 19. Bodily presence in a stewes, forced to behold the lewdness of whoredoms there committed, is no whoredom at all. No more is it spiritual whoredom to be compelled by force to go to mass.

Defending Hypocrisy

But (say you) it doth but make men hypocrites to compel men to conform the outward man for fear of punishment. If it did so, yet better to be hypocrites than profane persons. Hypocrites give God part of his due, the outward man, but the profane person giveth God neither outward nor inward man.

Your prayers for us we thankfully accept, and we hope God hath given us so much light and love (which you think we want) that if our native country were more zealous against horrid blasphemies and heresies than we be, we believe the Lord would look at it as a better improvement of all the great salvations he hath wrought for them than to set open a wide door to all abominations in religion. Do you think the Lord hath crowned the state with so many victories that they should suffer so many miscreants to pluck the crown of sovereignty from Christ's head? Some to deny his Godhead, some his manhood; some to acknowledge no Christ, nor heaven, nor hell, but what is in a man's self? Some to deny all churches and ordinances, and so to leave Christ no visible kingdom upon earth? And thus Christ by easing England of the yoke of a kingdom shall forfeit His own kingdom among the people of England. Now God forbid, God from heaven forbid, that the people and state of England should so ill requite the Lord Jesus. You know not if you think we came into this wilderness to practice those courses here which we fled from in England. We believe there is a vast difference between men's inventions and God's institutions. We fled from men's inventions, to which we else should have been compelled; we compel none to men's inventions.

If our ways (rigid ways as you call them) have laid us low in the hearts of God's people, yea and of the saints (as you style them), we do not believe it is any part of their saintship. Michal had a low esteem of David's zeal, but he was never a whit lower in the sight of God, nor she higher.

What you wrote out of Holland to our then governor, Mr. Dudley, in behalf of Anabaptists, Antinomians, Seekers, and the like, it seemeth met with a short answer from him, but zealous, for zeal will not bear such mixtures as coldness or lukewarmness will, Rev. 2:2, 14, 15, 20. Nevertheless, I tell you the truth, we have tolerated in our church some Anabaptists, some Antinomians, and some Seekers, and do so still at this day, though Seekers of all others have less reason to desire toleration in church fellowship. For they that deny all churches and church ordinances since the apostasy of Antichrist, they cannot continue in church fellowship but against their own judgment and conscience. And therefore four or five of them who openly renounced the church fellowship which they had long enjoyed, the church said amen to their act, and (after serious debate with them till they had nothing to answer) they were removed from their fellowship. Others carry their dissent more privately and inoffensively, and so are borne withal in much meekness. We are far from arrogating infallibility of judgment to ourselves or affecting uniformity; uniformity God never required, infallibility He never granted us. We content ourselves with unity in the foundation of religion and of church order. Superstructures we suffer to vary; we have here Presbyterian churches as well as Congregational, and have learned (through grace) to keep the unity of the spirit in the bond of peace. Only we are loath to be blown up and down (like chaff) by every wind of new notions.

You see how desirous we are to give you what satisfaction we may to your loving expostulation, which we pray you to accept with the same spirit of love wherewith it is indited. The Lord Jesus guide and keep your heart forever in the ways of His truth and peace. So humbly commending our due respect and hearty affection to your worship, we take leave and rest.

CHAPTER 3

Creating a Godly Community

Chapter Preface

In their efforts to create a "city on a hill" the Puritans went beyond banishing dissenters and religious heretics. They sought to create a community that followed God's laws as revealed in the Bible. Everything from trade procedures to the settlement of communities to drinking and card playing were guided by an overall goal of creating a godly community—or more accurately, a community of communities, for it was the individual town or village that was the social foundation of Puritan life. Historian Robert Kelley compares Massachusetts to the non-Puritan colony of Virginia in *The Shaping of the American Past*:

> Virginians settled as *individuals* upon the land they received from the Crown. New Englanders settled as *communities* upon land granted to each village by the General Court (the legislature) of the Massachusetts Bay Colony. Individuals got land only from the village, and then only if they were members of that community. That is, they would be looked over first by the members of the village to see if they were godly, if they were true Puritans. Then they would sign the covenant (common agreement) which the founders of the village had drawn up together at its founding. This covenant bound all people living in the town to "fear and reverence . . . Almighty God" and "profess and practice one truth . . . the foundation whereof is everlasting love."

Several factors helped facilitate the Puritans' efforts in creating a godly community. One was the vision of religious faith many Puritans shared—a vision inspired by biblical prophecies of the end-times and tempered by the experience of persecution in England that motivated their migration. Another factor was the demographic nature of the migration. Unlike most colonies, which were populated by single young men seeking their fortune, the typical unit of Puritan migration was two relatively educated parents in their thirties, with their children and, in a few cases, servants—a grouping that made for stable communities.

A third important factor was Massachusetts's colonial charter. Negotiated in 1629 by John Winthrop and other Puritan leaders, the charter provided for setting up the Massachusetts Bay Company to run the colony. Usually the headquarters of such a colonial corporation were in London, but this particular charter did not specify where the company was to be headquartered. Winthrop took the charter with him to Massachusetts and thus achieved an unprecedented degree of autonomy from England.

121

All of these factors helped foster the Puritan dream of communal utopia. With the passing of time, however, they proved as impermanent as did the dream itself. The religious ideas of the Puritan settlers became more diverse as people adapted to the new land and new generations developed that did not share the formative experiences in England. The new generation of Puritans sometimes seemed to their elders more concerned with trade and private wealth than with the church and the public good. Families became divided within churches as children of original members could not pass the strict guidelines for membership, which called for a saving conversion experience. The 1662 Half-Way Covenant, which established that upright churchgoers who were not "saved" could have their children baptized, ultimately failed to heal the rifts within the Puritan community. And by 1691, Massachusetts's charter, after several successful maneuvers of delay and prevention, was finally overturned. The new charter granted power to a Royal Governor appointed from England and increased religious tolerance by reducing the Puritans' authority to regulate and control religious minorities. Robert Kelley writes that, by 1700,

> New Englanders were not "saints" any more, and it became increasingly difficult to force people to live up to the moral and religious requirements of earlier times. New England, in contrast with the other colonies, would never lose its special, distinctively Puritan character, but it would no longer be what it had been in its first half-century.

VIEWPOINT 1

"If the people be governors, who shall be governed?"

Political Leadership Should Be Restricted to Church Members

John Cotton (1584-1652)

John Cotton was a leading Anglican minister who was forced to migrate to New England in 1633 because of his religious opinions. For the next twenty years he was one of the most prominent of the Puritan ministers as well as a prolific author of tracts, letters, and other writings explicating Puritan views. He became famous both in America and England as a spokesperson for New England Puritanism.

The following viewpoint is taken from a 1636 letter Cotton wrote to Lord Say and Seale, an English noble who had expressed interest in moving to the new colony but who wanted assurance that he would have a say in civic affairs. In the colony political power and the right to vote for political leaders was limited to full church members. To become a church member required more than good character and a desire to join. One had to persuade the congregation by testimony and action that one had been truly chosen to be transformed by God's grace. People were expected to attend church regardless of whether they had gone through this process, but only full members had official authority in civic

From John Cotton's letter to Lord Saye. In Thomas Hutchinson, *The History of the Colony of Massachusetts-Bay, from the First Settlement Thereof in 1628 Until 1691*, Boston, 1764.

affairs. It was such rules that Lord Say and Seale questioned and that John Cotton defends in this letter as being crucial to the godly community the Puritans were attempting to create. His views critical of democracy were representative of those held by John Winthrop and other Puritan leaders.

It is very suitable to Gods all-sufficient wisdom, and to the fullness and perfection of Holy Scriptures, not only to prescribe perfect rules for the right ordering of a private mans soul to everlasting blessedness with himself, but also for the right ordering of a mans family, yea, of the commonwealth too, so far as both of them are subordinate to spiritual ends, and yet avoid both the churches usurpation upon civil jurisdictions, *in ordine ad spiritualia*, and the commonwealths invasion upon ecclesiastical administrations, *in ordine* to civil peace, and conformity to the civil state. Gods institutions (such as the government of church and of commonwealth be) may be close and compact, and co-ordinate one to another, and yet not confounded. God hath so framed the state of church government and ordinances, that they may be compatible to any commonwealth, though never so much disordered in his frame. But yet when a commonwealth hath liberty to mold his own frame (*scriptura plenitudinem adoro*) I conceive the Scripture hath given full direction for the right ordering of the same, and that, in such sort as may best maintain the *euexia* of the church. Mr. Hooker doth often quote a saying out of Mr. Cartwright (though I have not read it in him) that no man fashioneth his house to his hangings, but his hangings to his house. It is better that the commonwealth be fashioned to the setting forth of Gods house, which is his church: than to accommodate the church frame to the civil state. Democracy, I do not conceive that ever God did ordain as a fit government either for church or commonwealth. If the people be governors, who shall be governed? As for monarchy, and aristocracy, they are both of them clearly approved, and directed in Scripture, yet so as referreth the sovereignty to himself, and setteth up Theocracy in both, as the best form of government in the commonwealth, as well as in the church.

The law, which your Lordship instanceth in [that none shall be chosen to magistracy among us, but a church member] was made and enacted before I came into the country; but I have hitherto wanted sufficient light to plead against it. The rule that directeth the choice of supreme governors, is of like equity and weight in all magistrates, that one of their brethren (not a stranger) should be set over them. Deut. 17. 15. and Jethro's counsel to Moses was approved of God, that the judges, and officers to be set over the people, should be men fearing God. Exod. 18. 21. and Solomon maketh it the joy of a commonwealth, when the righteous are in authority, and their mourning when the wicked rule, Prov. 29. 21. Job 34. 30. Your Lordship's fear, that this will bring in papal excommunication, is just, and pious: but let your Lordship be pleased again to consider whether the consequence be necessary. *Turpius ejictur quam non admittitur:* nonmembership may be a just cause of nonadmission to the place of magistracy, but yet, ejection out of his membership will not be a just cause of ejecting him out of his magistracy. A godly woman, being to make choice of an husband, may justly refuse a man that is either cast out of church fellowship, or is not yet received into it, but yet, when she is once given to him, she may not reject him then, for such defect. Mr. Humfrey was chosen for an assistant (as I hear) before the colony came over hither: and, though he be not as yet joined into church fellowship (by reason of the unsettledness of the congregation where he liveth) yet the commonwealth do still continue his magistracy to him, as knowing he waiteth for opportunity of enjoying church-fellowship shortly.

Church and State

When your Lordship doubteth, that this course will draw all things under the determination of the church, *in ordine ad spiritualia* (seeing the church is to determine who shall be members, and none but a member may have to do in the government of a commonwealth) be pleased (I pray you) to conceive, [that magistrates are neither chosen to office in the church, nor do govern by directions from the church, but by civil laws, and those enacted in general courts, and executed in courts of justice, by the governors and assistants.] In all which, the church (as the church) hath nothing to do: only, it prepareth fit instruments both to rule, and to choose rulers, which is no ambition in the church, nor dishonor to the commonwealth, the apostle, on the contrary, thought it a great dishonor and reproach to the church of Christ, if it were not able to yield able judges to hear and determine all causes amongst their brethren. *i, Cor.* 6. i. to 5. which place alone seemeth to me fully to decide this question: for it plainly holdeth forth this argument: It is a shame to the church to want able judges of civil matters (as v. 5.) and an audacious act in any church member voluntarily to go for judgment, other where than before the saints (as v. 1.) then it will be no arrogance nor folly in church members, nor prejudice to the commonwealth, if voluntarily they never choose any civil judges but from amongst the saints, such as church members are called to be. But the former is

Christian Liberty

John Winthrop's famous "Little Speech" was delivered to the General Court in July 1645 following his vindication against charges that he had curtailed the liberties of others by exceeding his authority. Historian George M. Waller writes that it is "a classic statement of the orthodox view of authority."

There is a twofold liberty, natural (I mean as our nature is now corrupt) and civil or federal. The first is common to man with beasts and other creatures. By this, man, as he stands in relation to man simply, hath liberty to do what he lists; it is a liberty to evil as well as to good. This liberty is incompatible and inconsistent with authority, and cannot endure the least restraint of the most just authority. The exercise and maintaining of this liberty makes men grow more evil, and in time to be worse than brute beasts. . . . This is that great enemy of truth and peace, that wild beast, which all the ordinances of God are bent against, to restrain and subdue it. The other kind of liberty I call civil or federal, it may also be termed moral, in reference to the covenant between God and man, in the moral law, and the politic covenants and constitutions, amongst men themselves. This liberty is the proper end and object of authority, and cannot subsist without it; and it is a liberty to that only which is good, just, and honest. This liberty you are to stand for, with the hazard (not only of your goods, but) of your lives, if need be. Whatsoever crosseth this, is not authority, but a distemper thereof. This liberty is maintained and exercised in a way of subjection to authority; it is of the same kind of liberty wherewith Christ hath made us free. The woman's own choice makes such a man her husband; yet being so chosen, he is her lord, and she is to be subject to him, yet in a way of liberty, not of bondage; and a true wife accounts her subjection her honor and freedom, and would not think her condition safe and free, but in her subjection to her husband's authority. Such is the liberty of the church under the authority of Christ, her king and husband; his yoke is so easy and sweet to her as a bride's ornaments; and if through forwardness or wantonness, etc., she shake it off, at any time, she is at no rest in her spirit, until she take it up again . . . If you stand for your natural corrupt liberties, and will do what is good in your own eyes, you will not endure the least weight of authority, but will murmur, and oppose, and be always striving to shake off that yoke; but if you will be satisfied to enjoy such civil and lawful liberties, such as Christ allows you, then will you quietly and cheerfully submit unto that authority which is set over you, in all the administrations of it, for your good. Wherein, if we fail at any time, we hope we shall be willing (by God's assistance) to hearken to good advice from any of you, or in any other way of God; so shall your liberties be preserved, in upholding the honor and power of authority amongst you.

clear: and how then can the latter be avoided. If this therefore be (as your Lordship rightly conceiveth one of the main objections if not the only one) which hindereth this commonwealth from the entertainment of the propositions of those worthy gentlemen, we entreat them, in the name of the Lord Jesus, to consider, in meekness of wisdom, it is not any conceit, or will of ours, but the holy counsel and will of the Lord Jesus (whom they seek to serve as well as we) that overruleth us in this case: and we trust will overrule them also, that the Lord only may be exalted amongst all his servants. What pity and grief were it, that the observance of the will of Christ should hinder good things from us!

But your Lordship doubteth, that if such a rule were necessary, then the church estate and the best ordered commonwealth in the world were not compatible. But let not your Lordship so conceive. For, the church submitteth itself to all the laws and ordinances of men, in what commonwealth soever they come to dwell. But it is one thing, to submit unto what they have no calling to reform: another thing, voluntarily to ordain a form of government, which to the best discerning of many of us (for I speak not of myself) is expressly contrary to rule. Nor need your Lordship fear (which yet I speak with submission to your Lordships, better judgment) that this course will lay such a foundation, as nothing but a mere democracy can be built upon it. Bodine confesseth, that though it be *status popularis*, where a people choose their own governors; yet the government is not a democracy, if it be administered, not by the people, but by the governors, whether one (for then it is a monarchy, though elective) or by many, for then (as you know) it is aristocracy. In which respect it is, that church government is justly denied (even by Mr. Robinson) to be democratical, though the people choose their own officers and rulers.

Three Aims

Nor need we fear, that this course will, in time, cast the commonwealth into distractions, and popular confusions. For (under correction) these three things do not undermine, but do mutually and strongly maintain one another (even those three which we principally aim at) authority in magistrates, liberty in people, purity in the church. Purity, preserved in the church, will preserve well-ordered liberty in the people, and both of them establish well-balanced authority in the magistrates. God is the author of all these three, and neither is himself the God of confusion, nor are the ways the ways of confusion, but of peace.

What our brethren (magistrates or ministers, or leading freeholders) will answer to the rest of the propositions, I shall better understand before the gentlemans return from Connecticut, who

127

brought them over. Mean while, two of the principal of them, the general court hath already condescended unto. (1) In establishing a standing council, who, during their lives, should assist the governor in managing the chiefest affairs of this little state. They have chosen, for the present, only two (Mr. Winthrop and Mr. Dudley) not willing to choose more, till they see what further better choice the Lord will send over to them, that so they may keep an open door, for such desirable gentlemen as your Lordship mentioneth. (2) They have granted the governor and assistants a negative voice, and reserved to the freemen the like liberty also. Touching other things, I hope to give your Lordship further account, when the gentleman returneth.

He being now returned, I have delivered to him an answer to the rest of your demands, according to the minds of such leading men amongst us, as I thought meet to consult withal, concealing your name from any, except two or three, who alike do concur in a joint desire of yielding to any such propositions as your Lordship demandeth, so far as with allowance from the word they may, beyond which I know your Lordship would not require any thing.

Now the Lord Jesus Christ (the prince of peace) keep and bless your Lordship, and dispose of all your times and talents to his best advantage: and let the covenant of his grace and peace rest upon your honourable family and posterity, throughout all generations.

Viewpoint 2

"We therefore desire that civil liberty ... be forthwith granted to all truly English, equal to the rest of their countrymen."

Political Leadership Restrictions Should Be Lifted

Robert Child (c. 1613-1654) et al.

Political leadership of the Massachusetts Bay Colony during the first years of its existence was limited to full church members—people who could demonstrate to others that their lives showed they were part of God's elect. Only church members could vote in elections for the Massachusetts General Court, the main governing body of the colony. These restrictions were stricter than those found in many Puritan parishes in England, and many people felt unfairly excluded.

In 1645 this arrangement came under attack from a small group of settlers led by Robert Child, a physician who had moved to Massachusetts in the late 1630s, then returned to England for a few years during the time the Puritan-dominated Parliament was gaining political control in England. He rejoined the Puritans in New England in 1645 "full of ideas for improving the place," according to historian Edmund S. Morgan.

In May 1645, Child and six others signed and sent a petition to the Massachusetts General Court. The petition argued that the

A petition to the Massachusetts General Court by Robert Child et al. In *Hutchinson Papers*. Volume 1. Albany, NY: Prince Society, 1865.

Bay Colony had violated their rights as Englishmen. Morgan writes in *The Puritan Dilemma:*

> Though in form a petition to the Massachusetts General Court, it was in fact a denunciation of the congregational organization of churches, of the limitation of political rights to church members, and of the independence which Massachusetts claimed in regard to England.

Perhaps most ominous to John Winthrop and other Puritan leaders was the group's threat to appeal to Parliament. Such an action might jeopardize the colony's charter and end the whole experiment of a theologically based community more or less autonomous from England. The Massachusetts General Court not only issued a rebuttal of the petition but took steps to prevent any of the signers from leaving for England to appeal. The court also wrote to Parliament defending its laws. By the time Child finally made it back to England, he found Parliament unresponsive to his arguments. Although he met with no personal success, Child's efforts did help liberalize the Massachusetts Bay Colony. A 1647 law permitted non-church members to vote for town officials, and a written code of laws, long sought by many but delayed by the colony's leaders, was finally produced in 1648.

We who in behalf of ourselves and divers of our countrymen, laying our hands upon our breasts and seriously considering that the hand of our good God, who through His goodness hath safely brought us and ours through the great ocean and planted us here, seems not now to be with us, yea rather against us, blasting all our designs—though contrived with much deliberation, undertaken with great care, and proceeding with more than ordinary probability of successful events—by which many of good estates are brought to the brink of extreme poverty, yea at this time laying His just hand upon our families, taking many away to Himself, striking others with unwanted malignant sicknesses, and with some shameful diseases, have thought it convenient with all respectiveness to present these our sincere requests and remonstrances to this honored court. . . .

English Liberties

1. Whereas this place hath been planted by the encouragement, next under God, of letters patents given and granted by His Majesty of England to the inhabitants thereof, with many privileges and immunities, viz.: incorporation into a company, liberty

of choosing governors, settling government, making laws not repugnant to the laws of England, power of administering the oath of allegiance to all, etc., as by the said letters patents more largely appeareth. Notwithstanding, we cannot according to our judgments discern a settled form of government according to the laws of England, which may seem strange to our countrymen, yea to the whole world, especially considering we are all English. Neither do we so understand and perceive our own laws or liberties, or any body of laws here so established, as that thereby there may be a sure and comfortable enjoyment of our lives, liberties, and estates, according to our due and natural rights as freeborn subjects of the English nation. By which many inconveniences flow into plantations, viz. jealousies of introducing arbitrary government—which many are prone to believe, construing the procrastination of such settled laws, to proceed from an overgreedy spirit of arbitrary power (which it may be is their weakness), such proceedings being detestable to our English nation and to all good men, and at present a chief cause of the intestine war in our dear country. Further, it gives cause to many to think themselves hardly dealt with, others too much favored, and the scale of justice too much bowed and unequally balanced. From when also proceedeth fears and jealousies of illegal commitments, unjust imprisonments, taxes, rates, customs, levies of ungrounded and undoing assessments, unjustifiable presses, undue fines, unmeasurable expenses and charges, of unconceivable dangers through a negative or destructive vote unduly placed and not well regulated, in a word, of a non-certainty of all things we enjoy, whether lives, liberties, or estates; and also of undue oaths, being subject to exposition according to the will of him or them that gives them, and not according to a due and unbowed rule of law, which is the true interpreter of all oaths to all men, whether judge or judged.

Wherefore our humble desire and request is that you would be pleased to consider of our present condition and upon what foundation we stand, and unanimously concur to establish the fundamental and wholesome laws of our native country, and such others as are no ways repugnant to them, unto which all of us are most accustomed. . . .

2. Whereas there are many thousands in these plantations, of the English nation, freeborn, quiet, and peaceable men, righteous in their dealings, forward with hand, heart, and purse to advance the public good, known friends to the honorable and victorious Houses of Parliament, lovers of their nation, etc., who are debarred from all civil employments (without any just cause that we know), not being permitted to bear the least office (though it cannot be denied but some are well qualified), no not so much as to have any vote in choosing magistrates, captains, or other civil

The Oath of Massachusetts Freemen

In addition to being a male church member of good standing, a Massachusetts voter had to subscribe to an oath, the second version of which is reprinted below. Approved by the Massachusetts General Court on May 14, 1634, this became in 1639 the first document printed on a printing press in America.

I . . . being by God's Providence an inhabitant and freeman within the jurisdiction of this commonwealth, do freely acknowledge myself to be subject to the government thereof; and therefore do swear by the great and dreadful name of the ever-living God that I will be true and faithful to the same, and will accordingly yield assistance and support thereunto with my person and estate, as in equity I am bound; and will also truly endeavor to maintain and preserve all the liberties and privileges thereof, submitting myself to the wholesome laws and orders made and established by the same. And further, that I will not plot or practise any evil against it, or consent to any that shall so do; but will timely discover and reveal the same to lawful authority now here established for the speedy preventing thereof.

Moreover, I do solemnly bind myself in the sight of God that, when I shall be called to give my voice touching any such matter of this state, in which freemen are to deal, I will give my vote and suffrage as I shall judge in my own conscience may best conduce and tend to the public weal of the body, without respect of persons or favor of any man. So help me God in the Lord Jesus Christ.

and military officers, notwithstanding they have here expended their youth, born the burthen of the day, wasted much of their estates for the subsistence of these poor plantations, paid all assessments, taxes, rates at least equal if not exceeding others. Yea when the late war was denounced against the Narragansett Indians without their consent, their goods were seized on for the service, themselves and servants especially forced and impressed to serve in that war, to the hazarding of all things most dear and near unto them, whence issue forth many great inconveniences, secret discontents, murmurings, rents in the plantations, discouragements in their callings, unsettledness in their minds, strife, contention, and the Lord only knows to what a flame in time it may kindle; also jealousies of too much unwarranted power and dominion on the one side and of perpetual slavery and bondage on the other, and—which is intolerable—even by those who ought to love and respect them as brethren.

We therefore desire that civil liberty and freedom be forthwith granted to all truly English, equal to the rest of their countrymen, as in all plantations is accustomed to be done and as all freeborn enjoy in our native country (we hoping here in some things to enjoy greater liberties than elsewhere, counting it no small loss of liberty to be as it were banished from our native home and enforced to lay our bones in a strange wilderness), without imposing any oaths or covenant on them, which we suppose cannot be warranted by the letters patents and seem not to concur with the oath of allegiance formerly enforced on all and later covenants lately imposed on many here present by the honorable Houses of Parliament, or at least to detract from our native country and laws—which by some are styled foreign and this place termed rather a free state than a colony or corporation of England. All of us [are] very willing to take such oaths and covenants as are expressions of our desires of advancing the glory of God and good of this place and of our duties to the state of England and love to our nation, being composed according to the laws and customs of other corporations of England. But all of us are exceeding unwilling by any policies whatsoever to be rent from our native country, though far distant from it, valuing our free derivations, the immunities and privileges which we and our posterity do and we hope shall always enjoy above the greatest honors of this country, not cemented to the state of England, and [we] glory to be accounted, though but as rushes of that land, yet that we may continue to write that we and ours are English; or lest we entreat that the bodies of us and ours (English subjects possessing here no privileges) may not be impressed, nor goods forcibly taken away, lest we, not knowing the justice of this war, may be ignorantly and unwillingly enforced upon our own destruction, and that all assessment, taxes, impositions—which are many and grievous (if civil liberty be not granted)—may be taken off, that in all things we may be strangers, otherwise we suppose ourselves in a worse case here and less free than the natives amongst whom we live, or any aliens. Further, that none of the English nation, who at this time are too forward to be gone and very backward to come hither, be banished, unless they break the known laws of England in so high a measure as to deserve so high a punishment, and that those few that come over may settle here without having two magistrates' hands, which sometimes not being possible to obtain hath procured a kind of banishment to some who might have been serviceable to this place, as they have been to the state of England, etc. And we likewise desire that no greater punishments be inflicted upon offenders than are allowed and set by the laws of our native country.

Church Membership Restrictions

3. Whereas there are divers sober, righteous, and godly men, eminent for knowledge and other gracious gifts of the holy spirit, no ways scandalous in their lives and conversation, members of

the Church of England (in all ages famous for piety and learning) not dissenting from the latest and best reformation of England, Scotland, etc., yet they and their posterity are detained from the seals of the covenant of free grace because, as it is supposed, they will not take these churches' covenants, for which as yet they see no light in God's word. Neither can they clearly perceive what they are, every church having their covenant differing from another's, at least in words—yea, some churches sometime adding, sometime detracting, calling it sometimes the covenant of grace, sometimes a branch of it, sometimes a profession of the free covenant, etc.— notwithstanding, they are compelled under a severe fine every Lord's day to appear at the congregation, and notice is taken of such who stay not till baptism be administered to other men's children, though denied to their own, and in some places forced to contribute to the maintenance of those ministers who vouchsafe not to take them into their flock, though desirous of the ordinances of God, etc., yet they are not accounted so much as brethren nor publicly so called, nor is Christian vigilancy (commanded to all) any way exercised to them. Whence, as we conceive, do abound an ocean of inconveniences, dishonor to God and to his ordinances, little profit by the ministry, increase of Anabaptism and of those that totally contemn all ordinances as vain, fading of Christian graces, decrease of brotherly love, heresies, schisms, etc., the whole body of the members of the Church of England, like sheep scattered in the wilderness, without a shepherd, in a forlorn condition.

We therefore humbly entreat you, in whose hands it is to help and whose judicious eyes discern these great inconveniences, for the glory of God and the comfort of your brethren and countrymen, to give liberty to the members of the Church of England not scandalous in their lives and conversations (as members of these churches) to be taken into your congregation and to enjoy with you all those liberties and ordinances Christ hath purchased for them and into whose name they are baptized, that the Lord may be one and His name one amongst us in this place; that the seals of the covenant may be applied to them and their posterity, as we conceive they ought to be, till inconveniences hereby be found prejudicial to the churches and colony (which we hope shall never be), not doubting but the same Christian favor will be shewed to all its members of these churches when they shall retire to our dear native country (if their conversations be righteous and holy), or otherwise to grant liberty to settle themselves here in a church way, according to the best reformations of England and Scotland. If not, we and they shall be necessitated to apply our humble desires to the honorable Houses of Parliament, who we hope will take our sad conditions into their serious considerations, to provide able ministers for us (this place not being so well provided as to spare any), or else out of their charity—many estates being wasted—to transport us to some other place where we may live like Christians and not be accounted burthens, but serviceable both to church and state.

Hopes for the Future

These things being granted, by the blessing of God to us in Christ, we hope to see the now contemned ordinances of God highly prized; the gospel much darkened break forth as the sun at noonday; Christian charity and brotherly love, almost frozen, wax warm; zeal and holy emulation more fervent; jealousy of arbitrary government (the bane of all commonwealths) quite banished; the wicked, if any such be found, in their courses disheartened; the righteous actors in their ways encouraged; secret discontents, fretting like cankers, remedied; merchandising and shipping, by special providence wasted, speedily increased; mines undertaken with more cheerfulness; fishing with more forwardness; husbandry, now withering, forthwith flourishing; villages and plantations, much deserted presently, more populous; all mechanical trades, the great enriching of all commonwealths, heartily going on; staple commodities, the life of trade, presently raised; our almost lost credit regained; our brethren of England's just indignation, and their force as a post flying from us, turned to embrace us; the honorable Houses of Parliament, patrons of piety, under their wings in these dangerous times with alacrity shrouding us; the privileges and immunities which we and ours enjoy in our native land more firmly settled; foreign enemies, daily threatening, totally discouraged; unsettled men, now abounding, firmly planted; that the prosperity of England may not be the ruin of this plantation but the contrary: hands, hearts, and purses, now straitened, freely opened for public and honorable services; strife and contention, now rife, abated; taxes and sesses lightened; the burthens of the state but pleasure, etc.

VIEWPOINT 3

"Some false principles were ... [t]hat a man might sell as dear as he can, and buy as cheap as he can."

Economic Exploitation Harms the Community

John Winthrop (1588-1649)

In their efforts to create a "city on a hill," the Puritans did not neglect the area of economics. The Puritan colonies passed many regulations on wages, prices, and business conditions in order to check inflation and "unfair" profits from buying and selling goods often in short supply. John Winthrop, the dominant political figure in the early history of the Massachusetts Bay Colony, recorded in his journal one example of the enforcement of the regulations. This 1639 case involved a Boston merchant named Robert Keayne, who was accused of amassing unfair profits by overcharging for his goods. Winthrop's account demonstrates how serious a matter such accusations were. Included in Winthrop's journal entry are notes he recorded from a sermon by John Cotton, one of the leading Puritan ministers, describing the "false principles" of some of the wealthier New England merchants and listing rules of proper business conduct.

From *Winthrop's Journal "History of New England," 1630-1649*. Edited by James K. Hosmer, New York, 1908.

[9 November 1639] At a general court holden at Boston, great complaint was made of the oppression used in the country in sale of foreign commodities; and Mr. Robert Keayne, who kept a shop in Boston, was notoriously above others observed and complained of. And, being convented, he was charged with many particulars; in some, for taking above six-pence in the shilling profit; in some above eight-pence; and, in some small things, above two for one; and being hereof convict (as appears by the records), he was fined £200, which came thus to pass. The deputies considered, apart, of his fine, and set it at £200; the magistrates agreed but to £100. So, the court being divided, at length it was agreed that his fine should be £200, but he should pay but £100, and the other should be respited to the further consideration of the next General Court. By this means the magistrates and deputies were brought to an accord which otherwise had not been likely, and so much trouble might have grown and the offender escaped censure. For the cry of the country was so great against oppression, and some of the elders and magistrates had declared such detestation of the corrupt practice of this man (which was the more observable because he was wealthy and sold dearer than most other tradesmen, and for that he was of ill report for the like covetous practice in England, that incensed the deputies very much against him). And sure the course was very evil, especial circumstances considered: (1) he being an ancient professor of the gospel; (2) a man of eminent parts; (3) wealthy, and having but one child; (4) having come over for conscience' sake and for the advancement of the gospel here; (5) having been formerly dealt with and admonished, both by private friends and also by some of the magistrates and elders, and having promised reformation, being a member of a church and commonwealth now in their infancy and under the curious observation of all churches and civil states in the world.

False Principles

These added much aggravation to his sin in the judgment of all men of understanding. Yet most of the magistrates (though they discerned of the offense clothed with all these circumstances) would have been more moderate in their censure: (1) because there was no law in force to limit or direct men in point of profit in their trade; (2) because it is the common practice in all countries for men to make use of advantages for raising the prices of their commodities; (3) because, though he were chiefly aimed at, yet he was not alone in this fault; (4) because all men through the country, in sale of cattle, corn, labor, etc., were guilty of the like excess

Enlargement Toward Others

In his famous sermon preached aboard the ship Arbella *during its 1630 voyage to America, John Winthrop exhorted his fellow Puritans to put the common good above private gain. He cites the Old Testament story of Nehemiah persuading moneylenders and others to sacrifice profits in order to rebuild Jerusalem.*

Question: What rule must we observe and walk by in cause of community of peril?

Answer: The same as before, but with more enlargement towards others and less respect towards ourselves and our own right. Hence it was that in the primitive church they sold all, had things in common, neither did any man say that which he possessed was his own. Likewise in their return out of the captivity, because the work was great for the restoring of the church and the danger of enemies was common to all, Nehemiah exhorts the Jews to liberality and readiness in remitting their debts to their brethren, and disposing liberally of his own to such as wanted, and stand not upon his own due, which he might have demanded of them. Thus did some of our forefathers in times of persecution in England, and so did many of the faithful of other churches, whereof we keep an honorable remembrance of them.

in prices; (5) because a certain rule could not be found out for an equal rate between buyer and seller, though much labor had been bestowed in it, and divers laws had been made, which, upon experience, were repealed, as being neither safe nor equal. Lastly, and especially, because the law of God appoints no other punishment but double restitution; and, in some cases, as where the offender freely confesseth and brings his offering, only half added to the principal. After the court had censured him, the church of Boston called him also in question, where (as before he had done in the court) he did, with tears, acknowledge and bewail his covetous and corrupt heart, yet making some excuse for many of the particulars which were charged upon him, as partly by pretense of ignorance of the true price of some wares, and chiefly by being misled by some false principles, as (1) that if a man lost in one commodity he might help himself in the price of another; (2) that if, through want of skill or other occasion, his commodity cost him more than the price of the market in England, he might then sell it for more than the price of the market in New England, etc. These things gave occasion to Mr. Cotton, in his public exercise the next lecture day, to lay open the error of such false principles, and to give some rules of direction in the case.

Some false principles were these:

1. That a man might sell as dear as he can, and buy as cheap as he can.

2. If a man lose by casualty of sea, etc., in some of his commodities, he may raise the price of the rest.

3. That he may sell as he bought, though he paid too dear, etc., and though the commodity be fallen, etc.

4. That, as a man may take the advantage of his own skill or ability, so he may of another's ignorance or necessity.

5. Where one gives time for payment, he is to take like recompense of one as of another.

The rules for trading were these:

1. A man may not sell above the current price, i.e., such a price as is usual in the time and place, and as another (who knows the worth of the commodity) would give for it, if he had occasion to use it; as that is called current money, which every man will take, etc.

2. When a man loseth in his commodity for want of skill, etc., he must look at it as his own fault or cross, and therefore must not lay it upon another.

3. Where a man loseth by casualty of sea, or, etc., it is a loss cast upon himself by providence, and he may not ease himself of it by casting it upon another; for so a man should seem to provide against all providences, etc., that he should never lose. But where there is a scarcity of the commodity, there men may raise their price, for now it is a hand of God upon the commodity and not the person.

4. A man may not ask any more for his commodity than his selling price, as Ephron to Abraham, the land is worth thus much.

The Church's Response

The cause being debated by the church, some were earnest to have him excommunicated; but the most thought an admonition would be sufficient. Mr. Cotton opened the causes, which required excommunication, out of that in 1 Cor. 5:11. The point now in question was whether these actions did declare him to be such a covetous person, etc. Upon which he showed that it is neither the habit of covetousness (which is in every man in some degree) nor simply the act that declares a man to be such, but when it appears that a man sins against his conscience, or the very light of nature, and when it appears in a man's whole conversation. But Mr. Keayne did not appear to be such, but rather upon an error in his judgment, being led by false principles; and, beside, he is otherwise liberal, as in his hospitality, and in church communion, etc. So, in the end, the church consented to an admonition.

VIEWPOINT 4

"Was the selling of 6 d. [pence] nails for 8 d. per lb. and 8 d. nails for 10 d. per lb. such a crying and oppressing sin?"

Making a Profit Does Not Harm the Community

Robert Keayne (c. 1595-1656)

Robert Keayne was one of the most successful and wealthiest of the merchants who bought and sold goods between England and the colonies. The first major philanthropist of Boston, his success was clouded in 1639 when he was charged with unethical trade practices and officially admonished by his church. When writing his will in 1653, Keayne sought to clear his name by giving his side of the story.

Keayne's motivation for defending himself lies in Puritan theology, which held that God's grace saved chosen people from eternal damnation. Such grace, or *justification*, could be demonstrated (but not achieved) by good works and success in life (sanctification). Thus, underlying the question of how Keayne obtained his wealth was the more significant question of whether it was evidence of God's grace or Satan's work.

From "The Apologia of Robert Keayne." In *Publications of the Colonial Society of Massachusetts.* Volume 42. Groton, MA: Colonial Society of Massachusetts, 1964. Reprinted with permission.

First and before all things, I commend and commit my precious soul into the hands of Almighty God. . . .

I do further desire from my heart to renounce all confidence or expectation of merit or desert in any of the best duties or services that ever I have, shall, or can be able to perform, acknowledging that all my righteousness, sanctification, and close walking with God, if it were or had been a thousand times more exact than ever yet I attained to, is all polluted and corrupt and falls short of commending me to God in point of my justification or helping forward my redemption or salvation. They deserve nothing at God's hand but hell and condemnation if He should enter into judgment with me for them. And though I believe that all my ways of holiness are of no use to me in point of justification, yet I believe they may not be neglected by me without great sin, but are ordained of God for me to walk in them carefully, in love to Him, in obedience to His commandments, as well as for many other good ends. They are good fruits and evidences of justification. Therefore, renouncing though not the acts yet all confidence in those acts of holiness and works of sanctification performed by me, I look for my acceptance with God and the salvation of my soul only from the merits or righteousness of the Lord Jesus Christ, and from the free, bountiful, and undeserved grace and love of God in Him. . . .

This faith in the Lord Jesus Christ hath been most plainly and sweetly taught in these churches of New England, in which place, though I met with many and deep sorrows and variety of exercises of spirit and hard measures offered to me, yet with unrepentant thoughts I desire to acknowledge it for a great blessing and undeserved favor of God that He hath brought me hither to enjoy His presence in the beauties of holiness, and to see His walkings in His holy sanctuary. And though there may be failings both in our civil government and churches (for all men have their weaknesses and the best societies of men have their imperfections, so that still there will be some things to be amended and reformed as God shall be pleased to discover new light and means to do it), yet I do unfeignedly approve of the way of the churches of Jesus Christ and the civil government that God hath here set up amongst us, and rejoice therein, as a way that both I pray for and doubt not but God will bless. According to that light that I have received or that which I ever read or heard of, it is one of the best and happiest governments that is this day in the world. . . .

The Judgment of God and of Men

I did not then nor dare not now go about to justify all my actions. I know God is righteous and doth all upon just grounds,

Boston's growing prosperity as a trading port led some ministers to question whether its people had lost sight of the religious ideals that had motivated its founding.

though men may mistake in their grounds and proceedings, counsel have erred and courts may err and a faction may be too hard and outvote the better or more discerning part. I know the errors of my life. The failings in my trade and otherwise have been many. Therefore from God (the censure) was most just. Though it had been much more severe I dare not so open my mouth against it, nor never did as I remember, [except to] justify Him. Yet I dare not say nor did I ever think (as far as I can call to mind) that the censure was just and righteous from men. Was the price of a bridle, not for taking but only asking, 2 s. [shillings] for [what] cost here 20 d. [pence] such a heinous sin? [Such bridles] have since been commonly sold and still are for 2 s. 6 d. and 3 s. or more, though worse in kind. Was it such a heinous sin to sell 2 or 3 dozen of great gold buttons for 2 s. 10 d. per dozen that cost 2 s. 2 d. ready money in London, bought at the best hand, as I showed to many by my invoice (though I could not find it at the instant when the Court desired to see it) and since was confirmed by special testimony from London? The buttons [were not even] paid for when the complaint was made, nor I think not yet; neither did the complaint come from him that bought and owed them nor with his knowledge or consent, as he hath since affirmed, but merely from the spleen and envy of another, whom it did nothing concern. Was this so great an offense? Indeed, that it might be made so, some out of their ignorance would needs say they were copper and not worth 9 d. per dozen. But these were weak grounds to pass heavy censures upon.

Was the selling of 6 d. nails for 8 d. per lb. and 8 d. nails for 10 d. per lb. such a crying and oppressing sin? And as I remember it was above two years before he that bought them paid me for them (and not paid for if I forgot not) when he made that quarreling exception and unrighteous complaint in the Court against me, (he then being of the Court himself) that I had altered and corrupted my book in adding more to the price than I had set down for them at first delivery. If I had set down 8 d. after 2 years' forbearance for what I would have sold for 7 d. if he had paid me presently, I think it had been a more honest act in me than it was in him that promised or at least pretended to pay me presently that he might get them at a lower price than a man could well live upon, and when he had got my goods into his hands to keep me 2 or 3 years without my money. All that while there was no fault found at the prices, but when he could for shame keep the money no longer, yet he will requite it with a censure in the Court. For my own part, as I did ever think it an ungodly act in him, so do I think in my conscience that it had been more just in the Court to have censured him than me for this thing, though this was the chiefest crime alleged and most powerfully carried against me. . . .

Now I leave it to the world or to any impartial man or any that hath understanding in trade to judge whether this was a just offense or so crying a sin for which I had such cause to be so penitent (this being the chief [accusation] and pressed on with so great aggravation by my opposers) [or whether] my actions, innocent in themselves, were misconstrued. I knew not how to help myself, especially considering it was no oppressing price but usual with others at that time to sell the like so and since [then] frequently for almost half as much more, as I think all know, and yet both given and taken without exception, or at least without public complaint. Yea, the same gentleman himself, since he hath turned merchant and trader, seems to have lost his former tenderness of conscience that he had when he was a buyer and is not so scrupulous in his own gains. . . .

I was much grieved and astonished to be complained of in Court and brought publicly to answer as a grievous malefactor only upon the displeasure of some that stirred in it more than properly did concern them and to be prosecuted so violently for such things as seemed to myself and others so trivial, and upon great outcries, as if the oppression had been unparalleled. And when all things were searched to the bottom nothing of moment was proved against me worthy of mention in a court but what I have here expressed. Yet no other way [was] left me for help, things being carried so highly against me by one party, as I had it by good informations, but by casting myself upon the favor or mercy of the Court, as some had counseled me. Since, though, I think they have had cause to be grieved for as well as I because it had an effect contrary to expectation. The means which should have procured the more clemency was by some made an argument of my greater guilt. If this should convince me of the equity and honesty of such men's moderation who delight to turn things not to the best but worst sense, the Lord help me to see that which yet I have not done. This was not the way to bow and melt my heart, but rather to provoke it to cry more earnestly to God to do me right in such a case.

A Shame and an Amazement

I confess still as I did then and as I have said before, that the newness and strangeness of the thing, to be brought forth into an open court as a public malefactor, was both a shame and an amazement to me. It was the grief of my soul (and I desire it may ever so be in a greater measure) that any act of mine (though not justly but by misconstruction) should be an occasion of scandal to the Gospel and profession of the Lord Jesus, or that myself should be looked at as one that had brought any just dishonor to God (which I have endeavored long and according to my weak ability desired to prevent), though God hath been pleased for causes best known to Himself to deny me such a blessing. And if it had been in my own power I should rather have chosen to have perished in my cradle than to have lived to such a time. But the good pleasure of God is to keep me low in my own eyes as well as in the eyes of others, and also to make me humble and penitent, lest such mercies should have lifted me up above what is meet. Yet I do say still as I have often done before, that those things for which I was questioned (in the best apprehension, guided by God's word, that I had then or have since attained to) did deserve no such proceedings as was carved out to me, though some blew up those sparks into a great flame. And I am not alone herein, though it was my own case, but many wise and godly servants of the Lord, as well as divers others were and still are of the same mind. Yea, some that were then much against me have confessed since to me that things were carried in a hurry.

Yea, and our own church, when they called all those complaints over again that was laid to my charge (as it was meet they should) to see how far there was equity in them and how far I was guilty of all those clamors and rumors that when I lay under, they heard my defense equally and patiently, and after all their exquisite search into them and attention to what others could allege or prove against me, they found no cause but only to give me an admonition. Less they could not do without some offense, considering what had passed in Court before against me. Now if the church had seen or apprehended or could have proved that I had been so justly guilty as others imagined, they could have done no less than to have excommunicated and cast me out of their society and fellowship as an unworthy member.

Viewpoint 5

"It is the righteous God [who] hath ... given commission to the barbarous heathen to rise up against us ... heereby speaking aloud to us to search ... and turne againe unto the Lord our God."

Stricter Laws Are Needed

The Massachusetts General Court

In 1675 the Puritans suffered their first major Indian attack in nearly forty years. Twelve frontier towns were eventually destroyed and some six hundred Puritan settlers were killed.

Many ministers and leaders interpreted the disaster as punishment of the Puritan colonies for breaching their covenant with God through immoral behavior. The General Court of Massachusetts in November 1675 issued a new series of rules and laws aimed to restore good behavior. Historian Edmund S. Morgan writes: "Nowhere in the records of seventeenth-century New England were the basic assumptions of Puritan political thought more explicitly exemplified in practice than in this effort of the government to restore the people to God's favor."

From *Records of the Governor and Company of the Massachusetts Bay in New England.* Volume 1. Edited by N.B. Shurtleff. Boston: William White, 1853.

Whereas the most wise & holy God, for severall yeares past, hath not only warned us by his word, but chastized us with his rods, inflicting upon us many generall (though lesser) judgments, but we have neither heard the word nor rod as wee ought, so as to be effectually humbled for our sinns to repent of them, reforme, and amend our wayes; hence it is the righteous God hath heightened our calamity, and given commission to the barbarous heathen to rise up against us, and to become a smart rod and severe scourge to us, in burning & depopulating severall hopefull plantations, murdering many of our people of all sorts, and seeming as it were to cast us off, and putting us to shame, and not going forth with our armies, heereby speaking aloud to us to search and try our wayes, and turne againe unto the Lord our God, from whom wee have departed with a great backsliding.

1. The Court, apprehending there is too great a neglect of discipline in the churches, and especially respecting those that are their children, through the non acknowledgment of them according to the order of the gospell; in watching over them, as well as chattechising of them, inquireing into theire spirittuall estates, that, being brought to take hold of the covenant, they may acknouledge & be acknouledged according to theire relations to God & to his church, and theire obligations to be the Lords, and to approove themselves so to be by a suiteable profession & conversation; and doe therefore solemnly recommend it unto the respective elders and brethren of the severall churches throughout this jurisdiction to take effectuall course for reformation herein.

Hair and Clothes

2. Whereas there is manifest pride openly appearing amongst us in that long haire, like weomens haire, is worne by some men, either their oune or others haire made into perewiggs, and by some weomen wearing borders of haire, and theire cutting, curling, & immodest laying out theire haire, which practise doeth prevayle & increase, especially amongst the younger sort,—

This Court doeth declare against this ill custome as offencive to them, and divers sober christians amongst us, and therefore doe hereby exhort and advise all persons to use moderation in this respect; and further, doe impower all grand juries to present to the County Court such persons, whither male or female, whom they shall judge to exceede in the premisses; and the County Courts are hereby authorized to proceed against such delinquents either by admonition, fine, or correction, according to theire good discretion.

3. Notwithstanding the wholesome lawes already made by this Court for restreyning excess in apparrell, yet through corruption

in many, and neglect of due execution of those lawes, the evill of pride in apparrell, both for costlines in the poorer sort, & vaine, new, strainge fashions, both in poore & rich, with naked breasts and armes, or, as it were, pinioned with the addition of superstitious ribbons both on haire & apparrell; for redresse whereof, it is ordered by this Court, that the County Courts, from time to time, doe give strict charge to present all such persons as they shall judge to exceede in that kinde, and if the grand jury shall neglect theire duty herein, the County Court shall impose a fine upon them at their discretion.

And it is further ordered, that the County Court, single magistrate, Commissioners Court in Boston, have heereby power to summon all such persons so offending before them, and for the first offence to admonish them, and for each offence of that kinde afterwards to impose a fine of tenn shillings upon them, or, if unable to pay, to inflict such punishment as shall be by them thought most suiteable to the nature of the offence; and the same judges above named are heereby impowred to judge of and execute the lawes already extant against such excesse.

Whereas it may be found amongst us, that mens thresholds are sett up by Gods thresholds, and mans posts besides Gods posts, espeacially in the open meetings of Quakers, whose damnable haeresies, abominable idolatrys, are hereby promoted, embraced, and practised, to the scandall of religion, hazard of souls, and provocation of divine jealousie against this people, for prevention & reformation whereof, it is ordered by this Court and the authority thereof, that every person found at a Quakers meeting shall be apprehended, ex officio, by the constable, and by warrant from a magistrate or commissioner shall be committed to the house of correction, and there to have the discipline of the house applied to them, and to be kept to worke, with bread & water, for three days, and then released, or else shall pay five pounds in money as a fine to the county for such offence; and all constables neglecting their duty in not faithfully executing this order shall incurr the penalty of four pounds, upon conviction, one third whereof to the informer.

And touching the law of importation of Quakers, that it may be more strictly executed, and none transgressing to escape punishment,—

It is heereby ordered, that the penalty to that law averred be in no case abated to lesse than twenty pounds.

5. Whereas there is so mutch profanes amongst us in persons turning their backs upon the publick worship before it be finished and the blessing pronounced,—

It is ordered by this Court, that the officers of the churches, or select-men, shall take care to prevent such disorders, by appointing persons to shutt the meeting house doores, or any other meete way to attaine the end.

Disorderly Youth

6. Whereas there is much disorder & rudenes in youth in many congregations in time of the worship of God, whereby sin & prophaness is greately increased, for reformation whereof,—

It is ordered by this Court, that the select men doe appoint such place or places in the meeting house for children or youth to sit in where they may be most together and in publick veiw, and that the officers of the churches, or select-men, doe appoint some grave & sober person or persons to take a particcular care of and inspection over them, who are heereby required to present a list of the names of such, who, by their oune observance or the information of others, shall be found delinquent, to the next magistrate or Court, who are impowred for the first offence to admonish them, for the second offence to impose a fine of five shillings on theire parents or governnors, or order the children to be whipt, and if incorrigible, to be whipt with ten stripes, or sent to the house of correction for three dayes.

Forbidding Dangerous Games

Massachusetts was not the only New England colony that attempted to foster virtue by strict laws. The prohibition reprinted below is taken from the 1650 Code of the Connecticut General Court.

Upon complaint of great disorder, by the use of the game called shuffleboard, in houses of common entertainment, whereby much precious time is spent unfruitfully, and much waste of wine and beer occasioned: *It is therefore ordered and enacted by the authority of this Court,* that no person shall henceforth use the said game of shuffleboard in any such house, nor in any other house used as common for such purpose, upon pain for every keeper of such house to forfeit for every such offense 20s.; and for every person playing at the said game in any such house, to forfeit for every such offense 5s.; the like penalty shall be for playing in any place at any unlawful game.

---

7. Whereas the name of God is prophaned by common swearing and cursing in ordinary communication, which is a sin that growes amongst us, and many heare such oathes and curses, and conceales the same from authority, for reformation whereof, it is ordered by this Court, that the lawes already in force against this sin be vigorously prosecuted; and, as addition thereunto, it is further ordered, that all such persons who shall at any time heare prophane oathes and curses spoken by any person or persons,

and shall neglect to disclose the same to some magistrate, commissioner, or constable, such persons shall incurr the same penalty provided in that law against swearers.

8. Whereas the shamefull and scandelous sin of excessive drinking, tipling, & company keeping in tavernes, &c, ordinarys, grows upon us, for reformation whereof,—

It is commended to the care of the respective County Courts not to license any more publick houses then are absolutely necessary in any toune, and to take care that none be licenst but persons of approoved sobriety and fidelity to law and good order; and that licensed houses be regulated in theire improovement for the refreshing & enterteinment of travailers & strangers only, and all toune dwellers are heereby strictly enjoyned & required to forbeare spending their time or estates in such common houses of enterteynment, to drincke & tiple, upon penalty of five shillings for every offence, or, if poore, to be whipt, at the discretion of the judge, not exceeding five stripes; and every ordinary keeper, permitting persons to transgress as above said, shall incurr the penalty of five shillings for each offence in that kinde; and any magistrate, commissioner, or select-men are impowred & required vigorously to putt the above-said law in execution.

And, ffurther, it is ordered, that all private, unlicensed houses of entertainment be diligently searched out, and the penalty of this law strictly imposed; and that all such houses may be the better discovered, the select-men of every toune shall choose some sober and discreete persons, to be authorized from the County Court, each of whom shall take the charge of ten or twelve families of his neighbourhood, and shall diligently inspect them, and present the names of such persons so transgressing to the magistrate, commissioners, or select-men of the toune, who shall returne the same to be proceeded with by the next County Court as the law directs; and the persons so chosen and authorized, and attending theire duty ffaithfully therein, shall have one third of the fines allowed them; but, if neglect of their duty, and shall be so judged by authority, they shall incurr the same penalty provided against unlicensed houses.

Contempt of Authority

9. Whereas there is a wofull breach of the fifth comandment to be found amongst us, in contempt of authority civil, ecclesiasticall, and domesticall, this Court doeth declare, that sin is highly provoaking to the Lord, against which he hath borne severe testimony in his word, especially in that remarkeable judgments upon Chorah and his company, and therefore doe strictly require & comand all persons under this goverment to reforme so great an evil, least God from heaven punish offenders heerin by some re-

markeable judgments. And it is further ordered, that all County Courts, magistrates, commissioners, select-men, and grand jurors, according to theire severall capacities, doe take strict care that the lawes already made & provided in this case be duely executed, and particcularly that evil of inferiours absenting themselves out of the families whereunto they belong in the night, and meeting with corrupt company without leave, and against the minde & to the great greife of theire superiours, which evil practise is of a very perrillous nature, and the roote of much disorder.

It is therefore ordered by this Court, that whatever inferiour shallbe legally convicted of such an evil practise, such persons shall be punished with admonition for the first offence, with fine not exceeding ten shillings, or whipping not exceeding five stripes, for all offences of like nature afterwards.

10. Whereas the sin of idlenes (which is a sin of Sodom) doeth greatly increase, notwithstanding the wholesome lawes in force against the same, as an addition to that law,—

This Court doeth order, that the constable, with such other person or persons whom the select-men shall appoint, shall inspect particcular families, and present a lyst of the names of all idle persons to the select-men, who are heereby strictly required to proceed with them as already the law directs, and in case of obstinacy, by charging the constable with them, who shall convey them to some magistrate, by him to be committed to the house of correction.

11. Whereas there is oppression in the midst of us, not only by such shopkeepers and merchants who set excessive prizes on their goods, also by mechanicks but *also by mechanicks* and day labourers, who are dayly guilty of that evill, for redress whereoff, & as an adition to the law, title Oppression, itt is ordered by this Court, that any person that judgeth himself oppressed by shopkeepers or merchants in setting excessive prizes on their goods, have heereby liberty to make theire complaint to the grand jurors, or otherwise by petition to the County Court immediately, who shall send to the person accused, and if the Court, upon examination, judge the person complayning injuried, they shall cause the offendor to returne double the overplus, or more then the equall price, to the injured person, and also impose a fine on the offendors at the discretion of the Court; and if any person judge himself oppressed by mechanicks or day labourers, they may make complaint thereof to the select-men of the toune, who if upon the examination doe find such complaint just, having respect to the quality of the pay, and the length or shortnes of the day labour, they shall cause the offendor to make double restitution to the party injuried, and pay a fine of double the value exceeding the due price.

12. Whereas there is a loose & sinfull custome of going or riding from toune to toune, and that oft times men & weomen together, upon pretence of going to lecture, but it appeares to be meerely to drincke & revell in ordinarys & tavernes, which is in itself scandalous, and it is to be feared a notable meanes to debauch our youth and hazard the chastity of such as are draune forth thereunto, for prevention whereof,—

It is ordered by this Court, that all single persons who, meerly for their pleasure, take such journeyes, & frequent such ordinaryes, shall be reputed and accounted riotous & unsober persons, and of ill behaviour, and shall be liable to be summoned to appeare before any County Court, magistrate, or commissioner, & being thereof convicted, shall give bond & sufficient sureties for the good behaviour in twenty pounds, and upon refusall so to doe, shall be committed to prison for ten days, or pay a fine of forty shillings for each offence.

VIEWPOINT 6

"Marvelous it may be to see and consider how some kind of wickedness did grow and break forth here, in a land where the same was so much witnessed against . . . and severely punished."

Stricter Laws Have Limited Effectiveness

William Bradford (1590-1657)

Plymouth Colony, much like the other New England colonies, faced the problem of people not living up to the moral standards prescribed by their religious leaders. The following viewpoint is by William Bradford, who served as governor of the colony for most of the years between 1621 and 1656. Under his leadership Plymouth Colony was generally more tolerant of religious differences than Massachusetts Bay Colony (though not as tolerant as Rhode Island). The colony did not restrict the voting franchise to church members, and it permitted a variety of church organizations.

The viewpoint is taken from Bradford's history of Plymouth, *Of Plymouth Plantation, 1620-1647*, which he began around 1630 and finished in 1651. This passage, written in 1642, describes the "wickedness" happening in the Massachusetts Bay Colony, Bradford's northern neighbor. It contrasts with similar writings of other Puritans in its recognition that human nature cannot be controlled simply by strict laws and that the behavior seen here might not be worse than in other parts of the world, just more noticeable in light of the colony's high ideals.

From *Of Plymouth Plantation* 1620-1647 by William Bradford, edit., Samuel Eliot Morison. Copyright 1952 by Samuel Eliot Morison and renewed 1980 by Emily M. Beck. Reprinted by permission of Alfred A. Knopf, Inc.

Marvelous it may be to see and consider how some kind of wickedness did grow and break forth here, in a land where the same was so much witnessed against and so narrowly looked unto, and severely punished when it was known, as in no place more, or so much, that I have known or heard of; insomuch that they have been somewhat censured even by moderate and good men for their severity in punishments. And yet all this could not suppress the breaking out of sundry notorious sins (as this year [1642], besides other, gives us too many sad precedents and instances), especially drunkenness and uncleanness. Not only incontinency between persons unmarried, for which many both men and women have been punished sharply enough, but some married persons also. But that which is worse, even sodomy and buggery (things fearful to name) have broken forth in this land oftener than once.

I say it may justly be marveled at and cause us to fear and tremble at the consideration of our corrupt natures, which are so hardly bridled, subdued, and mortified; nay, cannot by any other means but the powerful work and grace of God's Spirit. But (besides this) one reason may be that the devil may carry a greater spite against the churches of Christ and the Gospel here, by how much the more they endeavor to preserve holiness and purity among them and strictly punish the contrary when it arises either in church or commonwealth; that he might cast a blemish and stain upon them in the eyes of [the] world, who use to be rash in judgment. I would rather think thus, than that Satan has more power in these heathen lands, as some have thought, than in more Christian nations, especially over God's servants in them.

Limits of Strict Laws

Another reason may be that it may be in this case as it is with waters when their streams are stopped or dammed up. When they get passage they flow with more violence and make more noise and disturbance than when they are suffered to run quietly in their own channels; so wickedness being here more stopped by strict laws, and the same more nearly looked unto so as it cannot run in a common road of liberty as it would and is inclined, it searches everywhere and at last breaks out where it gets vent.

A third reason may be, here (as I am verily persuaded) is not more evils in this kind, nor nothing near so many by proportion as in other places; but they are here more discovered and seen and made public by due search, inquisition, and due punishment; for the churches look narrowly to their members, and the magistrates over all, more strictly than in other places. Besides, here the

154

God's Judgment and Mercy

Sermons and pamphlets decrying the evil and corruption of New England were fairly common late in the seventeenth century. Reacting in part to such dire pronouncements, Nicholas Noyes, a minister at Salem, wrote New England's Duty and Interest *in 1698.*

Some make as if *New-England* were already as sinful, as sinful can be; as bad, as bad can be. To which I reply, I have no design to speak diminutively of the Sins of the Countrey; I do acknowledge with grief, and shame, that they have been, and are very horrible; yet I think such Sayings are not justifyable in any. Some well-meaning holy men, being of dark melancholly Spirits, and little acquainted with the advances that Atheism, Idolatry, Superstition, Prophaneness, Iniquity and Sensuality have made in other professing parts of the World; are apt to *think so*, and in their indignation against sin & sinners to *say so*. But the truth is, Though we have cause to abhor our selves for being so bad as we are; and to meditate all ways possible to grow better; yet it cannot with truth be asserted, that as yet we are as bad as bad can be; for there is real danger of growing worse. There are other designing persons, that are of a vulture Spirit, that fly hastily over all the fair meadows and fields without eying of them; that they may pitch and prey upon some Carrion. These find nothing but faults in the *Government, Churches, Ministers,* and *Good people* of all ranks: & Sport themselves with the falls of here and there an Eminent Professor; or the infirmities, & real, or supposed mistakes of men much better than themselves; *These fools make a mock of sin*; and it serves their occasion, to blaspheme all the Work of God in the Wilderness; and traduce for Hypocrites, all those, that their evil example can't make loose or prophane. All I shall say to this latter sort is, That I have no design to justify our selves; Shame, and blushing, and confusion of face belongeth to us: for we are sinners. Yet if a comparative goodness would serve our turn (as it will not) we might possibly pass in this degenerate Age. We acknowledge we are very bad; but yet not so bad; but we are afraid of being worse.

people are but few in comparison of other places which are full and populous and lie hid, as it were, in a wood or thicket and many horrible evils by that means are never seen nor known; whereas here they are, as it were, brought into the light and set in the plain field, or rather on a hill, made conspicuous to the view of all.

CHAPTER 4

Puritans and Native Americans

Chapter Preface

Contrary to what might be implied by some Puritan writings, Puritan settlements were not in uninhabited wilderness but the home of several different tribes of native Americans. The four major tribes, all members of the Algonquian family, were the Wampanoags (who lived in what became Plymouth Colony), the Massachuset (Massachusetts Bay), the Narragansetts (present-day Rhode Island), and the Pequots (present-day Connecticut). The population of Indians in the New England area is estimated to have been around twenty-five thousand in 1615, but it was reduced drastically by two plagues caused by germs brought over by Europeans in 1616-19 and 1633-34. Some Puritans interpreted the plagues as a sign from God that the land was being vacated for them.

Historians have differed on how the Puritans treated the Indians. Winthrop D. Jordan and Leon F. Litwack write in *The United States* that

> the Puritans wished the Indians would become civilized or simply go away. Intent on establishing their holy commonwealths, the English settlers regarded the Indians with a combination of hostility, contempt, and indifference.

Francis J. Bremer writes in *The Puritan Experiment*, however, that Puritan actions and attitudes toward the Indians compare favorably with those of other European colonists:

> In their political, legal, and economic relations with the Algonquian tribes of the Northeast, the Puritans tried to deal with the Indian as an equal. Assuming that Indians were born white and became darker only from ceremonial staining and the sun, the New England colonists were free of racist attitudes toward them. This was due partly to the widespread belief that the Indian tribes were descendants of the lost tribes of the Jews, whose conversion would signal the advent of the millennium. But if they did not view the Indian as racially inferior, they certainly judged him culturally inferior and gradually mounted an effort to "raise" him to the level of Englishmen by bringing him the blessings of civilization and Christianity.

Despite the Puritans' strongly held beliefs that theirs was the only true religion, Puritans spent little effort in trying to convert the Indians. Historians have suggested several reasons for this. One is that the Puritans spent most of their energy, especially in the early years, on their own survival. Another relates to the

157

structure of their church. Ministers in New England were responsible for their own congregations; the decentralized Congregationalist church of the Puritans made no provision for ordaining special missionaries to the Indians. A third reason involved the nature of Puritan conversion. Becoming a full-fledged member of a Puritan church required more than professing faith in Christianity and leading a moral life; it demanded an intimate knowledge of the Bible, which did not appear in the Algonquian language until 1663. It also required convincing testimony to a meaningful conversion experience—a condition not only difficult for Indians, but one that only some of the English could meet.

Historian Larzer Ziff writes in *Puritanism in America* that another factor hampering the Puritan missionary effort was their belief that Indians had to adopt English culture (and create godly communities like the Puritans) in order to become Christians.

> Puritan missionaries . . . in relative innocence of the profundity of cultural patterns, took on the task of settling the Indians into European patterns in their everyday life as a necessary prelude to saving their souls. The Indians were to wear European dress, till the soil, and organize themselves into little commonwealths whence a congregation could finally be gathered. . . .

> The history of the efforts is, in the main, a history of a double defeat: the failure of the Puritans to win men to their God and the destruction of a people who could not otherwise be made to relinquish their culture.

Puritan-Indian relations were generally peaceful, with two noteworthy exceptions. The first major violent conflict between Puritans and Indians was the Pequot War of 1637. The Puritans succeeded in obliterating the Pequot tribe, although their massacres of women and children appalled their Indian allies. The overwhelming defeat of the Pequots probably helps explain the relative peace between Puritans and Indians for the next four decades. Colonial officials passed laws protecting the rights of Indians. Puritan missionaries such as John Eliot eventually helped found fourteen praying towns—communities of Indians who had accepted Puritan teachings—comprised of more than a thousand Indians.

In 1675 the peace was shattered by King Philip's War, the first large Indian uprising in the region's history. Metacom (or Metacomet), the chief of the Wampanoag tribe known to the colonists as King Philip, was upset over increasing white inroads into Indian lands and Indian subjection to English law and domination. When an Indian informant who told the colonists of Metacom's plans of resistance was later killed, the resulting retaliations and counterretaliations erupted into full-scale war. The colonists outnumbered the Indians and succeeded in quelling the uprising, but not until several thousand colonists and Indians (including Metacom) had perished. During the war, distinctions between tribes and between converted and nonconverted Indians were lost as the Puritans began to view all Indians as enemies. Bremer writes:

> King Philip's War was a turning point. While the earlier Pequot War had been essentially a conflict between the Puritans and a large segment of the Indians against a single tribe, the clash with Metacomet was far more of a race war in the eyes of the colonists, and it certainly was a graver threat to the survival of the English settlements. Because a large portion of the Indians turned against the English, and because the outlying settlements suffered fearfully from the atrocities of war, the pervasive attitudes among the Puritans turned bitter. During the war the praying Indians had to be relocated to an island in Boston harbor and guarded against the populace. And despite the aid of Christian Indians in bringing the uprising to an end, the broad support that had brought much success to the missionary effort could not be recaptured after the war. By 1700 the Puritans had begun to regard the Indians as a race apart. An emerging racism, based on fear of the Indian and a suspicion that he would never accept Christianity, justified a more callous treatment of the native tribes. . . . The charitable impulse of the earlier decades was all but forgotten.

VIEWPOINT 1

"If we took any lands from the natives, it was by way of purchase, and free consent."

Puritan Treatment of Indians Is Justified

John Cotton (1584-1652)

John Cotton, a Puritan clergyman, was one of the most famous of the New England ministers. He wrote numerous tracts and articles that were published in both England and America. Many of those tracts were debates with New England's most famous dissenter, Roger Williams. In the following viewpoint, taken from a tract first published in 1644, Cotton attacks Williams' views on the Indians. Williams had accused the Puritan colonies of illegally taking land away from the Indians, arguing that the king of England had no automatic right to grant American land. Cotton defends the legality of the colony's patent—the legal document by which the king of England secured the settlers' right to colonize the land. Cotton defends Puritan actions, in part by the doctrine of *vacuum domicilium* (the Indians had vacated the land, and thus had not truly possessed it).

From John Cotton, "A Reply to Mr. Williams His Examination" In *Publications of Narragansett Club*. Volume 2. Providence, 1867.

By the patent it is, that we [the settlers of Massachusetts Bay] received allowance from the King to depart his kingdom, and to carry our goods with us, without offense to his officers, and without paying custom to himself.

By the patent, certain select men (as magistrates, and freemen) have power to make laws, and the magistrates to execute justice, and judgment amongst the people, according to such laws.

By the patent we have power to erect such a government of the church, as is most agreeable to the Word, to the estate of the people, and to the gaining of natives (in God's time) first to civility and then to Christianity.

To this authority established by this patent, *Englishmen* do readily submit themselves: and foreign plantations (the *French*, the *Dutch*, and *Swedish*) do willingly transact their negotiations with us, as with a colony established by the royal authority of the state of *England*.

This patent, Mr. Williams publicly, and vehemently preached against, as containing matter of falsehood, and injustice: falsehood in making the King the first Christian prince who had discovered these parts: and injustice, in giving the country to his *English* subjects, which belonged to the native Indians. This therefore he pressed upon the magistrates and people, to be humbled for from time to time in days of solemn humiliation, and to return the patent back again to the King. It was answered to him, first, that it was neither the King's intendment, nor the *English* planters' to take possession of the country by murder of the natives, or by robbery; but either to take possession of the void places of the country by the law of nature, (for *vacuum domicilium cedit occupanti:*) or if we took any lands from the natives, it was by way of purchase, and free consent.

God Has Swept Them Away

A little before our coming, God had by pestilence, and other contagious diseases, swept away many thousands of the natives who had inhabited the Bay of *Massachusetts*, for which the patent was granted. Such few of them as survived were glad of the coming of the *English*, who might preserve them from the oppression of the *Narragansetts*. For it is the manner of the natives, the stronger nations to oppress the weaker.

This answer did not satisfy Mr. Williams, who pleaded, the natives, though they did not, nor could subdue the country, (but left it *vacuum domicilium*) yet they hunted all the country over, and for the expedition of their hunting voyages, they burnt up all the underwoods in the country, once or twice a year, and therefore as noble men in *England* possessed great parks, and the King great forests in *England* only for their game, and no man might lawfully invade their propriety: so might the natives challenge the like propriety of the country here.

It was replied unto him.

1. That the King, and noble men in *England*, as they possessed greater territories than other men, so they did greater service to church, and commonwealth.

2. That they employed their parks, and forests, not for hunting only, but for timber, and for the nourishment of tame beasts, as well as wild, and also for habitation to sundry tenants.

3. That our towns here did not disturb the huntings of the natives, but did rather keep their game fitter for their taking; for they take their deer by traps, and not by hounds.

4. That if they complained of any straits we put upon them, we gave satisfaction in some payments, or other, to their content.

5. We did not conceive that it is a just title to so vast a continent, to make no other improvement of millions of acres in it, but only to burn it up for pastime.

But these answers not satisfying him, this was still pressed by him as a national sin, to hold to the patent, yea, and a national duty to renounce the patent: which to have done, had subverted the fundamental state and government of the country.

VIEWPOINT 2

"I humbly pray your consideration, whether it be not only possible, but very easy, to live and die in peace with the natives of this country."

Puritan Treatment of Indians Is Not Justified

Roger Williams (1603-1683)

Roger Williams, one of America's first religious dissenters, was a minister who was banished from the Massachusetts Bay Colony in 1636 and subsequently founded the colony of Rhode Island. His banishment occurred in part because of his accusation that the colony's leaders were treating the Indians unfairly.

Williams was one of the few Puritans who learned the Indians' languages and studied their cultures. During the 1637 Pequot War he negotiated with several Indian tribes on behalf of all New England colonies. He wrote *A Key to the Language of America*, an examination of the language and customs of the Narragansett tribe, based on his experiences with them following his banishment.

Throughout his long life he wrote against the violent and unfair treatment many colonists perpetrated against the Indians. His view on Puritan mistreatment of the Indians is found in a 1654 letter to the General Court of Massachusetts. He speaks against the "seeming occasions for their destructions"—preemptive Puritan attacks on Indian villages—and argues against judging whole tribes on the basis of "a few inconsiderate pagans."

From Roger Williams's 1654 letter to the Massachusetts General Court. In *Records of the Colony of Rhode Island and Providence Plantations in New England*. Volume 1. Edited by John Russell Bartlett. Providence, 1856.

I never was against the righteous use of the civil sword of men or nations, but yet since all men of conscience or prudence ply to windward, to maintain their wars to be defensive (as did both King and Scotch, and English, and Irish too, in the late wars), I humbly pray your consideration, whether it be not only possible, but very easy, to live and die in peace with the natives of this country.

For, secondly, are not all the English of this land, generally, a persecuted people from their native soil? And hath not the God of peace and Father of mercies made these natives more friendly in this, than our native countrymen in our own land to us? Have they not entered leagues of love, and to this day continued peaceable commerce with us? Are not our families grown up in peace amongst them? Upon which I humbly ask, how it can suit with Christian ingenuity to take hold of some seeming occasions for their destructions, which, though the heads be only aimed at, yet, all experience tells us, falls on the body and on the innocent. . . .

Preserving the Name of God

Whether I have been and am a friend to the natives turning to civility and Christianity, and whether I have been instrumental, and desire so to be, according to my light, I will not trouble you with; only I beseech you consider, how the name of the most holy and jealous God may be preserved between the clashings of these two viz.: the glorious conversion of the Indians in New England, and the unnecessary wars and cruel destructions of the Indians in New England. . . .

I cannot yet learn, that it ever pleased the Lord to permit the Narragansetts to stain their hands with any English blood, neither in open hostilities nor secret murders, as both Pequots and Long Islanders did, and Mohegans, also, in the Pequot wars. It is true they are barbarians, but their greatest offenses against the English have been matters of money, or petty revenging of themselves on some Indians, upon extreme provocations, but God kept them clear of our blood. . . .

But, I beseech you, say your thoughts and the thoughts of your wives and little ones, and the thoughts of all English, and of God's people in England, and the thoughts of His Highness and Council (tender of these parts), if, for the sake of a few inconsiderable pagans, and beasts, wallowing in idleness, stealing, lying, whoring, treacherous witchcrafts, blasphemies, and idolatries, all that the gracious hand of the Lord hath so wonderfully planted in the wilderness, should be destroyed.

VIEWPOINT 3

"The Lord hath prepared this honor for you, oh you courageous soldiers of His, to execute vengeance upon the heathen."

Killing Indians Is Justified by God

Edward Johnson (1598-1672)

Edward Johnson, a trader who first came to New England in 1630 and moved his family there in 1636, wrote a history of the Massachusetts Bay Colony titled *Wonder-Working Providence of Sion's Savior in New England*. The work, first published in England in 1654, sought in part to paint a positive picture of the colony for the people of England.

In the section of the history dealing with the Pequot War, Johnson included a sample speech to illustrate what the Puritan clergymen preached to the soldiers before battle. The major battle in the Pequot War (in which Mohegan Indians joined the Puritans against the Pequot tribe) occurred on May 26, 1637, when Puritans attacked and burned a Pequot fort on the Mystic River, killing most of its several hundred inhabitants including women and children.

From Edward Johnson, *Wonder-Working Providence of Sion's Savior in New England,* published in England in 1654.

165

Fellow soldiers, countrymen, and companions in this wilderness work, who are gathered together this day by the inevitable providence of the great Jehovah, not in a tumultuous manner hurried on by the floating fancy of every high hot-headed brain, whose actions prove abortive, or if any fruit brought forth, it hath been rape, theft, and murder, things inconsisting with nature's light, then much less with a soldier's valor; but you, my dear hearts, purposely picked out by the godly grave fathers of this government, that your prowess may carry on the work, where there justice in her righteous course is obstructed, you need not question your authority to execute those whom God, the righteous Judge of all the world, hath condemned for blaspheming His sacred majesty, and murdering His servants: every common soldier among you is now installed a magistrate; then show yourselves men of courage. I would not draw low the height of your enemies' hatred against you, and so debase your valor. This you may expect, their swelling pride hath laid the foundation of large conceptions against you and all the people of Christ in this wilderness, even as wide as Babel's bottom but, my brave soldiers, it hath mounted already to the clouds, and therefore it is ripe for confusion; also their cruelty is famously known, yet all true-bred soldiers reserve this as a common maxim, cruelty and cowardice are unseparable companions; and in brief, there is nothing wanting on your enemies' part, that may deprive you of a complete victory, only their nimbleness of foot, and the unaccessible swamps and nut-tree woods, forth of which your small numbers may entice, and industry compel them. And now to you I put the question, who would not fight in such a cause with an agile spirit, and undaunted boldness? yet if you look for further encouragement, I have it for you; riches and honor are the next to a good cause eyed by every soldier, to maintain your own, and spoil your enemies' of theirs; although gold and silver be wanting to either of you, yet have you that to maintain which is far more precious, the lives, liberties, and new purchased freedoms, privileges, and immunities of the endeared servants of our Lord Christ Jesus, and of your second selves, even your affectionated bosommates, together with the chief pledges of your love, the comforting contents of harmless prattling and smiling babes; and in a word, all the riches of that goodness and mercy that attends the people of God in the enjoyment of Christ, in His ordinances, even in this life; and as for honor, David was not to be blamed for enquiring after it, as a due recompense of that true value the Lord hath bestowed on him: and now the Lord hath prepared this honor for you, oh you courageous soldiers of His, to execute vengeance upon the heathen, and correction among the people, to bind their kings in chains, and nobles in fetters of iron, that they may execute upon them the judgments that are written: this honor shall be to all His saints. But some of you may suppose death's stroke may cut you short of this: let every faithful soldier of Christ Jesus know, that the cause why some of His endeared servants are taken away by death in a just war (as this assuredly is) it is not because they should fall short of the honors accompanying such noble designs, but rather because earth's honors are too scant for them, and therefore the everlasting crown must be set upon their heads forthwith. Then march on with a cheerful Christian courage in the strength of the Lord and the power of His might, who will forthwith enclose your enemies in your hands, make their multitudes fall under your warlike weapons, and your feet shall soon be set on their proud necks.

VIEWPOINT 4

"I should think it requisite that convenient tracts of land should be set out to them."

The Indians Should Be Treated Charitably

Samuel Sewall (1652-1730)

Samuel Sewall was a leading Puritan judge and political figure. As judge he played a role in the Salem witch trials—a role he later confessed was in error. He served as Chief Justice of Massachusetts from 1718 to 1728.

Most of his career occurred after King Philip's War at a time when the threat of Indian warfare was relatively small. The following viewpoint is taken from a May 3, 1700, letter in which Sewall expressed his concerns on how the Indians were being treated. Among his suggestions for improved treatment are the ideas of recruiting Christian missionaries and teachers from Indian converts and fixing fair boundaries for Indian lands.

Last fall, I had notice of my being entrusted with a share in managing the Indian affairs, and presently upon it, the Commissioners were pleased to appoint me their secretary. As I account it an honor to be thus employed, so according to my mean ability, I shall endeavor faithfully to serve the Corporation and Commissioners, as I shall receive instructions from them.

From Samuel Sewall, "Accommodating the Indians." In *Collections of the Massachusetts Historical Society*. 6th series. Volume 1. Courtesy of the Massachusetts Historical Society.

I have met with an observation of some grave divines, that ordinarily when God intends good to a nation, He is pleased to make use of some of themselves to be instrumental in conveying of that good unto them. Now God has furnished several of the Indians with considerable abilities for the work of the ministry, and teaching school. And therefore I am apt to believe that if the Indians so qualified were more taken notice of in suitable rewards, it would conduce very much to the propagation of the Gospel among them. Besides the content they might have in a provision of necessary food and raiment, the respect and honor of it would quicken their industry and allure others to take pains in fitting themselves for a fruitful discharge of those offices.

A Grievous War

One thing more I would crave leave to suggest. We have had a very long and grievous war with the Eastern Indians, and it is of great concernment to His Majesty's interests here that a peace be concluded with them upon firm and sure foundations; which in my poor opinion cannot well be while our articles of accord with them remain so very general as they do. I should think it requisite that convenient tracts of land should be set out to them; and that by plain and natural boundaries, as much as may be—as lakes, rivers, mountains, rocks—upon which for any Englishman to encroach should be accounted a crime. Except this be done, I fear their own jealousies, and the French friars, will persuade them that the English, as they increase and think they want more room, will never leave till they have crowded them quite out of all their lands. And it will be a vain attempt for us to offer Heaven to them if they take up prejudices against us, as if we did grudge them a living upon their own earth.

The Savoy Confession of Faith, English on one side and Indian on the other, has been lately printed here; as also several sermons of the president's [of Harvard, Increase Mather] have been transcribed into Indian and printed; which I hope in God's time will have a very good effect. To see it and be employed in giving Your Honor an account of it would be a very desirable piece of service to [me].

VIEWPOINT 5

"The deepest estrangements of man from God is no hindrance to His Grace ... for what nation or people ever so deeply degenerated since Adam's fall as these Indians, and yet the Spirit of God is working upon them?"

A Missionary's View of Indians

John Eliot (1604-1690)

A Puritan minister who migrated to America in 1631, John Eliot shared ministerial duties in Roxbury, Massachusetts, with Thomas Welde. In the 1640s Eliot learned the Algonquian language from an Indian servant and began missionary work among the Indians. He continued his evangelizing until his death. Widely known both in America and in England as the "Apostle to the Indians," Eliot translated the Bible into the Algonquian language and wrote numerous pamphlets and tracts.

Eliot's views reflecting his hope of converting the Indians are preserved in a pamphlet first published in London in 1646. Part of its purpose was to elicit English support for his missionary efforts. The work, titled *The Day-Breaking, if not the Sun-Rising of the Gospell with the Indians in New-England*, is interesting for the information it provides on both Indians and their Puritan observers.

From John Eliot "The Day-Breaking, If Not the Sun-Rising, of the Gospell with the Indians in New-England." In *Collections of the Massachusetts Historical Society*. 3d series. Volume 3. Courtesy of the Massachusetts Historical Society.

Methinks now that it is with the Indians as it was with our New English ground when we first came over—there was scarce any man that could believe that English grain would grow, or that the plow could do any good in this woody and rocky soil. And thus they continued in this supine unbelief for some years, till experience taught them otherwise; and now all see it to be scarce inferior to Old English tillage, but bears very good burdens. So we have thought of our Indian people, and, therefore, have been discouraged to put plow to such dry and rocky ground, but God, having begun thus with some few, it may be they are better soil for the gospel than we can think.

I confess I think no great good will be done till they be more civilized. But why may not God begin with some few to awaken others by degrees? Nor do I expect any great good will be wrought by the English (leaving secrets to God, although the English surely begin and lay the first stones of Christ's kingdom and temple among them), because God is wont ordinarily to convert nations and peoples by some of their own countrymen who are nearest to them and can best speak, and, most of all, pity their brethren and countrymen. But yet, if the least beginnings be made by the conversion of two or three, it is worth all our time and travails, and cause of much thankfulness for such seeds, although no great harvests should immediately appear.

Surely this is evident, first, that they never heard heartbreaking prayer and preaching before now in their own tongue, that we know of. Second, that there were never such hopes of a dawning of mercy toward them as now. Certainly those abundant tears which we saw shed from their eyes argue a mighty and blessed presence of the Spirit of Heaven in their hearts, which when once it comes into such kind of spirits will not easily out again.

Hopeful Beginnings

The chief use that I can make of these hopeful beginnings, besides rejoicing for such shinings, is from Is. 2:5: "Oh, house of Israel, let us walk in the light of the Lord," considering that these blind natives begin to look toward God's mountain now.

The observations I have gathered by conversing with them are such as these:

1. That none of them . . . derided God's messenger: Woe unto those English that are grown bold to do that which Indians will not—heathens dare not.

2. That there is need of learning in ministers who preach to Indians, much more to Englishmen and gracious Christians, for these had sundry philosophical questions which some knowl-

edge of the arts must help to give answer to; and without which these would not have been satisfied. Worse than Indian ignorance has blinded their eyes that renounce learning as an enemy to gospel ministries.

3. That there is no necessity of extraordinary gifts nor miraculous signs always to convert heathens . . . for we see the Spirit of God working mightily upon the hearts of these natives in an ordinary way, and I hope will, they being but a remnant, the Lord using to show mercy to the remnant. For there be but few that are left alive from the plague and pox, which God sent into those parts; and, if one or two can understand, they usually talk of it as we do of news—it flies suddenly far and near, and truth scattered will rise in time, for ought we know.

A 1659 portrait of John Eliot, Puritan minister and missionary to the Indians.

4. If Englishmen begin to despise the preaching of faith and repentance and humiliation for sin, yet the poor heathens will be glad of it and it shall do good to them; for so they are and so it begins to do. The Lord grant that the foundation of our English woe be not laid in the ruin and contempt of those fundamental doctrines of faith, repentance, humiliation for sin, etc., but rather relishing the novelties and dreams of such men as are surfeited with the ordinary food of the Gospel of Christ. Indians shall weep to hear faith and repentance preached, when Englishmen shall

mourn, too late, that are weary of such truths.

5. That the deepest estrangements of man from God is no hindrance to His grace nor to the spirit of grace; for what nation or people ever so deeply degenerated since Adam's fall as these Indians, and yet the Spirit of God is working upon them?

Converting the Indians

6. That it is very likely if ever the Lord convert any of these natives that they will mourn for sin exceedingly and, consequently, love Christ dearly; for, if by a little measure of light such heartbreakings have appeared, what may we think will be when more is let in? They are some of them very wicked, some very ingenious. These latter are very apt and quick of understanding and naturally sad and melancholy (a good servant to repentance); and, therefore, there is the greater hope of great heartbreakings if ever God brings them effectually home, for which we should affectionately pray. . . .

We have cause to be very thankful to God who has moved the hearts of the General Court to purchase so much land for them to make their town in which the Indians are much taken with. And it is somewhat observable that, while the court were considering where to lay out their town, the Indians (not knowing of anything) were about that time consulting about laws for themselves, and their company who sit down with Waaubon. There were ten of them; two of them are forgotten.

Their laws were these:

1. That if any man be idle a week, at most a fortnight, he shall pay 5s [shillings].

2. If any unmarried man shall lie with a young woman unmarried, he shall pay 20s.

3. If any man shall beat his wife, his hands shall be tied behind him and [he shall be] carried to the place of justice to be severely punished.

4. Every young man, if not another's servant and if unmarried, he shall be compelled to set up a wigwam and plant for himself, and not live shifting up and down to other wigwams.

5. If any woman shall not have her hair tied up but hang loose or be cut as men's hair, she shall pay 5s.

6. If any woman shall go with naked breasts, [she] shall pay 2s. 6d [2 shillings 6 pence].

7. All those men that wear long locks shall pay 5s.

8. If any shall kill their lice between their teeth, they shall pay 5s. This law, though ridiculous to English ears, yet tends to preserve cleanliness among Indians.

It is wonderful in our eyes to understand by these two honest Indians what prayers Waaubon and the rest of them use to make, for he that preaches to them professes he never yet used any of their words in his prayers, from whom otherwise it might be thought that they had learned them by rote. One is this:

Amanaomen Jehovah tahassen metagh.

(Take away Lord my stony heart.)

Another:

Chechesom Jehovah kekowhogkew.

(Wash Lord my soul.)

Another:

(Lord lead me, when I die, to heaven.)

These are but a taste. They have many more, and these more en-larged than thus expressed, yet what are these but the sprinklings of the spirit and blood of Christ Jesus in their hearts?

And it is no small matter that such dry, barren, and long-accursed ground should yield such kind of increase in so small a time. I would not readily commend a fair day before night, nor promise much of such kind of beginnings, in all persons, nor yet in all of these, for we know the profession of very many is but a mere paint, and their best graces nothing but mere flashes and pangs, which are suddenly kindled and as soon go out and are extinct again. Yet God does not usually send His plow and seeds-man to a place but there is at least some little piece of good ground, although three to one be naught. And methinks the Lord Jesus would never have made so fit a key for their locks, unless He had intended to open some of their doors, and so to make way for His coming in. He that God has raised up and enabled to preach unto them is a man (you know) of a most sweet, humble, loving, gracious, and enlarged spirit, whom God hath blessed, and surely will still delight in and do good by.

Considerations

I did think never to have opened my mouth to any to desire those in England to further any good work here, but now I see so many things inviting to speak in this business that it were well if you did lay before those that are prudent and able these consider-ations:

1. That it is pretty heavy and chargeable to educate and train up those children which are already offered us, in schooling, cloth-ing, diet, and attendance, which they must have.

2. That in all probability, many Indians in other places, espe-cially under our jurisdiction, will be provoked by this example in these, both to desire preaching and also to send their children to us, when they see that some of their fellows fare so well among the English, and the civil authority here so much favoring and countenancing of these; and if many more come in, it will be more heavy to such as only are fit to keep them, and yet have

their hands and knees enfeebled so many ways besides.

3. That if any shall do anything to encourage this work, that it may be given to the college for such an end and use, that so from the college may arise the yearly revenue for their yearly maintenance. I would not have it placed in any particular man's hands for fear of cozenage or misplacing or careless keeping and improving; but at the college it is under many hands and eyes, the chief and best of the country who have been and will be exactly careful of the right and comely disposing of such things. And, therefore, if anything be given, let it be put in such hands as may immediately direct it to the president of the college, who you know will soon acquaint the rest with it; and for this end if any in England have thus given anything for this end, I would have them speak to those who have received it to send it this way, which if it be withheld I think it is no less than sacrilege. But if God moves no hearts to such a work, I doubt not then but that [weaker] means shall have the honor of it in the Day of Christ.

Instructing the Children

This day being December 9, the children being catechized, and that place of Ezekiel touching the dry bones being opened and applied to their condition, the Indians offered all their children to us to be educated among us and instructed by us, complaining to us that they were not able to give anything to the English for their education. For this reason, there are, therefore, preparations made toward the schooling of them, and setting up a school among them or very near unto them. Sundry questions also were propounded by them to us, and of us to them; one of them being asked, "What is sin?" He answered, "A naughty heart." Another old man complained to us of his fears, viz., that he was fully purposed to keep the Sabbath, but still he was in fear whether he should go to hell or heaven; and thereupon the justification of a sinner by faith in Christ was opened unto him as the remedy against all fears of hell. Another complained of other Indians that did revile them and call them rogues and suchlike speeches for cutting off their locks, and for cutting their hair in a modest manner as the New English generally do; for since the Word has begun to work upon their hearts, they have discerned the vanity and pride which they placed in their hair, and have, therefore, of their own accord (none speaking to them that we know of), cut it modestly. They were therefore encouraged by some there present of chief place and account with us not to fear the reproaches of wicked Indians, nor their witchcraft and powwows and poisonings; but let them know that if they did not dissemble but would seek God unfeignedly, that they would stand by them, and that God also would be with them.

They told us also of diverse Indians who would come and stay with them three or four days and one Sabbath, and then they would go from them. But as for themselves, they told us they were fully purposed to keep the Sabbath, to which we encouraged them; and, night drawing on, [we] were forced to leave them for this time.

VIEWPOINT 6

*"The enemy came upon our town like . . . so many
ravenous wolves, rending us and our lambs to death. But
what shall I say? God seemed to leave His people to
themselves and order all things for His own holy ends."*

A Captive's View
of Indians

Mary Rowlandson (c. 1635-c. 1678)

Mary Rowlandson was the author of one of the best selling and
widely read works of the colonial era—an account of her three-
month captivity by Indians during King Philip's War. *The
Soveraignty & Goodness of God . . . Being a Narrative of the Captivity
and Restauration of Mrs. Mary Rowlandson* is noteworthy for several reasons, including its gripping story of capture and imprisonment, its ruminations on God's power and His role in permitting such suffering, and its descriptions of Indian life. It provides
evidence of changing Puritan attitudes toward the Indians as
events like King Philip's War discouraged their hopes of conversion and peaceful coexistence.

Little is known of Rowlandson's life outside of what she tells in
her captivity narrative. She was the wife of Joseph Rowlandson,
the minister of Lancaster, a small village on the edge of the western frontier of Massachusetts. Her life as a minister's wife and
mother of three children was in all likelihood relatively unevent-
ful until February 10, 1676, when a band of Indians attacked the
village and captured her and her three children. (Joseph is believed to have been in Boston petitioning for more troops for Lan-

Reprinted by permission of the publishers from *Puritans Among the Indians: Accounts of
Captivity and Redemption, 1676-1724.* Edited by Alden T. Vaughn and Edward W. Clark.
Cambridge, MA: The Belknap Press of Harvard University Press, 1981. Copyright © 1981
by the President and Fellows of Harvard College.

caster, a circumstance which probably saved his life.) Her youngest child, wounded in the fighting, soon died, and her other children were soon separated from her. For almost three months the Indians held her prisoner, until on May 2 she was released for the sizable sum of twenty pounds of goods. She was shortly thereafter reunited with her husband and surviving children, who were also eventually released.

Rowlandson's account of her Indian captors is in some respects sympathetic, and she makes a point to mention that "not one of them ever offered me the least abuse of unchastity to me in word or action." However, her descriptions also reflect the change in Puritan attitudes. In the relatively peaceful decades before 1675 many Puritans viewed the Indians as unbelievers that needed to be converted, and they supported the efforts of missionaries such as John Eliot. With the coming of war, they began to perceive the Indians—including those who professed Christianity and lived in special Indian Christian communities—as enemies to be exterminated. Professors of English Richard Slotkin and James K. Folsom write in their book *So Dreadful a Judgment: Puritan Responses to King Philip's War*:

> Prior to 1675 opinion at least among the ministry had held that Indians were "heathens"; subsequently they became "savages." A "Praying Indian," according to Mary Rowlandson's eloquent witness, was no more than a hypocrite, totally enslaved still to his master Satan, the Prince of this world and the Father of Lies—and it should be remembered that she was by birth and by marriage part of the group that had previously most staunchly defended the enterprise of the "Apostle" Eliot in his attempts at converting the Indians to Christianity.

Rowlandson's account, with its descriptions of Indians gathering food, preparing for war, and asking her to sew things, combined with theological reflections on the goodness and nature of God, makes for revealing reading. Slotkin and Folsom conclude that Rowlandson's writing is

> a uniquely human and touching document, both as a record of incredible fortitude under hardship in which the inner life is as carefully observed as the outer and as an account of the Indians that couples genuine human sympathy with a hatred almost unimaginable to one who has not gone through her experiences.

On the tenth of February 1675 [1676 in modern reckoning] came the Indians with great numbers upon Lancaster. Their first coming was about sunrising. Hearing the noise of some guns, we looked out; several houses were burning and the smoke ascending to heaven. There were five persons taken in one house; the father and the mother and a sucking child they knocked on the head; the other two they took and carried away alive. There were two others, who being out of their garrison upon some occasion were set upon; one was knocked on the head, the other escaped. Another there was who running along was shot and wounded and fell down; he begged of them his life, promising them money (as they told me), but they would not hearken to him but knocked him in [the] head, stripped him naked, and split open his bowels. . . . Thus these murderous wretches went on, burning and destroying before them. . . .

The tenth edition of Mary Rowlandson's popular narrative was published in 1773. Its title page featured a woodcut and a secular title.

My eldest sister [Elizabeth] being yet in the house and seeing those woeful sights, the infidels hailing mothers one way and children another and some wallowing in their blood, and her elder son telling her that her son William was dead and myself was wounded, she said, "And, Lord, let me die with them." Which was no sooner said, but she was struck with a bullet and fell down dead over the threshold. I hope she is reaping the fruit of her good labors, being faithful to the service of God in her place. . . . But to return: the Indians laid hold of us, pulling me one way and the children another, and said, "Come go along with us." I told them they would kill me. They answered, if I were willing to go along with them they would not hurt me.

Oh, the doleful sight that now was to behold at this house! "Come, behold the works of the Lord, what desolation He has made in the earth." Of thirty-seven persons who were in this one house none escaped either present death or a bitter captivity save only one, who might say as he, Job 1:15, "And I only am escaped alone to tell the news." There were twelve killed, some shot, some stabbed with their spears, some knocked down with their hatchets. . . .

I had often before this said that if the Indians should come I should choose rather to be killed by them than taken alive, but when it came to the trial, my mind changed; their glittering weapons so daunted my spirit that I chose rather to go along with those (as I may say) ravenous beasts than that moment to end my days. And that I may the better declare what happened to me during that grievous captivity, I shall particularly speak of the several removes we had up and down the wilderness.

The First Remove

Now away we must go with those barbarous creatures with our bodies wounded and bleeding and our hearts no less than our bodies. About a mile we went that night up upon a hill within sight of the town where they intended to lodge. There was hard by a vacant house (deserted by the English before for fear of the Indians). I asked them whether I might not lodge in the house that night, to which they answered, "What, will you love English men still?" This was the dolefullest night that ever my eyes saw. Oh, the roaring and singing and dancing and yelling of those black creatures in the night, which made the place a lively resemblance of hell. And as miserable was the waste that was there made of horses, cattle, sheep, swine, calves, lambs, roasting pigs, and fowl (which they had plundered in the town), some roasting, some lying and burning, and some boiling to feed our merciless enemies who were joyful enough though we were disconsolate. To add to the dolefulness of the former day and the dismalness of the present night, my thoughts ran upon my losses and sad bereaved condition. All was gone: my husband gone (at least separated from me, he being in the Bay, and to add to my grief, the Indians told me they would kill him as he came homeward), my children gone, my relations and friends gone, our house and home and all our comforts within door and without, all was gone except my life, and I knew not but the next moment that might go too. There remained nothing to me but one poor wounded babe, and it seemed at present worse than death that it was in such a pitiful condition bespeaking compassion, and I had no refreshing for it nor suitable things to revive it. Little do many think what is the savageness and brutishness of this barbarous enemy, ay, even those that seem to profess more than others among them when the English have fallen into their hands. . . .

The morning being come, they prepared to go on their way. One of the Indians got up upon a horse, and they set me up behind him with my poor sick babe in my lap. A very wearisome and tedious day I had of it what with my own wound and my child's being so exceeding sick in a lamentable condition with her wound. It may be easily judged what a poor feeble condition we were in, there being not the least crumb of refreshing that came within either of our mouths from Wednesday night to Saturday night except only a little cold water. This day in the afternoon about an hour by sun we came to the place where they intended, *viz.* an Indian town called Wenimesset, nor[th]ward of Quabaug. When we were come, oh, the number of pagans (now merciless enemies) that there came about me that I may say as David, Psal. 27:13, "I had fainted, unless I had believed," etc. The next day was the Sabbath. I then remembered how careless I had been of God's holy time, how many Sabbaths I had lost and misspent and how evilly I had walked in God's sight, which lay so close unto my spirit that it was easy for me to see how righteous it was with God to cut the thread of my life and cast me out of His presence forever. Yet the Lord still showed mercy to me and upheld me, and as He wounded me with one hand, so He healed me with the other. . . .

Death of a Child

Nine days I sat upon my knees with my babe in my lap till my flesh was raw again; my child being even ready to depart this sorrowful world, they bade me carry it out to another wigwam (I suppose because they would not be troubled with such spectacles), whither I went with a heavy heart, and down I sat with the picture of death in my lap. About two hours in the night my sweet babe like a lamb departed this life on Feb. 18, 1675 [1676], it being about six years and five months old. It was nine days from the first wounding in this miserable condition without any refreshing of one nature or other except a little cold water. I cannot but take notice how at another time I could not bear to be in the room where any dead person was, but now the case is changed; I

181

must and could lie down by my dead babe side by side all the night after. I have thought since of the wonderful goodness of God to me in preserving me in the use of my reason and senses in that distressed time that I did not use wicked and violent means to end my own miserable life.

In the morning when they understood that my child was dead, they sent for me home to my master's wigwam. (By my master in this writing must be understood Quanopin who was a sagamore and married [to] King Philip's wife's sister, not that he first took me, but I was sold to him by another Narragansett Indian who took me when first I came out of the garrison.) I went to take up my dead child in my arms to carry it with me, but they bid me let it alone. There was no resisting, but go I must and leave it. When I had been at my master's wigwam, I took the first opportunity I could get to go look after my dead child. When I came, I asked them what they had done with it. Then they told me it was upon the hill. Then they went and showed me where it was, where I saw the ground was newly digged, and there they told me they had buried it. There I left that child in the wilderness and must commit it and myself also in this wilderness condition to Him who is above all. . . .

The next day, *viz.* to this, the Indians returned from Medfield all the company, for those that belonged to the other small company came through the town that now we were at. But before they came to us, oh, the outrageous roaring and whooping that there was! They began their din about a mile before they came to us. By their noise and whooping they signified how many they had destroyed, which was at that time twenty-three. Those that were with us at home were gathered together as soon as they heard the whooping, and every time that the other went over their number, these at home gave [such] a shout that the very earth rung again. And thus they continued till those that had been upon the expedition were come up to the sagamore's wigwam. And then, oh, the hideous insulting and triumphing that there was over some Englishmen's scalps that they had taken (as their manner is) and brought with them! . . .

The Eighth Remove

On the morrow morning we must go over the river, i.e. Connecticot, to meet with King Philip. . . .

We traveled on till night, and in the morning we must go over the river to Philip's crew. When I was in the canoe, I could not but be amazed at the numerous crew of pagans that were on the bank on the other side. When I came ashore, they gathered all about me, I sitting alone in the midst. I observed they asked one another questions and laughed and rejoiced over their gains and victories.

Then my heart began to fail and I fell a-weeping, which was the first time to my remembrance that I wept before them. Although I had met with so much affliction and my heart was many times ready to break, yet could I not shed one tear in their sight but rather had been all this while in a maze and like one astonished. But now I may say as Psal. 137:1, "By the rivers of Babylon there we sat down; yea, we wept when we remembered Zion." There one of them asked me why I wept; I could hardly tell what to say, yet I answered they would kill me. "No," said he, "none will hurt you." Then came one of them and gave me two spoonfuls of meal to comfort me, and another gave me half a pint of peas which was more worth than many bushels at another time. Then I went to see King Philip. He bade me come in and sit down and asked me whether I would smoke it (a usual compliment nowadays among saints and sinners), but this no way suited me. For though I had formerly used tobacco, yet I had left it ever since I was first taken. It seems to be a bait the devil lays to make men lose their precious time. I remember with shame how formerly when I had taken two or three pipes I was presently ready for another, such a bewitching thing it is. But I thank God He has now given me power over it; surely there are many who may be better employed than to lie sucking a stinking tobacco pipe.

The Torturing of Captives

John Kyles was captured by Indians at the age of ten in 1689. He was held by the Indians for six years and by the French for three years before being released. His Memoirs of Odd Adventures *was published in Boston in 1736. It featured often gruesome depictions of Indian tortures and practices.*

When any great number of Indians meet, or when any captives have been lately taken, or when any captives desert and are retaken, the Indians have a dance and at these dances torture the unhappy people who fall into their hands. My unfortunate brother [James], who was taken with me, after about three years' captivity deserted with an Englishman who was taken from Casco Bay and was retaken by the Indians at New Harbor and carried back to Penobscot Fort, where they were both tortured at a stake by fire for some time; then their noses and ears were cut off and they made to eat them, after which they were burned to death at the stake. The Indians at the same time declar[ed] that they would serve all deserters in the same manner. Thus they divert themselves in their dances!

Now the Indians gather their forces to go against Northampton. Overnight one went about yelling and hooting to give notice of the design, whereupon they fell to boiling of groundnuts and parching of corn (as many as had it) for their provision, and in the morning away they went. During my abode in this place Philip spoke to me to make a shirt for his boy, which I did, for which he gave me a shilling. I offered the money to my master, but he bade me keep it, and with it I bought a piece of horseflesh. Afterwards he asked me to make a cap for his boy, for which he invited me to dinner. I went, and he gave me a pancake about as big as two fingers; it was made of parched wheat, beaten and fried in bear's grease, but I thought I never tasted pleasanter meat in my life. There was a squaw who spoke to me to make a shirt for her *sannup* [husband], for which she gave me a piece of bear. Another asked me to knit a pair of stockings, for which she gave me a quart of peas. I boiled my peas and bear together and invited my master and mistress to dinner, but the proud gossip [i.e., companion], because I served them both in one dish, would eat nothing except one bit that he gave her upon the point of his knife. . . .

My son being now about a mile from me, I asked liberty to go and see him; they bade me go, and away I went. But quickly [I] lost myself, traveling over hills and through swamps, and could not find the way to him. And I cannot but admire at the wonderful power and goodness of God to me in that though I was gone from home and met with all sorts of Indians, and those I had no knowledge of, and there being no Christian soul near me, yet not one of them offered the least imaginable miscarriage to me. . . .

The Treachery of Praying Indians

Then came Tom and Peter [Christian Indians] with the second letter from the council about the captives. Though they were Indians, I got them by the hand and burst out into tears; my heart was so full that I could not speak to them, but recovering myself, I asked them how my husband did and all my friends and acquaintances. They said they [were] all very well but melancholy. . . .

When the letter was come, the sagamores met to consult about the captives and called me to them to inquire how much my husband would give to redeem me. When I came, I sat down among them as I was wont to do as their manner is. Then they bade me stand up and said they were the General Court. They bid me speak what I thought he would give. Now knowing that all we had was destroyed by the Indians, I was in a great strait. I thought if I should speak of but a little, it would be slighted and hinder the matter; if of a great sum, I knew not where it would be procured. Yet at a venture, I said twenty pounds yet desired them to take less, but they would not hear of that but sent that message to Boston that for twenty pounds I should be redeemed. It was a praying Indian that wrote their letter for them. . . .

There was another praying Indian who, when he had done all the mischief that he could, betrayed his own father into the English hands thereby to purchase his own life. Another praying Indian was at Sudbury fight, though, as he deserved, he was afterward hanged for it. There was another praying Indian so wicked and cruel as to wear a string about his neck strung with Christians' fingers. Another praying Indian, when they went to Sudbury fight, went with them and his squaw also with him with her papoose at her back. . . .

On Tuesday morning they called their General Court (as they call it) to consult and determine whether I should go home or no. And they all as one man did seemingly consent to it that I should go home except Philip who would not come among them.

Observations

But before I go any further, I would take leave to mention a few remarkable passages of providence which I took special notice of in my afflicted time.

1. Of the fair opportunity lost in the long march a little after the fort fight when our English army was so numerous and in pursuit of the enemy and so near as to take several and destroy them, and the enemy in such distress for food that our men might track them by their rooting in the earth for groundnuts while they were flying for their lives. I say that then our army should want provision and be forced to leave their pursuit and return homeward. And the very next week the enemy came upon our town like bears bereft of their whelps or so many ravenous wolves, rending us and our lambs to death. But what shall I say? God seemed to leave His people to themselves and order all things for His own holy ends. . . .

3. Which also I have hinted before when the English army with new supplies were sent forth to pursue after the enemy, and they, understanding it, fled before them till they came to Baquaug River where they forthwith went over safely, that that river should be impassable to the English. I can but admire to see the wonderful providence of God in preserving the heathen for further affliction to our poor country. They could go in great numbers over, but the English must stop. God had an overruling hand in all those things.

4. It was thought if their corn were cut down they would starve and die with hunger, and all their corn that could be found was destroyed, and they driven from that little they had in store into the woods in the midst of winter. And yet how to admiration did the Lord preserve them for His holy ends and the destruction of many still amongst the English! Strangely did the Lord provide for them that I did not see (all the time I was among them) one

man, woman, or child die with hunger. Though many times they would eat that that a hog or dog would hardly touch, yet by that God strengthened them to be a scourge to His people.

The chief and commonest food was groundnuts. They eat also nuts and acorns, artichokes, lily roots, groundbeans, and several other weeds and roots that I know not.

They would pick up old bones and cut them to pieces at the joints, and if they were full of worms and maggots, they would scald them over the fire to make the vermin come out and then boil them and drink up the liquor and then beat the great ends of them in a mortar and so eat them. They would eat horses' guts and ears, and all sorts of wild birds which they could catch; also bear, venison, beaver, tortoise, frogs, squirrels, dogs, skunks, rattlesnakes, yea, the very bark of trees, besides all sorts of creatures and provision which they plundered from the English. I can but stand in admiration to see the wonderful power of God in providing for such a vast number of our enemies in the wilderness where there was nothing to be seen but from hand to mouth. . . .

5. Another thing that I would observe is the strange providence of God in turning things about when the Indians [were] at the highest and the English at the lowest. I was with the enemy eleven weeks and five days, and not one weeks passed without the fury of the enemy and some desolation by fire and sword upon one place or other. They mourned (with their black faces) for their own losses, yet triumphed and rejoiced in their inhuman and many times devilish cruelty to the English. They would boast much of their victories, saying that in two hours' time they had destroyed such a captain and his company at such a place, and such a captain and his company in such a place, and such a captain and his company in such a place, and boast how many towns they had destroyed; and then scoff and say they had done them a good turn to send them to heaven so soon. Again they would say this summer that they would knock all the rogues in the head, or drive them into the sea, or make them fly the country, thinking surely Agag-like, "The bitterness of death is past." Now the heathen begins to think all is their own, and the poor Christians' hopes to fail (as to man), and now their eyes are more to God, and their hearts sigh heavenward and to say in good earnest, "Help Lord, or we perish." When the Lord had brought His people to this that they saw no help in anything but Himself, then He takes the quarrel into His own hand, and though they [the Indians] had made a pit in their own imaginations as deep as hell for the Christians that summer, yet the Lord hurled themselves into it. And the Lord had not so many ways before to preserve them, but now He hath as many to destroy them.

But to return again to my going home where we may see a remarkable change of providence. At first they were all against it except my husband would come for me, but afterwards they assented to it and seemed much to rejoice in it. Some asked me to send them some bread, others some tobacco, others shaking me by the hand, offering me a hood and scarf to ride in, not one moving hand or tongue against it. Thus hath the Lord answered my poor desire and the many earnest requests of others put up unto God for me. In my travels an Indian came to me and told me if I were willing, he and his squaw would run away and go home along with me. I told him no. I was not willing to run away but desired to wait God's time that I might go home quietly and without fear. And now God hath granted me my desire. O, the wonderful power of God that I have seen and the experience that I have had! I have been in the midst of those roaring lions and savage bears that feared neither God nor man nor the devil, by night and day, alone and in company, sleeping all sorts together, and yet not one of them ever offered me the least abuse of unchastity to me in word or action. Though some are ready to say I speak it for my own credit, I speak it in the presence of God and to His glory. God's power is as great now and as sufficient to save as when He preserved Daniel in the lion's den or the three children in the fiery furnace. I may well say as his Psal. 107:12, "Oh, give thanks unto the Lord for He is good, for His mercy endureth forever." Let the redeemed of the Lord say so whom He hath redeemed from the hand of the enemy, especially that I should come away in the midst of so many hundreds of enemies quietly and peaceably and not a dog moving his tongue.

CHAPTER 5

Crises and Renewal

Chapter Preface

The Puritans faced many crises and challenges to their faith. Two of these crises, though of relatively short duration, dramatically affected the Puritan community. The Salem witchcraft trials of 1692 were the most concentrated example of mass hysteria in New England history. They left a lingering shame in the minds and souls of those who allowed their reason to be carried away by drama and mob mentality. The Great Awakening, nearly a half-century later, was the final, desperate shudder of life before Puritanism forever died away, dissipated into new sects and lifestyles far from the theocracy envisioned by John Winthrop and his fellow journeyers.

In seventeenth-century Europe and America, people believed strongly in the works of God and just as strongly in the works of Satan. In Europe, executions of people—and animals—thought to be witches or agents of Satan numbered in the thousands. In New England the numbers were smaller, but it was not uncommon for an individual to be accused of witchcraft, and a few individuals were even executed for it. Then, in 1692, witchcraft hysteria struck the town of Salem, Massachusetts. A group of young girls began having sensational fits, and, pressed by adults, they accused an ever-increasing number of the town's citizens of causing their fits through witchcraft. During the following months accusations by the girls and others continued; arrests were made; and many people confessed, some voluntarily and some under extreme duress.

Over the ensuing months, several hundred individuals were accused of and tried for witchcraft; 55 confessed to being witches; 150 were imprisoned; 19 people and two dogs were hanged and one man was pressed to death.

Conditions were right for the people of Salem to panic and believe that their community was besieged by witches: Prosperity and materialism were challenging traditional Puritan values; debates over qualifications for church membership—and declining church attendance—were creating bitter factions and deep moral unease. The witch trials provided both a distraction and a scapegoat for the people's problems.

Even during the height of the witch trials, many Salem citizens felt unease—not at the idea of witchcraft in their village, but at the way the trials were conducted: Officials tortured accused persons in order to obtain confessions, and guilt was often ascertained by infamous "no-win" methods, such as the dunking stool (if the accused drowned, they were innocent; if they survived, it was because their satanic connection had saved them and thus they were guilty). By the end of 1692, a new governor had put a stop to the trials, and within the next five years many witnesses recanted their accusations and most of the judges of the Salem trials concluded that they had been wrong in their methods and had committed great injustices to those accused of being witches.

Although they had no direct bearing on Puritan religious belief, the Salem witch trials shook up the already tenuous unity of the Puritan community and left the people of Salem and its surrounding communities with deep fears and insecurities. Today this episode is one of the most strongly remembered from Puritan times, for the drama of the trials and the intrigue of the occult captured the American imagination in a way few other events of that day did. Writers continue to produce novels and movies about the Salem witches and their persecutors.

A scant thirty years after the Salem trials ended the Great Awakening began. A powerful religious revival movement that affected not only Puritans but most of the religions on the eastern seaboard of the country, the Great Awakening is often said to be the beginning of the religious revival movement in America.

Spanning the second through the fifth decades of the eighteenth century, the Great Awakening's peak was in the 1740s. It began with the powerful preachings of itinerant preachers who fervently admonished that religious faith and intensity were fading and that if religious ardor were not renewed, the wrath of God would fall upon the country. These preachers, mostly young and with theatrical preaching styles that contrasted greatly with the traditional staid style of most ministers of the time, created great enthusiasm in their listeners, an enthusiasm that some compared to the hysteria generated by the witch trials. These young preachers traveled from town to town delivering their stirring message of renewal and conversion to an ever-growing crowd of followers. Few who saw the thrilling itinerants preach were unaffected.

The Great Awakening responded directly to Puritan leaders' fears that their people's faith was weakening and that the religion of their fathers was in danger of dying out. Some illustrious ministers, such as Jonathan Edwards, welcomed the renewed interest in God and religion wrought by the intensity of the itinerant "awakeners." A few Puritans, however, did not perceive the dramatic and fiery preachers as positive influences. These critics spoke out against what they saw as unreasoning zealotry masquerading as religious fervor. The prominent Puritan minister Charles Chauncy, for one, urged his people to listen to reason, not emotion, and to stick to the traditional tenets of Puritanism.

By 1745, the Great Awakening had lost much of its momentum. The people's interests moved on to other things, including profit and the political rumblings that were to lead to the American Revolution. The movement had, say the editors of *The Reader's Companion to American History*, "extended the reach and scope of religion to the poor, to blacks who had been spurned by the established sects, to people in newly settled areas, and to women." It had also engendered serious divisions within Puritan and other religious communities and had further weakened the traditional Puritan faith.

The Great Awakening and the Salem witch trials both contributed to the expiration of pure Puritanism in America. The writers in the following chapter reflect the turmoil the Puritans experienced as their era came to an end.

VIEWPOINT 1

"Let them that have been guilty of Explicit Witchcraft, now also repent of their monstrous and horrid evil in it."

Witches Should Be Condemned

Cotton Mather (1662-1727)

Cotton Mather, the son of the prominent Puritan minister Increase Mather and grandson of John Cotton and Richard Mather, also important Puritan leaders, graduated from Harvard at age eighteen. He obtained his M.A. there as well and in 1685 was ordained a Congregational minister. (The Puritans were one branch of the Congregationalists; the Pilgrims were another.) Mather remained an influential Congregational minister and a prolific writer (more than 450 published works) in the city of Boston for the rest of his life.

Mather's sermons and writings contributed strongly to the witchcraft hysteria that affected Salem village. Although Mather urged caution in the prosecution of witches and spoke against the need for executions, he did not speak out against the executions during the time of the trials and he vocally defended the decisions of the court.

Cotton Mather's sermon *Memorable Providences, Related to Witchcrafts and Possessions*, from which the following viewpoint is taken, exemplifies the orthodox Puritan attitude toward witchcraft.

From a sermon of Cotton Mather published in 1689 in his *Memorable Providences, Relating to Witchcrafts and Possessions*.

Proposition I

Such an Hellish thing there is as Witchcraft in the World. There are Two things which will be desired for the advantage of this Assertion. It should first be showed,

WHAT Witchcraft is.

My Hearers will not expect from me an accurate definition of the vile Thing; since the Grace of God has given me the Happiness to speak without Experience of it. But from Accounts both by Reading and Hearing I have learn'd to describe it so.

WITCHCRAFT is the doing of strange (and for the most part ill) things by the help of evil Spirits, covenanting with (and usually Representing of) the woeful Children of Men.

This is the Diabolical Art that Witches are notorious for.

First, Witches are the Doers of strange Things. They cannot indeed perform any proper Miracles; those are things to be done only by the Favorites and Ambassadors of the LORD. But Wonders are often produced by them, though chiefly such Wonders as the Apostle calls in 2 Thes. 2. 9. Lying Wonders. There are wonderful Storms in the great World, and wonderful Wounds in the little World, often effected by these evil Causes. They do things which transcend the ordinary course of Nature, and which puzzle the ordinary Sense of Mankind. Some strange things are done by them in a way of Real Production. They do really Torment, they do really Afflict those that their Spite shall extend unto. Other strange things are done by them in a way of Crafty Illusion. They do craftily make of the Air, the Figures and Colors of things that never can be truly created by them. All men might see, but, I believe, no man could feel some of the Things which the Magicians of Egypt, exhibited of old.

Secondly, They are not only strange things, but ill things, that Witches are the Doers of. In this regard also they are not the Authors of Miracles: those are things commonly done for the good of Man, always done for the praise of GOD. But of these Hell-hounds it may in a special manner be said, as in Psal. 52. 3. Thou lovest evil more than good. For the most part they labor to rob Man of his Ease or his Wealth; they labor to wrong God of his Glory. There is mention of Creatures that they call White Witches, which do only Good-Turns for their Neighbors. I suspect that there are none of that sort; but rather think, There is none that doeth good no, not one. If they do good, it is only that they may do hurt.

The Aid of Evil Spirits

Thirdly, It is by virtue of evil Spirits that Witches do what they do. We read in Ephes. 22. about the Prince of the power of the Air.

There is confined unto the Atmosphere of our Air a vast Power, or Army of Evil Spirits, under the Government of a Prince who employs them in a continual Opposition to the Designs of GOD: The Name of that Leviathan who is the Grand Seignior of Hell, we find in the Scripture to be Beelzebub. Under the Command of that mighty Tyrant, there are vast Legions and Myriads of Devils, whose businesses and accomplishments are not all the same. Every one has his Post, and his Work; and they are all glad of an opportunity to be mischievous in the World. These are they by whom Witches do exert their devilish and malignant rage upon their Neighbors: And especially Two Acts concur hereunto. The First is, Their Covenanting with the Witches. There is a most hellish League made between them, with various Rites and Ceremonies. The Witches promise to serve the Devils, and the Devils promise to help the Witches; how? It is not convenient to be related. The Second is, Their Representing of the Witches. And hereby indeed these are drawn into Snares and Cords of Death. The Devils, when they go upon the Errands of the Witches, do bear their Names; and hence do Harms too come to be carried from the Devils to the Witches. We need not suppose such a wild thing as the Transforming of those Wretches into Brutes or Birds, as we too often do.

It should next be proved THAT Witchcraft is.

The Being of such a thing is denied by many that place a great part of their small wit in deriding the Stories that are told of it. Their chief Argument is, that they never saw any Witches, therefore there are none. Just as if you or I should say, we never met with any Robbers on the Road, therefore there was never any Padding there.

Indeed the Devils are loath to have true Notions of Witches entertained with us. I have beheld them to put out the Eyes of an Enchanted Child, when a Book that proves, There is Witchcraft, was laid before her. But there are especially two Demonstrations that Evince the Being of that Infernal mysterious thing.

Testimony as Proof

First, We have the Testimony of Scripture for it. We find Witchcrafts often mentioned, sometimes by way of Assertion, sometimes by way of Allusion, in the Oracles of God. Besides that, We have there the History of divers Witches in these infallible and inspired Writings. Particularly, the Instance of the Witch at Endor, in I Sam. 28. 7. is so plain and full that Witchcraft itself is not a more amazing thing than any Dispute about the Being of it, after this. The Advocates of Witches must use more Tricks to make Nonsense of the Bible, than ever the Witch of Endor used in her Magical Incantations, if they would Evade the Force of that

Famous History. They that will believe no Witches, do imagine that Jugglers only are meant by them whom the Sacred Writ calleth so. But what do they think of that Law in Exod. 22. 18. Thou shalt not suffer a Witch to live? Methinks 'tis a little too hard to punish every silly Juggler with so great severity.

Cotton Mather was one of a long line of Puritan leaders and was outspoken in favor of prosecution of witchcraft.

Secondly, We have the Testimony of Experience for it. What will those Incredulous, who must be the only Ingenious Men say to this? Many Witches have like those in Acts 19. 18. Confessed and showed their Deeds. We see those things done, that it is impossible any Disease, or any Deceit should procure. We see some hideous Wretches in hideous Horrors confessing, That they did the Mischiefs. This Confession is often made by them that are owners of as much Reason as the people that laugh at all Conceit of Witchcraft: The Exactest Scrutiny of Skillful Physicians cannot find any distraction in their minds. This Confession is often made by them that are apart one from another, and yet they agree in all the Circumstances of it. This Confession is often made by them that at the same time will produce the Engines and Ensigns of their Hellish Trade, and give the standers-by an Ocular Conviction of what they do, and how. There can be no Judgment left of any Human Affairs, if such Confessions must be Ridiculed: all

195

the Murders, yea, and all the Bargains in the World must be mere Imaginations if such Confessions are of no Account.

Proposition II

WITCHCRAFT is a most Monstrous and Horrid Evil. Indeed there is a vast Heap of Bloody Roaring Impieties contained in the Bowels of it. Witchcraft, is a Renouncing of God, and Advancing of a filthy Devil into the Throne of the Most High; 'tis the most nefandous High-Treason against the MAJESTY on High. Witchcraft, is a Renouncing of Christ, and preferring the Communion of a loathesome lying Devil before all the Salvation of the Lord Redeemer; 'tis a Trampling under foot that Blood which is more precious than Hills of Silver, or whole Mountains of Gold. There is in Witchcraft, a most explicit Renouncing of all that is Holy, and Just and Good. The Law given by God, the Prayer taught by Christ, the Creed left by the Apostles, is become Abominable where Witchcraft is Embraced: The very Reciting of those blessed things is commonly burdensome where Witchcraft is. All the sure Mercies of the New Covenant, and all the just Duties of it, are utterly abdicated by that cursed Covenant which Witchcraft is Constituted with. Witchcraft is a Siding with Hell against Heaven and Earth; and therefore a Witch is not to be endured in either of them. 'Tis a Capital Crime; and it is to be prosecuted as a piece of Devilism that would not only deprive God and Christ of all His Honor, but also plunder Man of all his Comfort. Witchcraft, it's an impotent, but an impudent Essay to make an Hell of the Universe, and to allow Nothing but a Tophet in the World. Witchcraft,—What shall I say of it! It is the furthest Effort of our Original Sin; and all that can make any Practice or Persons odious, is here in the Exalt[at]ion of it. . . .

What We Must Do

II. By way of Exhortation.

There is one thing to be now pressed upon us all.

Let us wisely endeavor to be preserved from the Molestations of all Witchcraft whatsoever. Since there is a thing so dangerous, defend yourselves, and shelter yourselves by all right means against the annoyance of it.

Consider the Multitudes of them, whom Witchcraft hath sometimes given Trouble to. Persons of all sorts have been racked and ruined by it; and not a few of them neither. It is hardly twenty years ago; that a whole Kingdom in Europe was alarmed by such potent Witchcrafts, that some hundreds of poor Children were invaded with them. Persons of great Honor have sometimes been cruelly bewitched. What lately befell a worthy Knight in Scotland, is well known unto the World. Persons of great Virtue too

Confessions of Witchcraft

At the time of the Salem witch trials, the Reverend John Hale was minister at Beverly, a parish just north of Salem. Hale was strongly interested in the trials and firmly believed the accounts of witchcraft reported there. Later, his own wife was accused and his opinions began to change. Ultimately, he came to believe the trials had been grossly unjust. In 1702 he wrote A Modest Enquiry into the Nature of Witchcraft, *an account of the witchcraft hysteria. The two excerpts here include an entry from his journal describing accused witch Ann Foster's acknowledgement of her evil doings and part of the "voluntary" confession of William Barker. Confessions such as these reinforced the people's belief in the need for the trials.*

I

Goody F. said . . . that she with two others (one of whom acknowledged the same) Rode from Andover to the same Village Witch meeting upon a stick above ground, and that in the way the stick brake, and gave the said F. a fall: whereupon, said she, I got a fall and hurt of which I am still sore. . . .

And some time after told me, she had some trouble upon her spirit, and when I enquired what? she said, she was in fear that G. B. and M. C. would kill her; for they appeared unto her (in Spectre, for their persons were kept in other Rooms in the Prison) and brought a sharp pointed iron like a spindle, but four square, and threatned to stab her to death with it; because she had confessed her Witchcraft, and told of them, that they were with her, and that M. C. above named was the person that made her a Witch.

II

The Devil brought my Shape to Salem, and did afflict M. S. and R. F. by clutching my Hand; and a Sabbath day my Shape afflicted A. M. and at night afflicted M. S. and A. M. E. I. and A. F. have been my Enticers to this great abomination, as one have owned and charged her to her Sister with the same. And the design was to Destroy Salem Village, and to begin at the Minister's House, and to destroy the Church of God, and to set up Satan's Kingdom, and then all will be well. And now I hope God in some measure has made me something sensible of my sin and apostasy, begging pardon of God, and of the Honorable Magistrates and all God's people, hoping and promising by the help of God, to set to my heart and hand to do what in me lieth to destroy such wicked worship, humbly begging the prayers of all God's People for me, I may walk humbly under this great affliction and that I may procure to myself, the sure mercies of David, and the blessing of Abraham.

have been bewitched, even into their Graves. But four years are passed since a holy Man was killed in this doleful way, after the Joy as well as the Grace of God had been wonderfully filling of him. This Consideration should keep us from censuring of those that Witchcraft may give disturbance to: But it should put us on studying of our own security. Suppose ye that the Enchanted Family in the Town, were sinners above all the Town, because they have suffered such things? I tell ye nay, but except ye repent, ye may all be so dealt withal. The Father of Lies uttered an awful Truth when he said through the Mouth of a possessed Man, If God would give me leave, I would find enough in the best of you all, to make you all mine.

Consider also, the Misery of them whom Witchcraft may be let loose upon. If David thought it a sad thing to fall into the hands of men, what is it to fall into the hands of Devils? The Hands of Turks, of Spaniards, of Indians, are not so dreadful as those hands that Witches do their works of Darkness by. O what a direful thing is it, to be pricked with Pins, and stabbed with Knives all over, and to be filled all over with broken Bones? 'Tis impossible to reckon up the varieties of miseries which those Monsters inflict where they can have a blow. No less than Death, and that a languishing and a terrible Death will satisfy the Rage of those formidable Dragons. Indeed Witchcraft sometimes grows up into Possession itself: the Devils that are permitted to torment, at last do possess the Bodies of the bewitched sufferers. But who can bear the thoughts of that! who can forbear crying out, O Lord, my flesh trembles for fear of Thee, and I am afraid of Thy Judgments. . . .

Let the Guilty Repent

Let them that have been guilty of Explicit Witchcraft, now also repent of their monstrous and horrid evil in it. If any of you have (I hope none of you have) made an Express Contract with Devils, know that your promise is better broke than kept; it concerns you that you turn immediately from the Power of Satan unto God. Albeit your sin be beyond all expression or conception heinous, yet it is not unpardonable. We read of Manasseh in 2 Chron. 33. 6. He used Enchantments, and used Witchcraft, and dealt with a Familiar Spirit, and wrought much Evil in the sight of the Lord. But that great Wizzard found Mercy with God, upon his deep Humiliation for it: Such a boundless thing is the Grace of our God! The Prey of Devils, may become the Joy of Angels: The Confederates of Hell, may become the Inhabitants of Heaven, upon their sincere turning unto God. A Witch may be penitent in this, and glorious in another World. There was one Hartford here, who did with much brokenness of Heart own her Witchcraft, and leave her Master, and expire, depending on the Free Grace of God in Christ, and on that word of his, Come to me, ye that labor and are heavy laden, and I will give you rest; and on that, There is a fountain open for sin and for uncleanness. Come then, renounce the

Slavery and the Interest of the Devils, renounce your mad League with 'em. Come and give up yourselves unto the Lord Jesus Christ, loathing yourselves exceedingly for your so siding with the black Enemies of his Throne. O come away from the doleful estate you are in. Come away from serving of the Devils that have ensnared your Souls. What Wages have you from those Hellish Taskmasters? Alas you are here among the poor and vile, and ragged Beggars upon Earth. When did Witchcraft ever make any person Rich? And hereafter you must be Objects for the intolerable insolence and cruelty of those Cannibals, and be broken sore in the place of Dragons for evermore. Betake yourselves then to Instant and Constant Prayer, and unto your old filthy Rulers now say, "Depart from me, ye Evil Spirits, for I will keep the Commandments of God."

VIEWPOINT 2

"This Salem philosophy ... I think it ... deserves the name of Salem superstition and sorcery, and it is not fit to be named in a land of such light as New England is."

"Witches" Have Been Unfairly Prosecuted

Thomas Brattle (1658-1713)

Not all Puritans were happy with the Salem prosecutions for witchcraft. Thomas Brattle, a prominent Boston merchant, strongly opposed the trials. Educated at Harvard, Brattle had deep interests in science and mathematics as well as commerce. He was liberal in his political and religious beliefs and opposed the Puritan orthodoxy.

The following viewpoint is excerpted from a letter Brattle wrote to an unknown English clergyman. The letter was not published in Brattle's day, but historians believe it may have been privately circulated, allowing Brattle to discreetly make his views of the witchcraft proceedings known.

I should be very loath to bring myself into any snare by my freedom with you, and therefore hope that you will put the best construction on what I write, and secure me from such as would interpret my lines otherwise than they are designed. Obedience to lawful authority I evermore accounted a great duty; and will-

From Thomas Brattle's letter of October 8, 1692, to an unknown English clergyman. In *Collections of the Massachusetts Historical Society.* Volume 5. Courtesy of the Massachusetts Historical Society.

ingly I would not practise anything that might thwart and contradict such a principle. Too many are ready to despise dominions, and speak evil of dignities; and I am sure the mischiefs which arise from a factious and rebellious spirit are very sad and notorious; insomuch that I would sooner bite my fingers' ends than willingly cast dirt on authority, or any way offer reproach to it. Far, therefore, be it from me to have anything to do with those men your letter mentions, whom you acknowledge to be men of a factious spirit, and never more in their element than when they are declaiming against men in public place, and contriving methods that tend to the disturbance of the common peace. I never accounted it a credit to my cause to have the good liking of such men. "My son! (says Solomon) fear thou the Lord and the king, and meddle not with them that are given to change" (Prov. 24:21).

However, sir, I never thought judges infallible, but reckoned that they, as well as private men, might err; and that when they were guilty of erring, standers-by, who possibly had not half their judgment, might, notwithstanding, be able to detect and behold their errors. And, furthermore, when errors of that nature are thus detected and observed, I never thought it an interfering with dutifulness and subjection for one man to communicate his thoughts to another thereabout, and with modesty and due reverence to debate the premised failings; at least, when errors are fundamental and palpably pervert the great end of authority and government; for as to circumstantial errors, I must confess my principle is that it is the duty of a good subject to cover with his silence a multitude of them.

But I shall no longer detain you with my preface, but pass to some things you look for, and whether you expect such freedom from me, yea or no, yet shall you find that I am very open to communicate my thoughts unto you, and in plain terms to tell you what my opinion is of the Salem proceedings.

The Judges' Methods

First, as to the method which the Salem justices do take in their examinations, it is truly this: A warrant being issued out to apprehend the persons that are charged and complained of by the afflicted children, as they are called; said persons are brought before the justices, the afflicted being present. The justices ask the apprehended why they afflict those poor children; to which the apprehended answer, they do not afflict them. The justices order the apprehended to look upon the said children, which accordingly they do; and at the time of that look (I dare not say *by* that look, as the Salem gentlemen do), the afflicted are cast into a fit. The apprehended are then blinded, and ordered to touch the afflicted; and at that touch, though not *by* the touch (as above), the afflicted ordinarily do come out of their fits. The afflicted persons then declare and affirm that the apprehended have afflicted them; upon which the apprehended persons, though of never so good repute, are forthwith committed to prison on suspicion for witchcraft.

An accused witch pleads with the judges for leniency as the hysterical witness avoids looking at her.

One of the Salem justices was pleased to tell Mr. Alden (when upon his examination) that truly he had been acquainted with him these many years, and had always accounted him a good man; but, indeed, now he should be obliged to change his opinion. This there are more than one or two did hear, and are ready to swear to, if not in so many words, yet as to its natural and plain meaning. He saw reason to change his opinion of Mr. Alden because that, at the time he touched the poor child, the poor child came out of her fit. I suppose His Honor never made the experiment whether there was not as much virtue in his own hand as there was in Mr. Alden's, to cure by a touch. I know a man that will venture two to one with any Salemite whatever that, let the matter be duly managed, and the afflicted person shall come out of her fit upon the touch of the most religious hand in Salem. It is worthily noted by some that at some times the afflicted will not presently come out of their fits upon the touch of the suspected;

and, then, forsooth, they are ordered by the justices to grasp hard, harder yet, etc., insomuch that at length the afflicted come out of their fits; and the reason is very good, because that a touch of any hand, and process of time, will work the cure; infallibly they will do it, as experience teaches.

I cannot but condemn this method of the justices, of making this touch of the hand a rule to discover witchcraft; because I am fully persuaded that it is sorcery, and a superstitious method, and that which we have no rule for, either from reason or religion. . . .

Superstition and Mockery

This Salem philosophy some men may call the new philosophy; but I think it rather deserves the name of Salem superstition and sorcery, and it is not fit to be named in a land of such light as New England is. I think the matter might be better solved another way; but I shall not make any attempt that way further than to say that these afflicted children, as they are called, do hold correspondence with the devil, even in the esteem and account of the Salem gentlemen; for when the black man, *i.e.*, say these gentlemen, the devil, does appear to them, they ask him many questions, and accordingly give information to the inquirer; and if this is not holding correspondence with the devil, and something worse, I know not what is. . . .

Second, with respect to the confessors, as they are improperly called, or such as confess themselves to be witches (the second thing you inquire into in your letter), there are now about fifty of them in prison, many of which I have again and again seen and heard; and I cannot but tell you that my faith is strong concerning them, that they are deluded, imposed upon, and under the influence of some evil spirit, and therefore unfit to be evidences, either against themselves or anyone else. I now speak of one sort of them, and of others afterward.

These confessors, as they are called, do very often contradict themselves, as inconsistently as is usual for any crazed, distempered person to do. This the Salem gentlemen do see and take notice of; and even the judges themselves have, at some times, taken these confessors in flat lies, or contradictions, even in the courts; by reason of which one would have thought that the judges would have frowned upon the said confessors, discarded them, and not minded one tittle of anything that they said. But instead thereof, as sure as we are men, the judges vindicate these confessors and salve their contradictions by proclaiming that the devil takes away their memory and imposes upon their brain. If this reflects anywhere, I am very sorry for it. I can but assure you that, upon the word of an honest man, it is truth, and that I can bring you many credible persons to witness it, who have been eye and ear witnesses to these things.

These confessors, then, at least some of them, even in the judges' own account, are under the influence of the devil; and the brain of these confessors is imposed upon by the devil, even in the judges' account. But now, if, in the judges' account, these confessors are under the influence of the devil, and their brains are affected and imposed upon by the devil so that they are not their own men, why then should these judges, or any other men, make such account of, and set so much by, the words of these confessors, as they do? In short, I argue thus:

If the devil does actually take away the memory of them at some times, certainly the devil, at other times, may very reasonably be thought to affect their fancies, and to represent false ideas to their imagination. But, now, if it be thus granted that the devil is able to represent false ideas (to speak vulgarly) to the imaginations of the confessors, what man of sense will regard the confessions, or any of the words, of these confessors?

The great cry of many of our neighbors now is—What, will you not believe the confessors? Will you not believe men and women who confess that they have signed to the devil's book? that they were baptized by the devil; and that they were at the mock sacrament once and again? What! will you not believe that this is witchcraft, and that such and such men are witches, although the confessors do own and assert it?

Thus, I say, many of our good neighbors do argue; but methinks they might soon be convinced that there is nothing at all in all these their arguings, if they would but duly consider of the premises.

In the meantime, I think we must rest satisfied in it, and be thankful to God for it, that all men are not thus bereft of their senses; but that we have here and there considerate and thinking men who will not thus be imposed upon, and abused, by the subtle endeavors of the crafty one.

In the next place, I proceed to the form of their indictments and the trials thereupon.

The indictment runs for sorcery and witchcraft, acted upon the body of such a one (say M. Warren), at such a particular time . . . and at diverse other times before and after, whereby the said M. W. is wasted and consumed, pined, etc.

Now for the proof of the said sorcery and witchcraft, the prisoner at the bar pleading not guilty.

1. The afflicted persons are brought into court, and, after much patience and pains taken with them, do take their oaths that the prisoner at the bar did afflict them. And here I think it very observable that often, when the afflicted do mean and intend only the appearance and shape of such a one (say G. Proctor), yet they

positively swear that G. Proctor did afflict them; and they have been allowed so to do, as though there was no real difference between G. Proctor and the shape of G. Proctor. This, methinks, may readily prove a stumbling block to the jury, lead them into a very fundamental error, and occasion innocent blood, yea, the innocentest blood imaginable, to be in great danger. Whom it belongs unto, to be eyes unto the blind and to remove such stumbling blocks, I know full well; and yet you, and everyone else, do

Spurious Trials Ended

Sir William Phips became the new governor of Massachusetts in May 1692. Upon his arrival, he was faced with much evidence of witchcraft in the colony, and he charged the judges to continue conducting trials. He then left the area to fight for several months in the French and Indian wars. When he returned, he discovered unreasoned and unjust treatment of those accused of witchcraft. He soon caused the trials to be stopped. This excerpt comes from his February 1693 letter to the Earl of Nottingham in England, reporting on what he observed in Salem.

I found people much dissatisfied at the proceedings of the Court, for about Twenty persons were condemned and executed of which number some were thought by many persons to be innocent. The Court still proceeded in the same method of trying them, which was by the evidence of the afflicted persons who when they were brought into the Court as soon as the suspected witches looked upon them instantly fell to the ground in strange agonies and grievous torments, but when touched by them upon the arm or some other part of their flesh they immediately revived and came to themselves, upon [which] they made oath that the Prisoner at the Bar did afflict them and that they saw their shape or specter come from their bodies which put them to such pains and torments: . . . at length I found that the Devil did take upon him the shape of Innocent persons and some were accused of whose innocency I was well assured and many considerable persons of unblameable life and conversation were cried out upon as witches and wizzards. The Deputy Govr. notwithstanding persisted vigorously in the same method, to the great dissatisfaction and disturbance of the people, until I put an end to the Court and stopped the proceedings, which I did because I saw many innocent persons might otherwise perish. . . . The stop put to the first method of proceedings hath dissipated the black cloud that threatened this Province with destruction; for whereas this delusion of the Devil did spread and its dismal effects touched the lives and estates of many of their Majesties' Subjects and the reputation of some of the principal persons here, and indeed unhappily clogged and interrupted their Majesties' affairs which hath been a great vexation to me, I have no new complaints but people's minds before divided and distracted by differing opinions concerning this matter are now well composed.

know as well as I who do not.

2. The confessors do declare what they know of the said prisoner; and some of the confessors are allowed to give their oaths, a thing which I believe was never heard of in this world, that such as confess themselves to be witches, to have renounced God and Christ and all that is sacred, should yet be allowed and ordered to swear by the name of the great God! This indeed seems to me to be a gross taking of God's name in vain. I know the Salem gentlemen do say that there is hope that the said confessors have repented; I shall only say that, if they have repented, it is well for themselves, but if they have not, it is very ill for you know who. But then,

3. Whoever can be an evidence against the prisoner at the bar is ordered to come into court; and here it scarce ever fails but that evidences, of one nature and another, are brought in; though, I think, all of them altogether alien to the matter of indictment, for they none of them do respect witchcraft upon the bodies of the afflicted, which is the alone matter of charge in the indictment.

4. They are searched by a jury; and as to some of them, the jury brought in, that on such or such a place there was a preternatural excrescence. And I wonder what person there is, whether man or woman, of whom it cannot be said but that, in some part of their body or other, there is a preternatural excrescence. The term is a very general and inclusive term.

Ignorance of Human Nature

Some of the Salem gentlemen are very forward to censure and condemn the poor prisoner at the bar because he sheds no tears; but such betray great ignorance in the nature of passion, and as great heedlessness as to common passages of a man's life. Some there are who never shed tears; others there are that ordinarily shed tears upon light occasions, and yet for their lives cannot shed a tear when the deepest sorrow is upon their hearts. And who is there that knows not these things? Who knows not that an ecstasy of joy will sometimes fetch tears, when as the quite contrary passion will shut them close up? Why then should any be so silly and foolish as to take an argument from this appearance? But this is by the by. In short, the prisoner at the bar is indicted for sorcery and witchcraft acted upon the bodies of the afflicted. Now, for the proof of this, I reckon that the only pertinent evidences brought in are the evidences of the said afflicted.

It is true that over and above the evidences of the afflicted persons there are many evidences brought in against the prisoner at the bar; either that he was at a witch meeting; or that he performed things which could not be done by an ordinary natural power; or that she sold butter to a sailor, which, proving bad at sea, and the seamen exclaiming against her, she appeared, and soon after there was a storm, or the like. But what if there were ten thousand evidences of this nature; how do they prove the matter of indictment? And if they do not reach the matter of indictment, then I think it is clear that the prisoner at the bar is brought in guilty and condemned, merely from the evidences of the afflicted persons. . . .

I cannot but admire that the justices, whom I think to be well-meaning men, should so far give ear to the devil, as merely upon his authority to issue out their warrants and apprehend people. Liberty was evermore accounted the great privilege of an Englishman; but certainly, if the devil will be heard against us and his testimony taken, to the seizing and apprehending of us, our liberty vanishes, and we are fools if we boast of our liberty. Now, that the justices have thus far given ear to the devil, I think may be mathematically demonstrated to any man of common sense. And for the demonstration and proof hereof, I desire, only, that these two things may be duly considered, viz.:

1. That several persons have been apprehended purely upon the complaints of these afflicted, to whom the afflicted were perfect strangers, and had not the least knowledge of [them] imaginable, before they were apprehended.

2. That the afflicted do own and assert, and the justices do grant, that the devil does inform and tell the afflicted the names of those persons that are thus unknown unto them. Now these two things being duly considered, I think it will appear evident to anyone that the devil's information is the fundamental testimony that is gone upon in the apprehending of the aforesaid people.

If I believe such or such an assertion as comes immediately from the minister of God in the pulpit, because it is the Word of the everliving God, I build my faith on God's testimony; and if I practise upon it, this my practice is properly built on the Word of God; even so in the case before us.

If I believe the afflicted persons as informed by the devil, and act thereupon, this my act may properly be said to be grounded upon the testimony or information of the devil. And now, if things are thus, I think it ought to be for a lamentation to you and me, and all such as would be accounted good Christians.

If any should see the force of this argument, and upon it say (as I heard a wise and good judge once propose) that they know not but that God Almighty, or a good spirit, does give this information to these afflicted persons, I make answer thereto and say that it is most certain that it is neither Almighty God, nor yet any good spirit, that gives this information; and my reason is good, because God is a God of truth, and the good spirits will not lie; whereas these informations have several times proved false, when the accused were brought before the afflicted.

VIEWPOINT 3

"That witches, when detected and convinced, ought to be exterminated and cut off, we have God's warrant for."

The Witch Trials Reflect the Spirit of God

Increase Mather (1639-1723)

Although Increase Mather and his son Cotton Mather are often credited with fanning the witchcraft hysteria in Salem, Massachusetts, in 1692, and although they actively participated in the trials, historians say that Increase Mather actually acted more as a restraining than an abetting influence. In fact, his 1693 work *Cases of Conscience Concerning Evil Spirits Personating Men* is credited with directly influencing the new governor, William Phips, to put a stop to the witchcraft trials.

The son of Richard Mather, a prominent Puritan leader, Increase Mather graduated from Harvard and earned a Masters' degree at Trinity College in Dublin, Ireland. He established himself in Boston and became acting president at Harvard for one year, followed by several years as the university's rector. While there, he promoted the study of science and the strength of Congregational (Puritan) influence.

Increase Mather took a cautious view of the witch trials, although he participated in their prosecution. He believed in the existence of witches and in the devil's work on earth. However, he urged careful examination of evidence before anyone would be convicted. The following excerpt from his *Cases of Conscience* reflects his views.

From Increase Mather, *Cases of Conscience Concerning Evil Spirits Personating Men*, Boston, 1693.

So Odious and Abominable is the Name of a Witch, to the Civilized, much more the Religious part of Mankind, that it is apt to grow up into a Scandal for any, so much as to enter some sober cautions against the over hasty suspecting, or too precipitant Judging of Persons on this account. But certainly, the more execrable the Crime is, the more critical care is to be used in the exposing of the Names, Liberties, and Lives of Men (especially of a Godly Conversation) to the imputation of it. The awful hand of God now upon us, in letting loose of evil Angels among us to perpetrate such horrid Mischiefs, and suffering of Hell's Instruments to do such fearful things as have been scarce heard of; hath put serious persons into deep Musings, and upon curious Inquiries what is to be done for the detecting and defeating of this tremendous design of the grand Adversary: And, tho' all that fear God are agreed, *That no evil is to be done, that good may come of it;* yet hath the Devil obtained not a little of his design, in the divisions of Reuben, about the application of this Rule.

Scriptural Proof

That there are Devils and Witches, the Scripture asserts, and experience confirms, That they are common enemies of Mankind, and set upon mischief, is not to be doubted: That the Devil can (by Divine Permission) and often doth vex men in Body and Estate, without the Instrumentality of Witches, is undeniable: That he often hath, and delights to have the concurrence of Witches, and their consent in harming men, is consonant to his native Malice to Man, and too lamentably exemplified: That Witches, when detected and convinced, ought to be exterminated and cut off, we have God's warrant for, *Exod.* 22. 18. Only the same God who hath said, *thou shalt not suffer a Witch to live;* hath also said, *at the Mouth of two Witnesses, or three Witnesses shall he that is worthy of Death, be put to Death: But at the Mouth of one Witness, he shall not be put to Death,* Deut. 17. 6. Much debate is made about *what is* sufficient Conviction, and some have (in their Zeal) supposed that a less clear evidence ought to pass in this than in other Cases, supposing that else it will be hard (if possible) to bring such to condign Punishment, by reason of the close conveyances that there are between the Devil and Witches; but this is a very dangerous and unjustifiable tenet. Men serve God in doing their Duty, he never intended that all persons guilty of Capital Crimes should be discovered and punished by men in this Life, though they be never so curious in searching after Iniquity. It is therefore exceeding necessary that in such a day as this, men be informed what is Evidence and what is not. It concerns men in point of

Charity; for tho' the most shining Professor may be secretly a most abominable Sinner, yet till he be detected, our Charity is bound to Judge according to what appears: and notwithstanding that a clear evidence must determine a case; yet presumptions must be weighed against presumptions, and Charity is not to be forgone as long as it has the most preponderating on its side. And it is of no less necessity in point of Justice; there are not only Testimonies required by God, which are to be credited according to the Rules given in his Word referring to witnesses: But there is also an Evidence supposed to be in the Testimony, which is thoroughly to be weighed, and if it do not infallibly prove the Crime against the person accused, it ought not to determine him guilty of it; for so a righteous Man may be Condemned unjustly. In the case of Witchcrafts we know that the Devil is the immediate Agent in the Mischief done, the consent or compact of the Witch is the thing to be Demonstrated. . . .

Increase Mather participated in the Salem witch trials. Although he urged cautious treatment of the suspects, he later regretted the part he had played in the hysteria.

There are Proofs for the Conviction of Witches which Jurors may with a safe Conscience proceed upon, so as to bring them in guilty. The Scripture which saith, *Thou shalt not suffer a Witch to live,* clearly implies, that some in the World may be known and proved to be Witches: For until they be so, they may and must be suffered to live. . . .

Q. But then the Inquiry is, *What is sufficient Proof?*

1. That a free and voluntary Confession of the Crime made by the Person suspected and accused after Examination, is a sufficient Ground of Conviction.

Indeed, if Persons are Distracted, or under the Power of *Phrenetic Melancholy*, that alters the Case; but the Jurors that examine them, and their Neighbors that know them, may easily determine that Case; or if Confession be extorted, the Evidence is not so clear and convictive; but if any Persons out of Remorse of Conscience, or from a Touch of God in their Spirits, confess and show their Deeds, as the Converted Magicians in *Ephesus* did, *Acts* 19.18, 19. nothing can be more clear. . . .

2. If two credible Persons shall affirm upon Oath that they have seen the party accused speaking such words, or doing things which none but such as have Familiarity with the Devil ever did or can do, that's a sufficient Ground for Conviction.

. . . The Devil never assists men to do supernatural things undesired. When therefore such like things shall be testified against the accused Party not by *Specters* which are Devils in the Shape of Persons either living or dead, but by real men or women who may be credited; it is proof enough that such an one has that Conversation and Correspondence with the Devil, as that he or she, whoever they be, ought to be exterminated from amongst men. This notwithstanding I will add; It were better that ten suspected Witches should escape, than that one innocent Person should be Condemned; that is an old saying, and true, *Prestat reum nocentem absolvi, quam ex prohibitis Indiciis & illegitima probatione condemnari.* It is better that a Guilty Person should be Absolved, than that he should without sufficient ground of Conviction be condemned. I had rather judge a Witch to be an honest woman, than judge an honest woman as a Witch. The Word of God directs men not to proceed to the execution of the most capital offenders, until such time as upon searching diligently, the matter is *found to be a Truth, and the thing certain*, Deut. 13. 14, 15. . . .

To Save Lives

The Design of the preceding *Dissertation*, is not to plead for Witchcrafts, or to appear as an Advocate for Witches. . . .

Nor is there designed any Reflection on those worthy Persons who have been concerned in the late Proceedings at *Salem*: They are wise and good Men, and have acted with all Fidelity according to their Light, and have out of tenderness declined the doing of some things, which in our own Judgments they were satisfied about: Having therefore so arduous a Case before them, Pity and Prayers rather than Censures are their due; on which account I am glad that there is published to the World (by my Son) a *Breviate of the Trials* of some who were lately executed, whereby I hope the thinking part of Mankind will be satisfied, that there was more than that which is called *Specter Evidence* for the Conviction of the Persons condemned. I was not myself present at any of the Trials, excepting one, *viz.* that of *George Burroughs;* had I been one of his Judges, I could not have acquitted him: For several Persons did upon Oath testify, that they saw him do such things as no Man that has not a Devil to be his Familiar could perform: And the Judges affirm, that they have not convicted anyone merely on the account of what *Specters* have said, or of what has been represented to the Eyes or Imaginations of the sick bewitched Persons. . . . It becomes those of my Profession to be very tender in Cases of Blood, and to imitate our Lord and Master, *Who came not to destroy the Lives of Men, but to save them.*

VIEWPOINT 4

"As long as the Devils Testimony, by the pretended afflicted, shall be received as more valid . . . than their Plea of Not Guilty to acquit . . . so long God will be Daily dishonoured."

The Witch Trials Reflect a Lack of Faith in God

Robert Calef (c. 1652-1719)

Historians know little about Robert Calef beyond the facts that he was born in England, was a Boston merchant, and was a friend of Thomas Brattle. Sharing Brattle's liberal political and religious views, Calef was a man "of good sense, and free from superstition," according to eighteenth-century historian Jeremy Belknap. Because of his views, Calef was outraged at the part played in the New England witch-hunts by such distinguished and influential clergy as Cotton and Increase Mather. In response to the witch trials, he wrote *More Wonders of the Invisible World*, from which the following viewpoint is excerpted. The title is a direct echo of the title of Cotton Mather's work *Wonders of the Invisible World*, in which Mather defends the verdicts at the Salem trials. In this excerpt, Calef suggests that the persecution of so-called witches is the opposite of a religious act; it is, he says, evidence of loss of faith in God.

From Robert Calef, *More Wonders of the Invisible World*. London, 1700.

As the Scriptures know nothing of a covenanting or commissioning Witch, so Reason cannot conceive how Mortals should by their Wickedness arrive at a power to Commissionate Angels, Fallen Angels, against their Innocent Neighbours. But the Scriptures are full in it, and the Instances numerous, that the Almighty, Divine Being has this prerogative to make use of what Instrument he pleaseth, in Afflicting any, and consequently to commissionate Devils: And tho this word commissioning, in the Authors former Books, might be thought to be by inadvertency; yet now after he hath been caution'd of it, still to persist in it seems highly Criminal. And therefore in the name of God, I here charge such belief as guilty of Sacriledge in the highest Nature, and so much worse than stealing Church Plate, etc., As it is a higher Offence to steal any of the glorious Attributes of the Almighty, to bestow them upon Mortals, than it is to steal the Utensils appropriated to his Service. And whether to ascribe such power of commissioning Devils to the worst of Men, be not direct Blasphemy, I leave to others better able to determine. When the Pharisees were so wicked as to ascribe to Beelzebub, the mighty works of Christ (whereby he did manifestly shew forth his Power and Godhead) then it was that our Saviour declar'd the Sin against the Holy Ghost to be unpardonable.

When the Righteous God is contending with Apostate Sinners, for their departures from him, by his Judgments, as Plagues, Earthquakes, Storms and Tempests, Sicknesses and Diseases, Wars, loss of Cattle, etc. Then not only to ascribe this to the Devil, but to charge one another with sending or commissionating those Devils to these things, is so abominable and so wicked, that it requires a better Judgment than mine to give it its just denomination.

Neighbor Pitted Against Neighbor

But that Christians so called should not only charge their fellow Christians therewith, but proceed to Tryals and Executions; crediting that Enemy to all Goodness, and Accuser of the Brethren, rather than believe their Neighbours in their own Defence; This is so Diabolical a Wickedness as cannot proceed, but from a Doctrine of Devils; how far damnable it is let others discuss. Tho such things were acting in this Country in Sir Williams time, yet there is a Discourse of a Guardian Angel, as then over-seeing it, which notion, however it may suit the Faith of Ethnicks [Pagans], or the fancies of Trithemius [a sixteenth-century German abbot and scholar who wrote about witches and angels]; it is certain that the Omnipresent Being stands not in need as Earthly Potentates do, of governing the World by Vicegerents. And if Sir William had such an Invisible pattern to imitate, no wonder tho some of his Actions were unaccountable, especially those relating to Witchcraft: For if there was in those Actions an Angel super-intending, there is little reason to think it was Gabriel or the Spirit of Mercury nor Hanael the Angel or Spirit of Venus, nor yet Samuel the Angel or Spirit of Mars; Names feigned by the said Trithemius, etc. It may rather be thought to be Apollyon, or Abaddon.

Recantation

Several years after the Salem trials, many of the judges and jurors concluded that their judgments at the time had been wrong. This excerpt comes from a recantation and plea for forgiveness signed by twelve of the Salem jurors.

We, whose names are under written, being in the year 1692 called to serve as jurors in court at Salem on trial of many, who were by some suspected guilty of doing acts of witchcraft upon the bodies of sundry persons:

We confess that we ourselves were not capable to understand, nor able to withstand, the mysterious delusions of the powers of darkness, and prince of the air; but were, for want of knowledge in ourselves, and better information from others, prevailed with to take up with such evidence against the accused, as, on further consideration and better information, we justly fear was insufficient for the touching the lives of any, (*Deut.* xvii. 6) whereby we fear we have been instrumental, with others, though ignorantly and unwittingly, to bring upon ourselves and this people of the Lord the guilt of innocent blood; which sin the Lord saith, in scripture, he would not pardon, (2 *Kings*, xxiv. 4) that is, we suppose, in regard of his temporal judgments. We do therefore hereby signify to all in general (and to the surviving sufferers in special) our deep sense of, and sorrow for, our errors, in acting on such evidence to the condemning of any person; and do hereby declare, that we justly fear that we were sadly deluded and mistaken; for which we are much disquieted and distressed in our minds; and do therefore humbly beg forgiveness, first of God for Christ's sake, for this our error.

Objection. But here it will be said, "What, are there no Witches? Do's not the Law of God command that they should be extirpated? Is the Command vain and Unintelligible?" *Solution.* For any to say that a Witch is one that makes a compact with, and Commissions Devils, etc., is indeed to render the Law of God vain and Unintelligible, as having provided no way whereby they might be detected, and proved to be such; And how the Jews waded thro this difficulty for so many Ages, without the Supplement of Mr. Perkins and Bernard thereto, would be very mysterious. But to him that can read the Scriptures without prejudice from Education, etc., it will manifestly appear that the Scripture is full and Intelligible, both as to the Crime and means to detect the culpable. He that shall hereafter see any person, who to confirm People in a false belief, about the power of Witches and Devils, pretending to a sign to confirm it, such as knocking off of invisible Chains with the hand, driving away Devils by brushing, striking with a Sword or Stick, to wound a person at a great distance, etc., may (according to that head of Mr. Gauls, quoted by Mr. C. M. and so often herein before recited, and so well proved by Scripture) conclude that he has seen Witchcraft performed.

If Baalam became a Sorcerer by Sacrifizing and Praying to the true God against his visible people; Then he that shall pray that the afflicted (by their Spectral Sight) may accuse some other Person (whereby their reputations and lives may be indangered) such will justly deserve the Name of a Sorcerer. If any Person pretends to know more than can be known by humane means, and professeth at the same time that they have it from the Black-Man, *i.e.* the Devil, and shall from hence give Testimony against the Lives of others, they are manifestly such as have a Familiar Spirit; and if any, knowing them to have their Information from the Black-Man, shall be inquisitive of them for their Testimony against others, they therein are dealing with such as have a Familiar Spirit.

And if these shall pretend to see the dead by their Spectral Sight, and others shall be inquisitive of them, and receive their Answers what it is the dead say, and who it is they accuse, both the one and the other are by Scripture Guilty of Necromancy.

These are all of them crimes as easily proved as any whatsoever, and that by such proof as the Law of God requires, so that it is no Unintelligible Law.

But if the Iniquity of the times be such, that these Criminals not only Escape Indemnified [unpunished], but are Incouraged in their Wickedness, and made use of to take away the Lives of others, this is worse than a making the Law of God Vain, it being a rendring of it dangerous, against the Lives of Innocents, and without all hopes of better, so long as these Bloody Principles remain.

Lack of Faith in God

As long as Christians do Esteem the Law of God to be Imperfect, as not describing that crime that it requires to be Punish'd by Death;

As long as men suffer themselves to be Poison'd in their Education, and be grounded in a False Belief by the Books of the Heathen;

As long as the Devil shall be believed to have a Natural Power, to Act above and against a course of Nature;

As long as the Witches shall be believed to have a Power to Commission him;

As long as the Devils Testimony, by the pretended afflicted, shall be received as more valid to Condemn, than their Plea of Not Guilty to acquit;

As long as the Accused shall have their Lives and Liberties confirmed and restored to them, upon their Confessing themselves Guilty;

As long as the Accused shall be forc't to undergo Hardships and Torments for their not Confessing;

As long as Tets for the Devil to Suck are searched for upon the Bodies of the accused, as a token of guilt;

As long as the Lords Prayer shall be profaned, by being made a Test, who are culpable;

As long as Witchcraft, Sorcery, Familiar Spirits, and Necromancy, shall be improved to discover who are Witches, etc.,

So long it may be expected that Innocents will suffer as Witches.

So long God will be Daily dishonoured, And so long his Judgments must be expected to be continued.

"There has been a happy and remarkable revival of religion in many parts of this land."

The Great Awakening Offers Hope of True Religious Revival

An Assembly of Pastors of Churches in New England

Unlike the staid preaching found in most early New England churches, the Great Awakening was characterized by flamboyant preaching and flamboyant reactions on the part of the listeners. Speaking in tongues, testimony of personal intimacy with God, lively singing, and dramatic conversions were exhibited at most of the religious functions of the awakeners. This enthusiasm seemed by some to be proof that devotion to God and to the Puritan and other Calvinistic religions was reawakening in New England and other parts of the country. Others, however, judged this enthusiasm as spurious and as evidence that the devil, not God, was influencing the people.

By the mid-1740s, the height of the Great Awakening, this issue deeply divided religious people. In the following viewpoint, a convention of ministers who met in July 1743 voice their support for the Great Awakening. Although largely supportive of the revival movement, they caution against the enthusiasts falling into the heresies of Antinomianism (emphasizing personal revelations and

The Testimony and Advice of an Assembly of Pastors of Churches in New England, at a meeting in Boston, July 7, 1743, occasioned by the late happy Revival of Religion in many parts of the Land.

grace from God rather than following God's—or human—laws as the key to salvation) and Arminianism (rejecting traditional Calvinistic beliefs, and particularly emphasizing humanity's ability to choose or reject salvation independent of God's will).

If it is the duty of every one capable of observation and reflection, to take a constant religious notice of what occurs in the daily course of common providence; how much more is it expected that those events in the divine economy, wherein there is a signal display of the power, grace and mercy of God in behalf of the church, should be observed with sacred wonder, pleasure, and gratitude! Nor should the people of God content themselves with a silent notice, but publish with the voice of thanksgiving, and tell of all his wondrous works.

More particularly, when Christ is pleased to come into his church in a plentiful effusion of his Holy Spirit, by whose powerful influences the ministration of the word is attended with uncommon success, salvation-work carried on in an eminent manner, and his kingdom, which is within men, and consists in righteousness and peace and joy in the Holy Ghost, is notably advanced, this is an event which, above all others, invites the notice and bespeaks the praises of the Lord's people, and should be declared abroad for a memorial of the divine grace; as it tends to confirm the divinity of a despised gospel, and manifests the work of the Holy Spirit in the application of redemption, which too many are ready to reproach; as it may have a happy effect, by the divine blessing, for the revival of religion in other places, and the enlargement of the kingdom of Christ in the world; and as it tends to enliven the prayers, strengthen the faith, and raise the hopes, of such as are waiting for the kingdom of God, and the coming on of the glory of the latter days.

But if it is justly expected of all who profess themselves the disciples of Christ, that they should openly acknowledge and rejoice in a work of this nature, wherein the honor of their divine Master is so much concerned; how much more is it to be looked for from those who are employed in the ministry of the Lord Jesus, and so stand in a special relation to him, as servants of his household, and officers in his kingdom! These stand as watchmen upon the walls of Jerusalem; and it is their business not only to give the alarm of war when the enemy is approaching, but to sound the trumpet of praise when the King of Zion cometh, in a meek triumph, having salvation.

For these and other reasons, we, whose names are hereunto annexed, pastors of churches in New England, met together in Boston, July 7, 1743, think it our indispensable duty, (without judging or censuring such of our brethren as cannot at present see things in the same light with us,) in this open and conjunct manner to declare, to the glory of sovereign grace, our full persuasion, either from what we have seen ourselves, or received upon credible testimony, that there has been a happy and remarkable revival of religion in many parts of this land, through an uncommon divine influence; after a long time of great decay and deadness, and a sensible and very awful withdraw of the Holy Spirit from his sanctuary among us.

Though the work of grace wrought on the hearts of men by the word and Spirit of God, and which has been more or less carried on in the church from the beginning, is always the same for substance, and agrees, at one time and another, in one place or person and another, as to the main strokes and lineaments of it, yet the present work appears to be remarkable and extraordinary,

Proof of God's Work

On account of the numbers wrought upon. We never before saw so many brought under soul concern, and with distress making the inquiry, What must we do to be saved? And these persons of all characters and ages. *With regard to the suddenness and quick progress of it.* Many persons and places were surprised with the gracious visit together, or near about the same time; and the heavenly influence diffused itself far and wide like the light of the morning. *Also in respect of the degree of operation*, both in a way of terror and in a way of consolation; attended in many with unusual bodily effects.

Not that all who are accounted the subjects of the present work, have had these extraordinary degrees of previous distress and subsequent joy. But many, and we suppose the greater number, have been wrought on in a more gentle and silent way, and without any other appearances than are common and usual at other times, when persons have been awakened to a solemn concern about salvation, and have been thought to have passed out of a state of nature into a state of grace.

As to those whose inward concern has occasioned extraordinary outward distresses, the most of them, when we came to converse with them, were able to give, what appeared to us, a rational account of what so affected their minds; viz., a quick sense of their guilt, misery, and danger; and they would often mention the passages in the sermons they heard, or particular texts of Scripture, which were set home upon them with such a powerful impression. And as to such whose joys have carried them into transports and extasies, they in like manner have accounted for them, from a lively sense of the danger they hoped they were freed from, and the happiness they were now possessed of; such clear views of divine and heavenly things, and particularly of the excellencies and loveliness of Jesus Christ, and such sweet tastes of redeeming love, as they never had before. The instances were very few in which we had reason to think these affections were produced by visionary or sensible representations, or by any other images than such as the Scripture itself presents unto us.

A New Godliness

Pastor Nathaniel Leonard of Plymouth, Massachusetts, was profoundly impressed with the impact of the Great Awakening on his town. His views of November 1744 were included in The Christian History, Containing Accounts of the Revival and Propagation of Religion in Great Britain and America, *edited by Thomas Prince Jr.*

After this, for some months together, you should scarcely see any body at the taverns, unless they were strangers, travellers, or some come there upon necessary business. The children foresook their plays in the streets, and persons of all denominations, except a few, gave themselves to reading the word of God, and other books of devotion, to meditation, prayer, conference, and other religious exercises, and refrained from their customary vices. And many that lived at a distance, being acquainted with this town in its former state, coming hither, beheld us now with admiration, saying, Surely the fear of God is in this place.

And here we think it not amiss to declare, that in dealing with these persons, we have been careful to inform them, that the nature of conversion does not consist in these passionate feelings; and to warn them not to look upon their state safe, because they have passed out of deep distress into high joys, unless they experience a renovation of nature, followed with a change of life, and a course of vital holiness. Nor have we gone into such an opinion of the bodily effects with which this work has been attended in some of its subjects, as to judge them any signs that persons who have been so affected, were then under a saving work of the Spirit of God. No; we never so much as called these bodily seizures, convictions; or spake of them as the immediate work of the Holy Spirit. Yet we do not think them inconsistent with a work of God upon the soul at that very time; but judge that those inward impressions which come from the Spirit of God, those terrors and consolations of which he is the author, may, according to the natural frame and constitution which some persons are of, occasion such bodily effects; and therefore that those extraordinary outward symptoms are not an argument that the work is delusive, or from the influence and agency of the evil spirit.

Becoming Real Christians

With respect to numbers of those who have been under the impressions of the present day, we must declare there is good ground to conclude they are become real Christians; the account they give of their conviction and consolation agreeing with the standard of the Holy Scriptures, corresponding with the experiences of the saints, and evidenced by the external fruits of holiness in their lives; so that they appear to those who have the nearest access to them, as so many epistles of Christ, written, not with ink, but by the Spirit of the living God, attesting to the genuineness of the present operation, and representing the excellency of it.

Indeed, many, who appeared to be under convictions, and were much altered in their external behaviour when this work began, and while it was most flourishing, have lost their impressions, and are relapsed into their former manner of life. Yet of those who were judged hopefully converted, and made a public profession of religion, there have been fewer instances of scandal and apostasy than might be expected. So that, as far as we are able to form a judgment, the face of religion is lately changed much for the better in many of our towns and congregations; and together with a reformation observable in divers instances, there appears to be more experimental godliness and lively Christianity, than the most of us can remember we have ever seen before.

Thus we have freely declared our thoughts as to the work of God, so remarkably revived in many parts of this land. And now, we desire to bow the knee in thanksgiving to the God and Father of our Lord Jesus Christ, that our eyes have seen and our ears heard such things. And while these are our sentiments, we must necessarily be grieved at any accounts sent abroad, representing this work as all enthusiasm, delusion and disorder.

Indeed, it is not to be denied, that in some places many irregularities and extravagances have been permitted to accompany it, which we would deeply lament and bewail before God, and look upon ourselves obliged, for the honor of the Holy Spirit, and of his blessed operations on the souls of men, to bear a public and faithful testimony against; though at the same time it is to be acknowledged with much thankfulness, that in other places, where the work has greatly flourished, there have been few, if any, of these disorders and excesses. But who can wonder, if at such a time as this, Satan should intermingle himself, to hinder and blemish a work so directly contrary to the interests of his own kingdom? Or if, while so much good seed is sowing, the enemy should be busy to sow tares? We would therefore, in the bowels of Jesus, beseech such as have been partakers of this work, or are zealous to promote it, that they be not ignorant of Satan's devices; that they watch and pray against errors and misconduct of every kind, lest they blemish and hinder that which they desire to honor and advance.

Cautions

Particularly,

That they do not make secret impulses on their minds, without a due regard to the written word, the rule of their duty: a very dangerous mistake, which, we apprehend, some in these times have gone into. That to avoid Arminianism, they do not verge to the opposite side of Antinomianism; while we would have others take good heed to themselves, lest they be by some led into, or fixed in, Arminian tenets, under the pretense of opposing Antinomian errors. That laymen do not invade the ministerial office, and, under a pretense of exhorting, set up preaching; which is very contrary to gospel order, and tends to introduce errors and confusion into the church. That ministers do not invade the province of others, and in ordinary cases preach in another's parish without his knowledge, and against his consent; nor encourage raw and indiscreet young candidates, in rushing into particular places, and preaching publicly or privately, as some have done, to the no small disrepute and damage of the work in places where it once promised to flourish. Though at the same time we would have ministers show their regard to the spiritual welfare of their people, by suffering them to partake of the gifts and graces of able, sound and zealous preachers of the word, as God in his providence may give opportunity therefor; being persuaded God has in this day remarkably blessed the labors of some of his servants who have travelled in preaching the gospel of Christ. That people beware of entertaining prejudices against their own pastors, and do not run into unscriptural separations. That they do not indulge a disputatious spirit, which has been attended with mischievous effects; nor discover a spirit of censoriousness, uncharitableness, and rash judging the state of others; than which scarce any thing has more blemished the work of God amongst us. And while we would meekly exhort both ministers and Christians, so far as is consistent with truth and holiness, to follow the things that make for peace; we would most earnestly warn all sorts of persons not to despise these outpourings of the Spirit, lest a holy God be provoked to withhold them, and instead thereof, to pour out upon this people the vials of his wrath, in temporal judgments and spiritual plagues; and would call upon every one to improve this remarkable season of grace, and put in for a share of the heavenly blessings so liberally dispensed.

Finally, we exhort the children of God to continue instant in prayer, that He with whom is the residue of the Spirit, would grant us fresh, more plentiful and extensive effusions, that so this wilderness, in all the parts of it, may become a fruitful field; that the present appearances may be an earnest of the glorious things promised to the church in the latter days; when she shall shine with the glory of the Lord arisen upon her, so as to dazzle the eyes of beholders, confound and put to shame all her enemies, rejoice the hearts of her solicitous and now saddened friends, and have a strong influence and resplendency throughout the earth. Amen! Even so. Come, Lord Jesus; come quickly!

"Some in our land look upon what are called secret impulses upon their minds, without due regard to the written word [of the Bible]."

The Great Awakening Offers Errors in Religious Thinking

Pastors of the Churches in the Province of Massachusetts Bay

Many of the most orthodox Puritans scorned and feared the Great Awakening, believing it to be unreasoning hysteria rather than true religious renewal. In the following viewpoint a group of Massachusetts ministers voice their opinion that the awakeners are promulgating several false doctrines and practices.

We, the pastors of the churches of Christ in the province of Massachusetts Bay, in New England, at our Annual Convention, May 25, 1743, taking into consideration several errors in doctrine and disorders in practice that have of late obtained in various parts of the land, look upon ourselves bound, in duty to our great Lord and Master, Jesus Christ, and in concern for the purity and

From "The Testimony of the Pastors of the Churches in the Province of Massachusetts Bay, in New England, at Their Annual Convention in Boston, May 25, 1743, Against Several Errors in Doctrine and Disorders in Practice, Which Have of Late Obtained in Various Parts of the Land." In Joseph Tracy, *A History of the Revival of Religion in the Time of Edwards and Whitefield*, Boston, 1842.

welfare of these churches, in the most public manner to bear our testimony against them.

I. As to errors in doctrine; we observe that some in our land look upon what are called secret impulses upon their minds, without due regard to the written word, the rule of their conduct; that none are converted but such as know they are converted, and the time when; that assurance is of the essence of saving faith; that sanctification is no evidence of justification; with other Antinomian and Familistical errors which flow from these; all which, as we judge, are contrary to the pure doctrines of the Gospel, and testified against and confuted in the Acts of the Synod of August, 1637; as printed in a book entitled "The Rise, and Reign, and Ruin, of Antinomianism, &c., in New England."

II. As to disorders in practice, we judge,

1. The itinerancy, as it is called, by which either ordained ministers or young candidates go from place to place, and without the knowledge, or contrary to the leave of the stated pastors in such places, assemble their people to hear themselves preach,—arising, we fear, from too great an opinion of themselves, and an uncharitable opinion of those pastors, and a want of faith in the great Head of the churches, is a breach of order, and contrary to the Scriptures, 1 Pet. 4: 15; 2 Cor. 10: 12, to the end, and the sentiments of our fathers expressed in their Platform of Church Discipline, chap. 9, sect. 6.

2. Private persons of no education and but low attainments in knowledge and in the great doctrines of the gospel, without any regular call, under a pretence of exhorting, taking upon themselves to be preachers of the word of God, we judge to be a heinous invasion of the ministerial office, offensive to God, and destructive to these churches; contrary to Scripture, Numb. 16; 1 Cor. 28, 29, and testified against in a "Faithful Advice to the Churches of New England" by several of our venerable fathers.

3. The ordaining or separating of any persons to the work of the evangelical ministry at large, and without any relation to a particular charge, which some of late have unhappily gone into, we look upon as contrary to the Scriptures, and directly opposite to our Platform, chap. 6, sect. 3, and the practice of the Protestant churches; as may be seen in "The order of the Churches Vindicated," by the very Reverend Dr. Increase Mather.

4. The spirit and practice of separation from the particular flocks to which persons belong, to join themselves with, and support lay exhorters or itinerants, is very subversive of the churches of Christ, opposite to the rule of the gospel, Gal. 5: 19, 20; Jude 19; 1 Cor. 12: 25; 1 Cor. 3: 3, and utterly condemned by our Platform, chap. 13, sect. 1, 5, and contrary to their covenant engagements.

5. Persons assuming to themselves the prerogatives of God, to

look into and judge the hearts of their neighbours, censure and condemn their brethren, especially their ministers, as Pharisees, Arminians, blind and unconverted, &c., when their doctrines are agreeable to the gospel and their lives to their Christian profession, is, we think, most contrary to the spirit and precepts of the gospel and the example of Christ, and highly unbecoming the character of those who call themselves the disciples of the meek and lowly Jesus. John 13: 34, 35; 1 Sam. 16: 7; Mat. 7: 1; Rom. 14: 10.

Visions of the Weak and Ignorant

In 1742, a long anonymously written tract called The Wonderful Narrative *was published in Boston. It compared the awakeners to past religious zealots, concluding that "solid Christians" did not undergo the dramatic events experienced by the awakeners.*

Who are the Persons who see VISIONS and fall into TRANCES, and make Pretences to the *Spirit* in an *extraordinary* Manner? Look back into the History of former Days, and you will presently find who they are; not the *sober* and *judicious* among Christians, those who place Religion in that which is the *Life* and *Essence* of it: No, but the *weak* and *ignorant*, or those who are naturally of a *warm Imagination*. *Visions* and *Revelations* are to be met with *chiefly*, if not only, among those who have been esteemed *Enthusiasts*, and have proved themselves to be so: They were common among the *Montanists*, but not among the other Christians in that Day; among the FRENCH PROPHETS, and those in *that Way* in *England*, but not among the Christians of established Character in the Nation. It is a STRONG PRESUMPTION therefore against any, that they have a *strange Fire* working in them, when they are seized with SWOONINGS, and have bodily Representations of those Things, which are *spiritually* to be discerned; because these *Sights* have been common among *Enthusiasts* of all Sorts, but seldom or never among *solid* Christians.

---

6. Though we deny not that the human mind, under the operations of the Divine Spirit, may be overborne with terrors and joys; yet the many confusions that have appeared in some places, from the vanity of mind and ungoverned passions of people, either in the excess of sorrow or joy, with the disorderly tumults and indecent behaviour of persons, we judge to be so far from an indication of the special presence of God with those preachers that have industriously excited and countenanced them, or in the assemblies where they prevail, that they are a plain evidence of the weakness of human nature; as the history of the enthusiasms that have appeared in the world, in several ages, manifests. Also, 1 Cor. 14: 23, 40. At the same time we bear our testimony against the impious spirit of those that from hence take occasion to reproach the work

of the Divine Spirit in the hearts of the children of God.

Upon the whole, we earnestly recommend the churches of this country to the gracious care and conduct of the great Shepherd of the sheep, with our thankful acknowledgments for his merciful regard to them in supplying them with faithful pastors, and protecting them from the designs of their enemies, and advancing his spiritual kingdom in the souls of so many, from the foundation of this country to this day; and where there is any special revival of pure religion in any parts of our land at this time, we would give unto God all the glory. And we earnestly advise all our brethren in the ministry carefully to endeavour to preserve their churches pure in their doctrine, discipline and manners, and guard them against the intrusion of itinerants and exhorters, to uphold a spirit of love towards one another, and all men; which, together with their fervent prayers, will be the most likely means, under God, to promote the true religion of the holy Jesus, and hand it, uncorrupt, to succeeding generations.

VIEWPOINT 7

"There is the clearest evidence ... that this is the work of God. ... a very great and wonderful, and exceeding glorious work of God."

Religious Fervor Should Be Praised

Jonathan Edwards (1703-1758)

Jonathan Edwards was one of the most important and influential religious thinkers and writers of his day. He graduated from Yale at age seventeen and after two more years of theological study there became a minister, first in New York and later in Northampton, Massachusetts. Edwards' early preaching started the revival movement in New England, and Edwards became one of the few non-itinerant preachers to wield extensive influence in the Great Awakening. His preaching, fusing rationalism and mysticism, encouraged the conservation of Calvinist religious values. It was his stress on the mystical that was most controversial among the conservative orthodox and liberal Puritans and that led eventually to his ouster from Northampton. He moved to Stockbridge, Massachusetts, where he was a church pastor and missionary to the Indians. It was there that he wrote many of his most important religious works.

The following viewpoint, taken from a three-hundred-page work he wrote supporting the Great Awakening, responds to critics of the revival movement who were particularly put off by the dramatic fervor shown by the participants in the movement. Edwards says that such enthusiasm, even when sometimes misguided, is evidence that the movement is indeed a work of God.

Excerpted from Jonathan Edwards, *Some Thoughts Concerning the Present Revival of Religion in New-England*, Boston, 1742.

The error of those who have ill thoughts of the great religious operation on the minds of men, that has been carried on of late in New England (so far as the ground of such an error has been in the understanding, and not in the disposition), seems fundamentally to lie in three things: *first*, in judging of this work a priori; *secondly*, in not taking the Holy Scriptures as an whole rule whereby to judge of such operations; *thirdly*, in not justly separating and distinguishing the good from the bad.

The Revival Not To Be Judged A Priori

They have greatly erred in the way in which they have gone about to try this work, whether it be a work of the Spirit of God or no, viz. in judging of it a priori; from the way that it began, the instruments that have been employed, the means that have been made use of, and the methods that have been taken and succeeded in carrying it on. Whereas, if we duly consider the matter, it will evidently appear that such a work is not to be judged of a priori, but a posteriori: we are to observe the effect wrought; and if, upon examination of that, it be found to be agreeable to the Word of God, we are bound without more ado to rest in it as God's work; and shall be like to be rebuked for our arrogance, if we refuse so to do till God shall explain to us how he has brought this effect to pass, or why he has made use of such and such means in doing of it. Those texts are enough to cause us with trembling to forbear such a way of proceeding in judging of a work of God's Spirit, Isa. 40:13-14, "Who hath directed the Spirit of the Lord, or being his counselor hath taught him? With whom took he counsel, and who instructed him; and who taught him in the path of judgment, and taught him knowledge, and shewed to him the way of understanding?" John 3:8, "The wind bloweth where it listeth; and thou hearest the sound thereof; but canst not tell whence it cometh, and whither it goeth." We hear the sound, we perceive the effect, and from thence we judge that the wind does indeed blow; without waiting, before we pass this judgment, first to be satisfied what should be the cause of the wind's blowing from such a part of the heavens, and how it should come to pass that it should blow in such a manner, at such a time. To judge a priori is a wrong way of judging of any of the works of God. We are not to resolve that we will first be satisfied how God brought this or the other effect to pass, and why he hath made it thus, or why it has pleased him to take such a course, and to use such and such means, before we will acknowledge his work, and give him the glory of it. This is too much for the clay to take upon it with respect to the potter. . . .

Indeed God has not taken that course, nor made use of those means, to begin and carry on this great work, which men in their wisdom would have thought most advisable, if he had asked their counsel; but quite the contrary. But it appears to me that the great God has wrought like himself, in the manner of his carrying on this work; so as very much to show his own glory, and exalt his own sovereignty, power and all-sufficiency, and pour contempt on all that human strength, wisdom, prudence and sufficiency, that men have been wont to trust, and to glory in; and so as greatly to cross, rebuke and chastise the pride and other corruptions of men; in a fulfilment of that [verse,] Isa. 2:17, "And the loftiness of man shall be bowed down, and the haughtiness of men shall be made low, and the Lord alone shall be exalted in that day." God doth thus, in intermingling in his providence so many stumbling blocks with this work; in suffering so much of human weakness and infirmity to appear; and in ordering so many things that are mysterious to men's wisdom: in pouring out his Spirit chiefly on the common people, and bestowing his greatest and highest favors upon them, admitting them nearer to himself than the great, the honorable, the rich and the learned. . . .

Scripture as a Whole the Criterion

Another foundation error of those that don't acknowledge the divinity of this work, is not taking the Holy Scriptures as an whole, and in itself a sufficient rule to judge of such things by. They that have one certain consistent rule to judge by, are like to come to some clear determination; but they that have half a dozen different rules to make the thing they would judge of agree to, no wonder that instead of justly and clearly determining, they do but perplex and darken themselves and others. They that would learn the true measure of anything, and will have many different measures to try it by, and find in it a conformity to, have a task that they will not accomplish. . . .

If we take the Scriptures for our rule, then the greater and higher are the exercises of love to God, delight and complacence in God, desires and longings after God, delight in the children of God, love to mankind, brokenness of heart, abhorrence of sin, and self-abhorrence for sin; and the "peace of God which passeth all understanding" [Phil. 4:7], and "joy in the Holy Ghost" [Rom. 14:17], "joy unspeakable and full of glory" [I Pet. 1:8]; admiring thoughts of God, exulting and glorying in God; so much the higher is Christ's religion, or that virtue which he and his apostles taught, raised in the soul.

It is a stumbling to some that religious affections should seem to be so powerful, so that they should be so violent (as they express it) in some persons: they are therefore ready to doubt whether it can be the Spirit of God, or whether this vehemence ben't rather a sign of the operation of an evil spirit. But why should such a doubt arise from no other ground than this? What is represented in Scripture as more powerful in its effects than the Spirit of God, which is therefore called "the power of the highest," Luke 1:35? And its saving effect in the soul [is] called "the power of godliness." So we read of the "demonstration of the Spirit and of power," I Cor. 2:4. And it is said to operate in the minds of men with "the exceeding greatness of divine power," and "according to the working of God's mighty power," Eph. 1:19. So we read of "the effectual working of his power," Eph. 3:7; and of "the power that worketh in" Christians, vs. 20; and of the "glorious power" of God in the operations of the Spirit, Col. 1:11; and of "the work of faith," its being wrought "with power," II Thess. 1:11; and in II Tim. 1:7 the Spirit of God is called the Spirit of "power, and [of] love, and of a sound mind." So [also] the Spirit is represented by a mighty wind, and by fire [Acts 2:2-3], things most powerful in their operation. . . .

The Need for Discrimination

Another foundation error of those that reject this work, is their not duly distinguishing the good from the bad, and very unjustly judging of the whole by a part; and so rejecting the work in general, or in the main substance of it, for the sake of some things that are accidental to it, that are evil. They look for more in men that are divinely influenced, because subject to the operations of a good spirit, than is justly to be expected from them for that reason, in this imperfect state and dark world, where so much blindness and corruption remains in the best. When any profess to have received light and influence and comforts from heaven, and to have had sensible communion with God, many are ready to expect that now they appear like angels, and not still like poor, feeble, blind and sinful worms of the dust. There being so much corruption left in the hearts of God's own children, and its prevailing as it sometimes does, is indeed a mysterious thing, and always was a stumbling block to the world; but won't be so much wondered at by those that are well versed in, and duly mindful of, two things: viz. *first*, the Word of God, which teaches us the state of true Christians in this world; and *secondly*, their own hearts, at least if they have any grace, and have experience of its conflicts with corruption. They that are true saints are most inexcusable in making a great difficulty of a great deal of blindness, and many sinful errors in those that profess godliness. If all our

232

conduct, both open and secret, should be known, and our hearts laid open to the world, how should we be even ready to fly from the light of the sun, and hide ourselves from the view of mankind! And what great allowances would it be found that we should need, that others should make for us?—perhaps much greater than we are willing to make for others.

The great weakness of the bigger part of mankind, in any affair that is new and uncommon, appears in not distinguishing, but either approving or condemning all in the lump. They that highly approve of the affair in general, can't bear to have anything at all found fault with. . . .

Historical Pictures/Stock Montage

Jonathan Edwards, fiery minister who led the Great Awakening in New England.

True disciples of Christ may have a great deal of false zeal, such as the disciples had of old, when they would have fire called for from heaven to come down on the Samaritans, because they did not receive them. [Luke 9:51-56] And even so eminently holy and great and divine a saint as Moses, who conversed with God from time to time as a man speaks with his friend, and concerning whom God gives his testimony, that he "was very meek, above any man upon the face of the earth" [Num. 12:3], yet may be rash and sinful in his zeal, when his spirit is stirred by the hard-heartedness and opposition of others, so as to speak very "unad-

233

visedly with his lips," and greatly to offend God, and shut himself out from the possession of the good things that God is about to accomplish for his church on earth; as Moses was excluded [from] Canaan, though he had brought the people out of Egypt, Ps. 106:32-33 [cf. also Num. 20:7-12]. And men, even in those very things wherein they are influenced by a truly pious principle, yet, through error and want of due consideration and caution, may be very rash with their zeal. It was a truly good spirit that animated that excellent generation of Israel that was in Joshua's time, in that affair that we have an account of in the 22d chapter of Joshua; and yet they were rash and heady with their zeal, to go about to gather all Israel together to go up so furiously to war with their brethren of the two tribes and [a] half, about their building the altar *Ed*, without first inquiring into the matter, or so much as sending a messenger to be informed. So [also] the Christians that were of the circumcision, with warmth and contention condemned Peter for receiving Cornelius, as we have account, Acts 11. This their heat and censure was unjust, and Peter was wronged in it; but there is all appearance in the story that they acted from a real zeal and concern for the will and honor of God. So the primitive Christians, from their zeal for and against unclean meats, censured and condemned one another: this was a bad effect, and yet the Apostle bears them witness, or at least expresses his charity towards them, that both sides acted from a good principle, and true respect to the Lord, Rom. 14:6. The zeal of the Corinthians with respect to the incestuous man, though the Apostle highly commends it, yet at the same time saw that they needed a caution lest they should carry it too far, to an undue severity, and so as to fail of Christian meekness and forgiveness, II Cor. 2:6-11 and chap. 7:11 to the end. Luther, the great Reformer, had a great deal of bitterness with his zeal.

It surely cannot be wondered at by considerate persons, that at a time when multitudes all over the land have their affections greatly moved, that great numbers should run into many errors and mistakes with respect to their duty, and consequently into many acts and practices that are imprudent and irregular. I question whether there be a man in New England, of the strongest reason and greatest learning, but what would be put to it to keep master of himself, thoroughly to weigh his words, and consider all the consequences of his behavior, so as to behave himself in all respects prudently, if he were so strongly impressed with a sense of divine and eternal things, and his affections so exceedingly moved, as has been frequent of late among the common people. How little do they consider human nature, who look upon it so insuperable a stumbling block, when such multitudes of all kinds of capacities, natural tempers, educations, customs and manners of life, are so greatly and variously affected, that imprudences and irregularities of conduct should abound; especially in a state of things so uncommon, and when the degree, extent, swiftness and power of the operation is so very extraordinary, and so new, that there has not been time and experience enough to give birth to rules for people's conduct, and so unusual in times past, that the writings of divines don't afford rules to direct us in such a state of things?

Tumult Is to Be Expected

A great deal of noise and tumult, confusion and uproar, and darkness mixed with light, and evil with good, is always to be expected in the beginning of something very extraordinary, and very glorious in the state of things in human society, or the church of God. As after nature has long been shut up in a cold dead state, in time of winter, when the sun returns in the spring, there is, together with the increase of the light and heat of the sun, very dirty and tempestuous weather, before all is settled calm and serene, and all nature rejoices in its bloom and beauty. It is in the new creation as it was in the old: the Spirit of God first moved upon the face of the waters, which was an occasion of great uproar and tumult, and things were gradually brought to a settled state, till at length all stood forth in that beautiful, peace-, ful order, when the heavens and the earth were finished, and God saw everything that he had made; "and behold, it was very good" [cf. Gen. 1]. When God is about to bring to pass something great and glorious in the world, nature is in a ferment and struggle, and the world as it were in travail. As when God was about to introduce the Messiah into the world, and that new and glorious dispensation that he set up, he shook the heavens and the earth, and shook all nations [Hag. 2:6-7]. There is nothing that the church of God is in Scripture more frequently represented by than vegetables; as a tree, a vine, corn, etc., which gradually bring forth their fruit, and are first green before they are ripe. A great revival of religion is expressly compared to this gradual production of vegetables, Isa. 61:11, "As the earth bringeth forth her bud, and as the garden causeth the things that are sown in it to spring forth; so the Lord God will cause righteousness and praise to spring forth before all the nations." The church is in a special manner compared to a palm tree, Cant. 7:7-8; Exod. 15:27; I Kings 6:29; Ps. 92:12. Of which tree this peculiar thing is observed, that the fruit of it, though it be very sweet and good when it is ripe, yet before it has had time to ripen, has a mixture of poison.

The weakness of human nature has always appeared in times of great revival of religion, by a disposition to run to extremes and get into confusion; and especially in these three things—

enthusiasm, superstition, and intemperate zeal. So it appeared in the time of the Reformation, very remarkably; and also in the days of the apostles; many were then exceedingly disposed to lay weight on those things that were very notional and chimerical, giving heed to fables and whimsies, as appears by I Tim. 1:4 and 4:7; II Tim. 2:16 and vs. 23; and Tit. 1:14 and 3:9. . . .

We have long been in a strange stupor; the influences of the Spirit of God upon the heart have been but little felt, and the nature of them but little taught; so that they are in many respects new to great numbers of those that have lately fallen under them. And is it any wonder that they that never before had experience of the supernatural influence of the divine Spirit upon their souls, and never were instructed in the nature of these influences, don't so well know how to distinguish one extraordinary new impression from another, and so (to themselves insensibly) run into enthusiasm, taking every strong impulse or impression to be divine? How natural is it to suppose, that among the multitudes of illiterate people (most of which are in their youth) that find themselves so wonderfully changed, and brought into such new, and before (to them) almost unheard of circumstances, that many should pass wrong and very strange judgments of both persons and things that are about them; and that now they behold them in such a new light, they in their surprise should go further from the judgment that they were wont to make of them than they ought, and in their great change of sentiments, should pass from one extreme to another? And why should it be thought strange, that those that scarce ever heard of any such thing as an outpouring of the Spirit of God before; or if they did, had no notion of it; don't know how to behave themselves in such a new and strange state of things? And is it any wonder that they are ready to hearken to those that have instructed them, that have been the means of delivering them from such a state of death and misery as they were in before, or have a name for being the happy instruments of promoting the same work among others? Is it unaccountable that persons in these circumstances are ready to receive everything they say, and to drink down error as well as truth from them? And why should there be all indignation and no compassion towards those that are thus misled?

When these persons are extraordinarily affected with a new sense, and recent discovery they have received of the greatness and excellency of the divine Being, the certainty and infinite importance of eternal things, the preciousness of souls, and the dreadful danger and madness of mankind, together with a great sense of God's distinguishing kindness and love to them; no wonder that now they think they must exert themselves, and do something extraordinary for the honor of God and the good of the souls of their fellow creatures, and know not how to sit still, and forbear speaking and acting with uncommon earnestness and vigor. . . .

Awareness of Their Own Sins

Great numbers under this influence have been brought to a deep sense of their own sinfulness and vileness; the sinfulness of

Against the True Prophets

Samuel Finley, a minister and educator, staunchly defended the Great Awakening against its critics. In this excerpt from a letter to a friend, written in 1741, Finley compares those who speak against the awakeners to those deluded or evil people who spoke against Christ and other great prophets.

It is a lamentable Truth, that when ever the Gospel is preach'd with such Power and Purity as to shake the strong Holds of Satan, and rouse a World lying securely in Wickedness then those who ought, and seem'd to be Pillars of God's House, and Religion's only Friends, do always make the most violent Opposition against it. The Church of God has always had its Ebbings and Flowings; sometimes flourishing, and again declining; and whoever will look into the History of it, with any Care and Attention, will be oblig'd to grant the Truth of the following Observations among many others. *First*, that, in whatever State it was, there was always such People, such Priests. . . . And *Secondly*, we may observe, that whenever God would reform his Church and revive his People, he always did something extraordinary. . . . *Thirdly*, we may observe, that these were always opposed and rejected, by that Set of Priests who were then established when a Reformation began: It was the Builders, who always set at nought the Chief Corner Stone. No wonder then, that a rushing mighty Wind should make their House reel and totter and fall to the Ground. Thus the false Prophets persecuted the true Ones. . . . *Fourthly*, we may observe that Pride and Interest always hinder'd the Generality of these Ecclesiasticks from Embracing Christ; they would not humble themselves so far as to own their Ignorance or Prejudice; and their Interests made them always strive to stir up the People against Christ and his Gospel, that so they might keep them on their own Side; and thus, by insensible Degrees, they have stop'd their Ears and Shut their Eyes, and would neither see nor hear; and have still, alas! turn'd away much People from the Lord, being neither willing to enter into the Kingdom of Heaven themselves, nor yet to suffer those who were entering to go in. . . . And *Lastly*, we may observe, that the common People do generally hear Christ gladly, to the great Dissatisfaction of the Scribes and Pharisees: *Have any of the Rulers or Pharisees believ'd on him? No, but this People who know not the Law are accursed.*

their lives, the heinousness of their disregard of the authority of the great God, and the heinousness of their living in contempt of a Saviour: they have lamented their former negligence of their souls and neglecting and losing precious time. Their sins of life have been extraordinarily set before them: and they have also had a great sense of their sins of heart; their hardness of heart, and enmity against that which is good, and proneness to all evil; and also of the worthlessness of their own religious performances, how unworthy their prayers, praises, and all that they did in religion, was to be regarded of God. And it has been a common thing that persons have had such a sense of their own sinfulness, that they have thought themselves to be the worst of all, and that none ever was so vile as they. And many seem to have been greatly convinced that they were utterly unworthy of any mercy at the hands of God, however miserable they were, and though they stood in extreme necessity of mercy; and that they deserved nothing but eternal burnings: and have been sensible that God would be altogether just and righteous in inflicting endless damnation upon them, at the same time that they have had an exceeding affecting sense of the dreadfulness of such endless torments, and have apprehended themselves to be greatly in danger of it. And many have been deeply affected with a sense of their own ignorance and blindness, and exceeding helplessness, and so of their extreme need of the divine pity and help. And so far as we are worthy to be credited one by another, in what we say (and persons of good understanding and sound mind, and known and experienced probity, have a right to be believed by their neighbors, when they speak of things that fall under their observation and experience), multitudes in New England have lately been brought to a new and great conviction of the truth and certainty of the things of the Gospel; to a firm persuasion that Christ Jesus is the Son of God, and the great and only Saviour of the world; and that the great doctrines of the Gospel touching reconciliation by his blood, and acceptance in his righteousness, and eternal life and salvation through him, are matters of undoubted truth; together with a most affecting sense of the excellency and sufficiency of this Saviour, and the glorious wisdom and grace of God shining in this way of salvation; and of the wonders of Christ's dying love, and the sincerity of Christ in the invitations of the Gospel, and a consequent affiance and sweet rest of soul in Christ, as a glorious Saviour, a strong rock and high tower, accompanied with an admiring and exalting apprehension of the glory of the divine perfections, God's majesty, holiness, sovereign grace, etc.; with a sensible, strong and sweet love to God, and delight in him, far surpassing all temporal delights, or earthly pleasures; and a rest of soul in him as a portion and the fountain of all good, attended with an abhorrence of sin, and self-loathing for it, and earnest longings of soul after more holiness and conformity to God, with a sense of the great need of God's help in order to holiness of life; together with a most dear love to all that are supposed to be the children of God, and a love to mankind in general, and a most sensible and tender compassion for the souls of sinners, and earnest desires of the advancement of Christ's kingdom in the world. And these things have appeared to be in many of them abiding now for many months, yea, more than a year and [a] half; with an abiding concern to live an holy life, and great complaints of remaining corruption, longing to be more free from the body of sin and death [cf. Rom. 6:6, 7:24, 8:2].

Joyous Renewal

And not only do these effects appear in new converts, but great numbers of those that were formerly esteemed the most sober and pious people have, under the influence of this work, been greatly quickened, and their hearts renewed with greater degrees of light, renewed repentance and humiliation, and more lively exercises of faith, love and joy in the Lord. Many, as I am well knowing, have of late been remarkably engaged to watch, and strive, and fight against sin, and cast out every idol, and sell all for Christ, and give up themselves entirely to God, and make a sacrifice of every worldly and carnal thing to the welfare and prosperity of their souls. And there has of late appeared in some places an unusual disposition to bind themselves to it in a solemn covenant with God. And now instead of meetings at taverns and drinking houses, and meetings of young people in frolics and vain company, the country is full of meetings of all sorts and ages of persons, young and old, men, women and little children, to read and pray, and sing praises, and to converse of the things of God and another world. In very many places the main [subject] of the conversation in all companies turns on religion, and things of a spiritual nature. Instead of vain mirth amongst young people, there is now either mourning under a sense of the guilt of sin, or holy rejoicing in Christ Jesus; and instead of their lewd songs, are now to be heard from them songs of praise to God, and [to] the Lamb that was slain to redeem them by his blood [cf. Rev. 5:6, 9, and 12]. And there has been this alteration abiding on multitudes all over the land, for a year and [a] half, without any appearance of a disposition to return to former vice and vanity. And under the influences of this work, there have been many of the remains of those wretched people and dregs of mankind, the poor Indians, that seemed to be next to a state of brutality, and with whom, till now, it seemed to be to little more purpose to use endeavors for their instruction and awakening, than with the beasts; whose minds have now been strangely opened to receive instruction, and have been deeply affected with the concerns of their precious souls, and have reformed their lives, and forsaken their former stupid, barbarous and brutish way of living; and particularly that sin to which they have been so exceedingly addicted, their drunkenness; and are become devout and serious persons; and many of them to appearance brought truly and greatly to delight in the things of God, and to have their souls very much engaged and entertained with the great things of the Gospel. And many of the poor Negroes also have been in like manner wrought upon and changed. And the souls of very many little children have been remarkably enlightened, and their hearts wonderfully affected and enlarged, and their mouths opened, expressing themselves in a manner far beyond their years, and to the just astonishment of those that have heard them; and some of them from time to time, for many months, greatly and delightfully affected with the glory of divine things, and the excellency and love of the Redeemer, with their hearts greatly filled with love to and joy in him, and have continued to be serious and pious in their behavior.

The divine power of this work has marvelously appeared in some instances I have been acquainted with, in supporting and fortifying the heart under great trials, such as the death of children, and extreme pain of body; wonderfully maintaining the serenity, calmness and joy of the soul, in an immovable rest in God, and sweet resignation to him. There also have been instances of some that have been the subjects of this work, that under the blessed influences of it have, in such a calm, bright and joyful frame of mind, been carried through the valley of the shadow of death.

And now let us consider—Is it not strange that in a Christian, orthodox country, and such a land of light as this is, there should be many at a loss whose work this is, whether the work of God or the work of the Devil? Is it not a shame to New England that such a work should be much doubted of here? . . .

The Work of God

As there is the clearest evidence, from those things that have been observed, that this is the work of God, so it is evident that it is a very great and wonderful, and exceeding glorious work of God. This is certain that it is a great and wonderful event, a strange revolution, an unexpected, surprising overturning of things, suddenly brought to pass; such as never has been seen in New England, and scarce ever has been heard of in any land. Who that saw the state of things in New England a few years ago, the state that it was settled in, and the way that we had been so long going on in, would have thought that in so little a time there would be such a change? This is undoubtedly either a very great work of God, or a great work of the Devil, as to the main substance of it. For though undoubtedly, God and the Devil may work together at the same time, and in the same land; and when God is at work, especially if he be very remarkably at work, Satan will do his utmost endeavor to intrude, and by intermingling his work, to darken and hinder God's work; yet God and the Devil don't work together in producing the same event, and in effecting the same change in the hearts and lives of men: but 'tis apparent that there are some things wherein the main substance of this work consists, a certain effect that is produced, and alteration that is made in the apprehensions, affections, dispositions and behavior of men, in which there is a likeness and agreement everywhere. Now this I say, is either a wonderful work of God, or a mighty work of the Devil; and so is either a most happy event, greatly to be admired and rejoiced in, or a most awful calamity. Therefore if what has been said before, be sufficient to determine it to be as to the main, the work of God, then it must be acknowledged to be a very wonderful and glorious work of God.

VIEWPOINT 8

"Many have fancied themselves acting by immediate warrant from heaven, while they have been committing the most undoubted wickedness."

Religious Zealotry Should Be Avoided

Charles Chauncy (1705-1787)

Although the dramatic preaching of Jonathan Edwards and the itinerant revival ministers was evidence to some Puritans that religion was being strengthened, many others thought the awakeners were charlatans, actors, deceivers, workers of the devil—anything but good religious influences on the people. Most critics of the revival movement criticized it on the basis of its emotionalism and mysticism. The eighteenth century was, after all, the Age of Reason, and the awakeners did not appeal to participants' intellect or reason. Some critics would like to have banished the awakeners; others, like Charles Chauncy, urged reasoned compassion. Some of the awakeners, they said, could be sincere even though misled, and the more "sober" true believers should be the ones to lead these miscreants back to the right path.

Chauncy, one of Jonathan Edwards's staunchest theological foes during the period of the Great Awakening, was a Boston pastor of liberal leanings. In the following viewpoint he describes the dangers of "enthusiasm" and tells how to avoid that evil.

From Charles Chauncy, *Enthusiasm Described and Caution'd Against*, Boston, 1742.

I COR. XIV. xxxvii.

If any Man among you think himself to be a Prophet, or Spiritual, let him acknowledge that the Things that I write unto you are the Commandments of the Lord.

Many Things were amiss in the Church of Corinth, when Paul wrote this Epistle to them. There were envyings, strife and divisions among them, on account of their ministers. Some cried up one, others another: one said, I am of PAUL, another I am of APPOLLOS. They had form'd themselves into parties, and each party so admired the teacher they followed, as to reflect unjust contempt on the other.

Nor was this their only fault. A spirit of pride prevailed exceedingly among them. They were conceited of their gifts, and too generally dispos'd to make an ostentatious shew of them. From this vain glorious temper proceeded the forwardness of those that had the gift of tongues, to speak in languages which others did not understand, to the disturbance, rather than edification of the church: And from the same principle it arose, that they spake not by turns, but several at once, in the same place of worship, to the introducing such confusion, that they were in danger of being tho't mad.

Nor were they without some pretence to justify these disorders. Their great plea was, that in these things they were guided by the Spirit, acted under his immediate influence and direction. This seems plainly insinuated in the words I have read to you. If any man think himself to be a prophet, or spiritual, let him acknowledge that the things that I write unto you are the commandments of the Lord. As if the apostle had said, you may imagine your selves to be spiritual men, to be under a divine afflatus in what you do; but 'tis all imagination, meer pretence, unless you pay a due regard to the commandments I have here wrote to you; receiving them not as the word of man, but of GOD. Make trial of your spiritual pretences by this rule: If you can submit to it, and will order your conduct by it, well; otherwise you only cheat yourselves, while you think yourselves to be spiritual men, or prophets: You are nothing better than Enthusiasts; your being acted by SPIRIT, immediately guided and influenced by him, is meer pretence; you have no good reason to believe any such thing.

From the words thus explained, I shall take occasion to discourse to you upon the following Particulars.

I. I shall give you some account of Enthusiasm, in its nature and influence.

II. Point you to a rule by which you may judge of persons,

whether they are under the influence of Enthusiasm.

III. Say what may be proper to guard you against this unhappy turn of mind.

The whole will then be follow'd with some suitable Application.

I am in the first place, to give you some account of Enthusiasm. And as this a thing much talk'd of at present, more perhaps than at any other time that has pass'd over us, it will not be tho't unseasonable, if I take some pains to let you into a true understanding of it.

The word, from its Etymology, carries in it a good meaning, as signifying inspiration from GOD: in which sense, the prophets under the old testament, and the apostles under the new, might properly be called Enthusiasts. For they were under a divine influence, spake as moved by the HOLY GHOST, and did such things as can be accounted for in no way, but by recurring to an immediate extraordinary power, present with them.

The Bad Side of Enthusiasm

But the word is more commonly used in a bad sense, as intending an imaginary, not a real inspiration: according to which sense, the Enthusiast is one, who has a conceit of himself as a person favoured with the extraordinary presence of the Deity. He mistakes the workings of his own passions for divine communications, and fancies himself immediately inspired by the SPIRIT of GOD, when all the while, he is under no other influence than that of an over-heated imagination.

The cause of this enthusiasm is a bad temperament of the blood and spirits; 'tis properly a disease, a sort of madness: And there are few; perhaps none at all, but are subject to it, tho' none are so much in danger of it as those, in whom melancholy is the prevailing ingredient in their constitution. In these it often reigns; and sometimes to so great a degree, that they are really beside themselves, acting as truly by the blind impetus of a wild fancy, as tho' they had neither reason nor understanding.

And various are the ways in which their enthusiasm discovers itself.

Sometimes, it may be seen in their countenance. A certain wildness is discernable in their general look and air; especially when their imaginations are mov'd and fired.

Sometimes, it strangely loosens their tongues, and gives them such an energy, as well as fluency and volubility in speaking, as they themselves, by their utmost efforts, can't so much as imitate, when they are not under the enthusiastick influence.

Sometimes, it affects their bodies, throws them into convulsions and distortions, into quakings and tremblings. This was formerly common among the people called Quakers. I was myself, when a

Lad, an eye witness to such violent agitations and foamings, in a boisterous female speaker, as I could not behold but with surprize and wonder.

Sometimes, it will unaccountably mix itself with their conduct, and give it such a tincture of that which is freakish or furious, as none can have an idea of, but those who have seen the behaviour of a person in a phrenzy.

Charles Chauncy, a leading New England speaker against the Great Awakening, urged reason instead of emotion as a guide to God's work.

Sometimes, it appears in their imaginary peculiar intimacy with heaven. They are, in their own opinion, the special favourites of GOD, have more familiar converse with him than other good men, and receive immediate, extraordinary communications from him. The tho'ts, which suddenly rise up in their minds, they take for suggestions of the SPIRIT; their very fancies are divine illuminations; nor are they strongly inclin'd to any thing, but 'tis an impulse from GOD, a plain revelation of his will.

And what extravagances, in this temper of mind, are they not capable of, and under the specious pretext too of paying obedience to the authority of GOD? Many have fancied themselves acting by immediate warrant from heaven, while they have been committing the most undoubted wickedness. There is indeed scarce any thing so wild, either in speculation or practice, but they have given into it: They have, in many instances, been blasphemers of GOD, and open disturbers of the peace of the world.

But in nothing does the enthusiasm of these persons discover it self more, than in the disregard they express to the Dictates of reason. They are above the force of argument, beyond conviction from a calm and sober address to their understandings. As for them, they are distinguish'd persons; GOD himself speaks inwardly and immediately to their souls. "They see the light infused into their understandings, and cannot be mistaken; 'tis clear and visible there, like the light of bright sunshine; shews it self and needs no other proof but its own evidence. They feel the hand of GOD moving them within, and the impulses of his SPIRIT; and cannot be mistaken in what they feel. Thus they support themselves, and are sure reason hath nothing to do with what they see and feel. What they have a sensible experience of, admits no doubt, needs no probation." And in vain will you endeavour to convince such persons of any mistakes they are fallen into. They are certainly in the right, and know themselves to be so. They have the SPIRIT opening their understandings and revealing the truth to them. They believe only as he has taught them: and to suspect they are in the wrong is to do dishonour to the SPIRIT; 'tis to oppose his dictates, to set up their own wisdom in opposition to his, and shut their eyes against that light with which he has shined into their souls. They are not therefore capable of being argued with; you had as good reason with the wind. . . .

This is the nature of Enthusiasm, and this its operation, in a less or greater degree, in all who are under the influence of it. 'Tis a kind of religious Phrenzy, and evidently discovers it self to be so, whenever it rises to any great height.

And much to be pitied are the persons who are seized with it. Our compassion commonly works towards those, who, while under distraction, fondly imagine themselves to be Kings and Emperors: And the like pity is really due to those, who, under the power of enthusiasm, fancy themselves to be prophets; inspired of GOD, and immediately called and commissioned by him to deliver his messages to the world: And tho' they should run into disorders, and act in a manner that cannot but be condemned, they should notwithstanding be treated with tenderness and lenity; and the rather, because they don't commonly act so much under the influence of a bad mind, as a deluded imagination. And who more worthy of christian pity than those, who, under the notion of serving GOD and the interest of religion, are filled with zeal, and exert themselves to the utmost, while all the time they are hurting and wounding the very cause they take so much pains to advance. 'Tis really a pitiable case: And tho' the honesty of their intentions won't legitimate their bad actions, yet it very much alleviates their guilt: We should think as favourably of them as may be, and be dispos'd to judge with mercy, as we would hope to obtain mercy. . . .

But as the most suitable guard against the first tendencies to-wards enthusiasm, let me recommend to you the following words of counsel.

1. Get a true understanding of the proper work of the SPIRIT; and don't place it in those things wherein the gospel does not make it to consist. The work of the SPIRIT is different now from what it was in the first days of christianity. Men were then favored with the extraordinary presence of the SPIRIT. He came upon them in miraculous gifts and powers; as a spirit of prophecy, of knowl-edge, of revelation, of tongues, of miracles: But the SPIRIT is not now to be expected in these ways. His grand business lies in preparing men's minds for the grace of GOD, by true humiliation, from an apprehension of sin, and the necessity of a Saviour; then in working in them faith and repentance, and such a change as shall turn them from the power of sin and satan unto GOD; and in fine, by carrying on the good work he has begun in them; assist-ing them in duty, strengthening them against temptation, and in a word, preserving them blameless thro' faith unto salvation: And all this he does by the word and prayer, as the great means in the accomplishment of these purposes of mercy.

Herein, in general, consists the work of the SPIRIT. It does not lie in giving men private revelations, but in opening their minds to understand the publick ones contained in the scripture. It does not lie in sudden impulses and impressions, in immediate calls and extraordinary missions. Men mistake the business of the SPIRIT, if they understand by it such things as these. And 'tis, probably, from such unhappy mistakes, that they are at first be-trayed into enthusiasm. Having a wrong notion of the work of the SPIRIT, 'tis no wonder if they take the uncommon sallies of their own minds for his influences.

You cannot, my brethren, be too well acquainted with what the bible makes the work of the HOLY GHOST, in the affair of salva-tion: And if you have upon your minds a clear and distinct un-derstanding of this, it will be a powerful guard to you against all enthusiastical impressions.

2. Keep close to the scripture, and admit of nothing for an im-pression of the SPIRIT, but what agrees with that unerring rule. Fix it in your minds as a truth you will invariably abide by, that the bible is the grand test, by which every thing in religion is to be tried; and that you can, at no time, nor in any instance, be under the guidance of the SPIRIT of GOD, much less his extraordinary guidance, if what you are led to, is inconsistent with the things there revealed, either in point of faith or practice. And let it be your care to compare the motions of your minds, and the work-ings of your imaginations and passions, with the rule of GOD's word. And see to it, that you be impartial in this matter: Don't

make the rule bend to your pre-conceiv'd notions and inclinations; but repair to the bible, with a mind dispos'd, as much as may be, to know the truth as it lies nakedly and plainly in the scripture it self. And whatever you are moved to, reject the motion, esteem it as nothing more than a vain fancy, if it puts you upon any method of thinking, or acting, that can't be evidently reconcil'd with the revelations of GOD in his word.

Shocking Convulsions

Charles Brockwell, an Anglican missionary in Salem, was appalled by the "enthusiasm" exhibited by participants in the Great Awakening. This excerpt comes from a February 1742 letter he sent home to England.

It is impossible to relate the convulsions into which the whole Country is thrown by a set of Enthusiasts that strole about harangueing the admiring Vulgar in *extempore* nonsense, nor is it confined to these only, for Men, Women, Children, Servants, & Nigros are now become (as they phrase it) Exhorters. Their behaviour is indeed as shocking, as uncomon, their groans, cries, screams, & agonies must affect the Spectators were they never so obdurate & draw tears even from the most resolute, whilst the ridiculous & frantic gestures of others cannot but excite both laughter & contempt, some leaping, some laughing, some singing, some clapping one another upon the back, &c. The tragic scene is performed by such as are entering into the pangs of the New Birth; the comic by those who are got thro' and those are so truly enthusiastic, that they tell you they saw the Joys of Heaven, can describe its situation, inhabitants, employments, & have seen their names entered into the Book of Life & can point out the writer, character & pen. And like the Papists support their fraud by recommending every dream as a Divine Vision & every idle untruth as a revelation to the admiring multitude. Their works may justly be called the works of darkness as acted in the Night & often continued to the noon of the next day & the sleep of children depriv'd of their natural rest is called a trance, & their uncouth dreams (occasion'd from the awfulness of the place, the number of Lights, the variety of action among the People, some praying, some exhorting, some swooning, &c) are deemed no less than heavenly discoveries. In Connecticut, the next Government, 'tis said many have laid their Bibles aside; and some have burnt them, as useless to those who are so plenteously fill'd with the Spirit, as to cry out Enough Lord! In short Sir, such confusion, disorder, & irregularity Eye never beheld.

This adherence to the bible, my brethren is one of the best preservatives against enthusiasm. If you will but express a due reverence to this book of GOD, making it the great rule of judgment, even in respect of the SPIRIT's influences and operations, you will not be in much danger of being led into delusion. Let that be your inquiry under all suppos'd impulses from the SPIRIT, What saith the scripture? To the law, and to the testimony: If your impressions, and imagined spiritual motions agree not therewith, 'tis because there is no hand of the SPIRIT of GOD in them: They are only the workings of your own imaginations, or something worse; and must at once, without any more ado, be rejected as such.

Make Use of Reason

3. Make use of the Reason and Understanding GOD has given you. This may be tho't an ill-advis'd direction, but 'tis as necessary as either of the former. Next to the scripture, there is no greater enemy to enthusiasm, than reason. 'Tis indeed impossible a man shou'd be an enthusiast, who is in the just exercise of his understanding; and 'tis because men don't pay a due regard to the sober dictates of a well inform'd mind, that they are led aside by the delusions of a vain imagination. Be advised then to shew yourselves men, to make use of your reasonable powers; and not act as the horse or mule, as tho' you had no understanding.

'Tis true, you must not go about to set up your own reason in opposition to revelation: Nor may you entertain a tho't of making reason your rule instead of scripture. The bible, as I said before, is the great rule of religion, the grand test in matters of salvation: But then you must use your reason in order to understand the bible: Nor is there any other possible way, in which, as a reasonable creature, you shou'd come to an understanding of it. . . .

4. You must not lay too great stress upon the workings of your passions and affections. These will be excited, in a less or greater degree, in the business of religion: And 'tis proper they shou'd. The passions, when suitably mov'd, tend mightily to awaken the reasonable powers, and put them upon a lively and vigorous exercise. And this is their proper use: And when address'd to, and excited to this purpose, they may be of good service: whereas we shall mistake the right use of the passions, if we place our religion only or chiefly, in the heat and fervour of them. The soul is the man: And unless the reasonable nature is suitably wro't upon, the understanding enlightned, the judgment convinc'd, the will perswaded, and the mind intirely chang'd, it will avail but to little purpose; tho' the passions shou'd be set all in a blaze. This therefore you shou'd be most concern'd about. And if while you are sollicitous that you may be in transports of affection, you neglect your more noble part, your reason and judgment, you will be in great danger of being carried away by your imaginations. This indeed leads directly to Enthusiasm: And you will in vain, endeavour to preserve yourselves from the influence of it, if you a'nt duly careful to keep your passions in their proper place, under

the government of a well inform'd understanding. While the passions are uppermost, and bear the chief sway over a man, he is in an unsafe state: None knows what he may be bro't to. You can't therefore be too careful to keep your passions under the regimen of a sober judgment. 'Tis indeed a matter of necessity, as you would not be led aside by delusion and fancy. . . .

Real, Sober Religion

There is such a thing as real religion, let the conduct of men be what it will; and 'tis, in its nature, a sober, calm, reasonable thing: Nor is it an objection of any weight against the sobriety or reasonableness of it, that there have been enthusiasts, who have acted as tho' it was a wild, imaginary business. We should not make our estimate of religion as exhibited in the behaviour of men of a fanciful mind; to be sure, we should not take up an ill opinion of it, because in the example they give of it, it don't appear so amiable as we might expect. This is unfair. We shou'd rather judge of it from the conduct of men of a sound judgment; whose lives have been such a uniform, beautiful transcript of that which is just and good, that we can't but think well of religion, as display'd in their example.

Chapter 6

Historians View the Puritans

Chapter Preface

The portrayal of Puritans by American historians has changed frequently over the years. They have been depicted as heroic founders and as humorless religious fanatics, as both pioneers and enemies of American democracy. The nature of Puritanism remains an area of historical investigation and dispute even today.

The earliest historians of Puritanism were the Puritans themselves. Such leading early figures as William Bradford, governor of the Plymouth Colony for most of its early years, and John Winthrop, Bradford's counterpart at the Massachusetts Bay Colony, kept extensive journals. Their writings, part personal diaries and part social histories of the colonies they led, are still used by historians seeking information on the early years of New England.

Perhaps the most noteworthy of the early historians was Cotton Mather, the prominent Puritan minister and scholar who in 1702 wrote *Magnalia Christi Americana* (or "The Great Achievements of Christ in America"), a seven-volume history of New England. Everett Emerson writes in *Puritanism in America* that Mather's work belongs in the category of myth as much as history:

> The jeremiads of the second generation had told of the Golden Age of New England's founders. Mather makes them larger-than-life epic heroes. He tells of the New Englanders' departure from England as an exile from depravity and corruption, an exile from Babylon. . . . His account of their crossing the Atlantic likewise becomes amplified, mythologized. . . . His work is the ultimate jeremiad, reminding New Englanders again and again of their backsliding from the glorious tradition from which they had departed.

Mather's description of Puritans as true American heroes prevailed up to the nineteenth century through the writings of such historians as George Bancroft and John Gorham Palfrey. Bancroft argued that New England and its Puritan tradition was the source of American democracy. As for character, he wrote that "Puritanism was a life-giving spirit; activity, thrift, intelligence, followed in its train."

The historians of the later nineteenth and early twentieth centuries were notably less admiring of the Puritans. The brothers Brooks and Charles Francis Adams each wrote a series of works attacking the Puritans as being intolerant and intellectually sterile. Charles Francis Adams referred to the Puritan era, from the

1630s to the 1760s, as the "theologicoglacial period" of Massachusetts history, relieved only when the more secular and rational leaders of the American Revolution attained prominence.

In the early twentieth century Charles A. Beard, James Truslow Adams, and other "progressive" historians also downplayed the importance of Puritan influence on American history and culture. They argued that economic interests rather than Puritan ideas on theology or society were the determining factors in New England history. H. L. Mencken's mocking definition of a Puritan as someone "haunted by the fear that someone, somewhere, may be happy" seemed to be shared by most historians and Americans in general in the early twentieth century.

The past few decades have seen a remarkable renaissance in the historical interpretations of Puritanism. A primary factor has been the work of Perry Miller, a history professor at Harvard University whose writings from the 1930s to his death in 1963 are credited by many for resurrecting the study of Puritanism and its ideas. Miller along with such historians as Kenneth Murdock and Samuel Eliot Morison painted a new picture of the Puritans that, as Alden T. Vaughan writes in *The Puritan Tradition in America*, was

> at once more flattering than that offered by the Progressive historians yet without hiding the characteristics and episodes that deservedly drew criticism from earlier generations. . . . More importantly, the historians offered convincing evidence of the Puritans' impressive accomplishments in education, law, and literature, . . . a far cry from C. F. Adams's view of a society "singularly barren—almost inconceivably sombre."

The depiction of Puritans by Miller and his contemporaries has been both challenged and deepened by subsequent historical study. Historians such as Darrett B. Rutman have challenged Miller's emphasis on intellectual history as reflected by documents written by the Puritan elite. Rutman and others argue that the everyday life of most Puritans was not necessarily reflected in Puritan writings. Newer studies have focused on specific villages and towns, the Puritans' relationship with Indians, and domestic and family matters. Currently Puritan studies remains far from a state of consensus. Vaughan writes:

> Now, three and a half centuries after the first arrival of the Puritan tradition in America, our understanding of that tradition remains far from complete. Symptomatic is Professor Michael McGiffert's conclusion, based on extensive correspondence with forty-six scholars working on the topic, "At present Puritan and New England historiography is remarkable more for vitality than coherence." The explanation may lie less with the historians than with the subject itself. Puritanism, like any "ism," is difficult to pin down; it encompasses divergent, even contradictory, qualities and personalities; it changes over time;

it has subtle and far-reaching ramifications. Perhaps its very illusiveness helps to account for the vitality and longevity of the Puritan tradition in America.

The two historians in this chapter, Perry Miller and Theodore Dwight Bozeman, debate an aspect of Puritanism that was the theme of the opening chapter of this book and an underlying concern of the other chapters as well. It is the nature of the Puritan vision that caused them to leave their home and settle into an unknown land and how their experiences in this new land shaped and melded their vision. In examining many of the same primary sources, the two men come to different conclusions, thus further illustrating the continuing vitality—and disagreement—that remains an enduring hallmark of the study of Puritanism.

VIEWPOINT 1

"While the first aim was ... to realize in America the due form of government. ... the aim behind that aim was to vindicate the most rigorous ideal of the Reformation, so that ultimately all Europe would imitate New England."

The Puritans Saw Themselves as a Model for the World

Perry Miller (1905-1963)

Perry Miller is regarded as one of the foremost authorities on American Puritanism. From the 1930s to the 1960s he taught at Harvard University in Cambridge, Massachusetts, and wrote numerous books and articles on Puritanism, including *The New England Mind: The Seventeenth Century, Orthodoxy in Massachusetts,* and *The Puritans,* an anthology of Puritan writings. George M. Waller of Butler University writes in *Puritanism in Early America* that Miller

> is the acknowledged leader of the "Harvard school" who have attempted to know the meaning of "Puritanism" for New England. . . . Miller sought to rebut those who had found the Puritans repressive, intellectually stale, and altogether an adverse influence on later America.

Much of Miller's work focused on the intellectual history of the Puritans as revealed in the writings of key leaders. His careful

Reprinted by permission of the publishers from *Errands into the Wilderness* by Perry Miller. Cambridge, MA: The Belknap Press of Harvard University Press, 1956. Copyright © 1956 by the President and Fellows of Harvard College.

study and belief in the importance of Puritan ideas greatly influenced future historical studies. "A self-proclaimed atheist, Miller almost single-handedly revitalized historians' scholarly interest in the Puritans," according to history teachers James R. Giese and Laurel R. Singleton.

The following viewpoint is taken from one of Miller's most famous essays, "Errand into the Wilderness," first published in 1952. In it Miller examines the motivations that led the Puritans to settle in New England. He argues that they saw themselves on a dual errand—to create a Christian society and to serve as a model for England and the rest of the world. Such an understanding of the Puritans who came to America is essential, Miller argues, if one is to fully understand their actions in America and their legacy to American history since.

It was a happy inspiration that led the staff of the John Carter Brown Library to choose as the title of its New England exhibition of 1952 a phrase from Samuel Danforth's election sermon, delivered on May 11, 1670: *A Brief Recognition of New England's Errand into the Wilderness*. It was of course an inspiration, if not of genius at least of talent, for Danforth to invent his title in the first place. But all the election sermons of this period—that is to say, the major expressions of the second generation, which, delivered on these forensic occasions, were in the fullest sense community expression—have interesting titles; a mere listing tells the story of what was happening to the minds and emotions of the New England people: John Higginson's *The Cause of God and His People in New-England* in 1663, William Stoughton's *New England's True Interest, Not to Lie* in 1668, Thomas Shepard's *Eye-Salve* in 1672, Urian Oakes's *New England Pleaded With* in 1673, and, climactically and most explicitly, Increase Mather's *A Discourse Concerning the Danger of Apostasy* in 1677.

All of these show by their title pages alone—and, as those who have looked into them know, infinitely more by their contents—a deep disquietude. They are troubled utterances, worried, fearful. Something has gone wrong. As in 1662 Wigglesworth already was saying in verse, God has a controversy with New England; He has cause to be angry and to punish it because of its innumerable defections. They say, unanimously, that New England was sent on an errand, and that it has failed.

To our ears these lamentations of the second generation sound strange indeed. We think of the founders as heroic men—of the towering stature of Bradford, Winthrop, and Thomas Hooker—who braved the ocean and the wilderness, who conquered both, and left to their children a goodly heritage. Why then this whimpering? . . .

Two Meanings of Errand

Since Puritan intellectuals were thoroughly grounded in grammar and rhetoric, we may be certain that Danforth was fully aware of the ambiguity concealed in his word "errand." It already had taken on the double meaning which it still carries with us. Originally, as the word first took form in English, it meant exclusively a short journey on which an inferior is sent to convey a message or to perform a service for his superior. In that sense we today speak of an "errand boy"; or the husband says that while in town on his lunch hour, he must run an errand for his wife. But by the end of the Middle Ages, errand developed another connotation: it came to mean the actual business on which the actor goes, the purpose itself, the conscious intention in his mind. In this signification, the runner of the errand is working for himself, is his own boss; the wife, while the husband is away at the office, runs her own errands. Now in the 1660's the problem was this: which had New England originally been—an errand boy or a doer of errands? In which sense had it failed? Had it been despatched for a further purpose, or was it an end in itself? Or had it fallen short not only in one or the other, but in both of the meanings? If so, it was indeed a tragedy, in the primitive sense of a fall from a mighty designation.

If the children were in grave doubt about which had been the original errand—if, in fact, those of the founders who lived into the later period and who might have set their progeny to rights found themselves wondering and confused—there is little chance of our answering clearly. Of course, there is no problem about Plymouth Colony. That is the charm about Plymouth: its clarity. The Pilgrims, as we have learned to call them, were reluctant voyagers; they had never wanted to leave England, but had been obliged to depart because the authorities made life impossible for Separatists. They could, naturally, have stayed at home had they given up being Separatists, but that idea simply did not occur to them. Yet they did not go to Holland as though on an errand; neither can we extract the notion of a mission out of the reasons which, as [William] Bradford tells us, persuaded them to leave Leyden for "Virginia." The war with Spain was about to be resumed, and the economic threat was ominous; their migration was not so much an errand as a shrewd forecast, a plan to get out while the getting was good, lest, should they stay, they would be "intrapped or surrounded by their enemies, so as they should neither be able to fight nor flie." . . . We are bound, I think, to see in Bradford's account the prototype of the vast majority of subsequent immigrants—of those Oscar Handlin calls "The Uprooted": they came for better advantage and for less danger, and to give their posterity the opportunity of success.

The Great Migration

The Great Migration of 1630 is an entirely other story. True, among the reasons John Winthrop drew up in 1629 to persuade himself and his colleagues that they should commit themselves to the enterprise, the economic motive frankly figures. Wise men thought that England was over-populated and that the poor would have a better chance in the new land. But Massachusetts Bay was not just an organization of immigrants seeking advantage and opportunity. It had a positive sense of mission—either it was sent on an errand or it had its own intention, but in either case the deed was deliberate. It was an act of will, perhaps of willfulness. These Puritans were not driven out of England (thousands of their fellows stayed and fought the Cavaliers)—they went of their own accord.

So, concerning them, we ask the question, why? If we are not altogether clear about precisely how we should phrase the answer, this is not because they themselves were reticent. They spoke as fully as they knew how, and none more magnificently or cogently than John Winthrop in the midst of the passage itself, when he delivered a lay sermon aboard the flagship *Arabella* and called it "A Modell of Christian Charity." It distinguishes the motives of this great enterprise from those of Bradford's forlorn retreat, and especially from those of the masses who later have come in quest of advancement. Hence, for the student of New England and of America, it is a fact demanding incessant brooding that John Winthrop selected as the "doctrine" of his discourse, and so as the basic proposition to which, it then seemed to him, the errand was committed, the thesis that God had disposed mankind in a hierarchy of social classes, so that "in all times some must be rich, some poor, some highe and eminent in power and dignitie; others mean and in subjeccion." It is as though, preternaturally sensing what the promise of America might come to signify for the rank and file, Winthrop took the precaution to drive out of their heads any notion that in the wilderness the poor and the mean were ever so to improve themselves as to mount above the rich or the eminent in dignity. Were there any who had signed up under the mistaken impression that such was the purpose of their errand, Winthrop told them that, although other peoples, lesser breeds, might come for wealth or pelf, this migration was specifically dedicated to an avowed end that had nothing to do with incomes. We have entered into an explicit covenant with God, "we haue professed to enterprise these Accions vpon these and these ends"; we have drawn up indentures with the Almighty, wherefore if we succeed and do not let ourselves get diverted into making money, He will reward us. Whereas if we fail, if we "fall to embrace this present world and prosecute our carnall intencions, seeking greate things for our selves and our posterity, the Lord wil surely breake out in wrathe against us be revenged of such a perjured people and make us knowe the price of the breache of such a Covenant."

Puritans and Tolerance

Perry Miller discusses in his 1956 book Errand into the Wilderness *why the American Puritan vision did not include ideas of religious tolerance.*

Every respectable state in the Western world assumed that it could allow only one church to exist within its borders, that every citizen should be compelled to attend it and conform to its requirements, and that all inhabitants should pay taxes for its support. When the Puritans came to New England the idea had not yet dawned that a government could safely permit several creeds to exist side by side within the confines of a single nation. They had not been fighting in England for any milk-and-water toleration, and had they been offered such religious freedom as dissenters now enjoy in Great Britain they would have scorned to accept the terms. Only a hypocrite, a person who did not really believe what he professed, would be content to practice his religion under those conditions. The Puritans were assured that they alone knew the exact truth, as it was contained in the written word of God, and they were fighting to enthrone it in England and to extirpate utterly and mercilessly all other pretended versions of Christianity. When they could not succeed at home, they came to America, where they could establish a society in which the one and only truth should reign forever.

Well, what terms were agreed upon in this covenant? Winthrop could say precisely—"It is by a mutual consent through a specially overruleing providence, and a more than ordinary approbation of the Churches of Christ to seeke out a place of Cohabitation and Consorteshipp under a due forme of Government both civill and ecclesiasticall." If it could be said thus concretely, why should there be any ambiguity? There was no doubt whatsoever about what Winthrop meant by a due form of ecclesiastical government: he meant the pure Biblical polity set forth in full detail by the New Testament, that method which later generations, in the days of increasing confusion, would settle down to calling Congregational, but which for Winthrop was no denominational peculiarity but the very essence of organized Christianity. What a due form of civil government meant, therefore, became crystal clear: a political regime, possessing power, which would consider its main function to be the erecting, protecting, and preserving of this form of polity. This due form would have, at the very beginning of its list of responsibilities, the duty of suppressing heresy, of subduing or somehow getting rid of dissenters—of being, in short, deliberately, vigorously, and consistently intolerant.

Regarded in this light, the Massachusetts Bay Company came on an errand in the second and later sense of the word: it was, so to speak, on its own business. What it set out to do was the sufficient reason for its setting out. About this Winthrop seems to be perfectly certain, as he declares specifically what the due forms will be attempting: the end is to improve our lives to do more service to the Lord, to increase the body of Christ, and to preserve our posterity from the corruptions of this evil world, so that they in turn shall work out their salvation under the purity and power of Biblical ordinances. Because the errand was so definable in advance, certain conclusions about the method of conducting it were equally evident: one, obviously, was that those sworn to the covenant should not be allowed to turn aside in a lust for mere physical rewards; but another was, in Winthrop's simple but splendid words, "we must be knit together in this worke as one man, wee must entertaine each other in brotherly affection." We must actually delight in each other, "always having before our eyes our Commission and community in the worke, our community as members of the same body." This was to say, were the great purpose kept steadily in mind, if all gazed only at it and strove only for it, then social solidarity (within a scheme of fixed and unalterable class distinctions) would be an automatic consequence. A society despatched upon an errand that is its own reward would want no other rewards: it could go forth to possess a land without ever becoming possessed by it; social gradations would remain eternally what God had originally appointed; there would be no internal contention among groups or interests, and though there would be hard work for everybody, prosperity would be bestowed not as a consequence of labor but as a sign of approval upon the mission itself. For once in the history of humanity (with all its sins), there would be a society so dedicated to a holy cause that success would prove innocent and triumph not raise up sinful pride or arrogant dissension.

God's Punishments

Or, at least, this would come about if the people did not deal falsely with God, if they would live up to the articles of their bond. If we do not perform these terms, Winthrop warned, we may expect immediate manifestations of divine wrath; we shall perish out of the land we are crossing the sea to possess. And here in the 1660's and 1670's, all the jeremiads (of which Danforth's is one of the most poignant) are castigations of the people for having defaulted on precisely these articles. They recite the long list of afflictions an angry God had rained upon them, surely enough to prove how abysmally they had deserted the covenant: crop failures, epidemics, grasshoppers, caterpillars, torrid summers, arctic winters, Indian wars, hurricanes, shipwrecks, accidents, and (most grievous of all) unsatisfactory children. The solemn work of the election day, said William Stoughton in 1668, is "Foundation-work"—not, that is, to lay a new one, "but to continue, and strengthen, and beautifie, and build upon that which has been laid." It had been laid in the covenant before even a foot was set ashore, and thereon New England should rest. Hence the terms of survival, let alone of prosperity, remained what had first been propounded:

> If we should so frustrate and deceive the Lords Expectations, that his Covenant-interest in us, and the Workings of his Salvation be made to cease, then All were lost indeed; Ruine upon Ruine, Destruction upon Destruction would come, until one stone were not left upon another.

Since so much of the literature after 1660—in fact just about all of it—dwells on this theme of declension and apostasy, would not the story of New England seem to be simply that of the failure of a mission? Winthrop's dread was realized: posterity had not found their salvation amid pure ordinances but had, despite the ordinances, yielded to the seductions of the good land. Hence distresses were being piled upon them, the slaughter of King Philip's War and now the attack of a profligate king upon the sacred charter. By about 1680, it did in truth seem that shortly no stone would be left upon another, that history would record of New England that the founders had been great men, but that their children and grandchildren progressively deteriorated.

This would certainly seem to be the impression conveyed by the assembled clergy and lay elders who, in 1679, met at Boston in a formal synod, under the leadership of Increase Mather, and there prepared a report on why the land suffered. The result of their deliberation, published under the title *The Necessity of Reformation*, was the first in what has proved to be a distressingly long succession of investigations into the civic health of Americans, and it is probably the most pessimistic. The land was afflicted, it said, because corruption had proceeded apace; assuredly, if the people did not quickly reform, the last blow would fall and noth-

ing but desolation be left. Into what a moral quagmire this dedicated community had sunk, the synod did not leave to imagination; it published a long and detailed inventory of sins, crimes,
misdemeanors, and nasty habits, which makes, to say the least,
interesting reading. . . .

I have elsewhere endeavored to argue that, while the social or
economic historian may read this literature for its contents—and
so construct from the expanding catalogue of denunciations a
record of social progress—the cultural anthropologist will look
slightly askance at these jeremiads; he will exercise a method-
ological caution about taking them at face value. If you read them
all through, the total effect, curiously enough, is not at all de-
pressing: you come to the paradoxical realization that they do not
bespeak a despairing frame of mind. There is something of a ritu-
alistic incantation about them; whatever they may signify in the
realm of theology, in that of psychology they are purgations of
soul; they do not discourage but actually encourage the community to persist in its heinous conduct. The exhortation to a reformation which never materializes serves as a token payment upon
the obligation, and so liberates the debtors. Changes there had to
be: adaptations to environment, expansion of the frontier, man-
sions constructed, commercial adventures undertaken. These activities were not specifically nominated in the bond Winthrop had
framed. They were thrust upon the society by American experience; because they were not only works of necessity but of excite-
ment, they proved irresistible—whether making money, haunting
taverns, or committing fornication. Land speculation meant not
only wealth but dispersion of the people, and what was to stop
the march of settlement? The covenant doctrine preached on the
Arabella has been formulated in England, where land was not to
be had for the taking; its adherents had been utterly oblivious of
what the fact of a frontier would do for an imported order, let
alone for a European mentality. Hence I suggest that under the
guise of this mounting wail of sinfulness, this incessant and never
successful cry for repentance, the Puritans launched themselves
upon the process of Americanization. . . .

Who Are We?

The titles alone of productions in the next generation show how
concentrated have become emotion and attention upon the interest of New England. . . . Their range is sadly constricted, but every effort, no matter how brief, is addressed to the persistent
question: what is the meaning of this society in the wilderness? If
it does not mean what Winthrop said it must mean, what under
Heaven is it? Who, they are forever asking themselves, who are
we?—and sometimes they are on the verge of saying, who the

Devil are we, anyway?

This brings us back to the fundamental ambiguity concealed in the word "errand," that *double entente* of which I am certain Danforth was aware when he published the words that give point to the exhibition. While it was true that in 1630, the covenant philosophy of a special and peculiar bond lifted the migration out of the ordinary realm of nature, provided it with a definite mission which might in the secondary sense be called its errand, there was always present in Puritan thinking the suspicion that God's saints are at best inferiors, despatched by their Superior upon particular assignments. Anyone who has run errands for other people, particularly for people of great importance with many things on their minds, such as army commanders, knows how real is the peril that, by the time he returns with the report of a message delivered or a bridge blown up, the Superior may be interested in something else; the situation at headquarters may be entirely changed, and the gallant errand boy . . . may be told that he is too late. . . . He has been sent, as the devastating phrase has it, upon a fool's errand, than which there can be a no more shattering blow to self-esteem.

God's Promise

The Great Migration of 1630 felt insured against such treatment from on high by the covenant. . . . Winthrop and his colleagues believed fully in the covenant, but because they could see in the pattern of history that their errand was not a mere scouting expedition: it was an essential maneuver in the drama of Christendom. The Bay Company was not a battered remnant of suffering Separatists thrown up on a rocky shore; it was an organized task force of Christians, executing a flank attack on the corruptions of Christendom. These Puritans did not flee to America; they went in order to work out that complete reformation which was not yet accomplished in England and Europe, but which would quickly be accomplished if only the saints back there had a working model to guide them. It is impossible to say that any who sailed from Southampton really expected to lay his bones in the new world; were it to come about—as all in their heart of hearts anticipated—that the forces of righteousness should prevail . . . that England after all should turn toward reformation, where else would the distracted country look for leadership except to those who in New England had perfected the ideal polity and who would know how to administer it? This was the large unspoken assumption in the errand of 1630: if the conscious intention were realized, not only would a federated Jehovah bless the new land, but He would bring back these temporary colonials to govern England.

In this respect, therefore, we may say that the migration was running an errand in the earlier and more primitive sense of the word—performing a job not so much for Jehovah as for history, which was the wisdom of Jehovah expressed through time. Winthrop was aware of this aspect of the mission—fully conscious of it. "For wee must Consider that wee shall be as a Citty upon a Hill, the eies of all people are uppon us." More was at stake than just one little colony. If we deal falsely with God, not only will He descend upon us in wrath, but even more terribly, He will make us "a story and a by-word through the world, wee shall open the mouthes of enemies to speake evill of the wayes of god and all professours for Gods sake." No less than John Milton was New England to justify God's ways to man, though not, like him, in the agony and confusion of defeat but in the confidence of approaching triumph. This errand was being run for the sake of Reformed Christianity; and while the first aim was indeed to realize in America the due form of government, both civil and ecclesiastical, the aim behind that aim was to vindicate the most rigorous ideal of the Reformation, so that ultimately all Europe would imitate New England. If we succeed, Winthrop told his audience, men will say of later plantations, "the lord make it like that of New England." There was an elementary prudence to be observed: Winthrop said that the prayer would arise from subsequent plantations, yet what was England itself but one of God's plantations? In America, he promised, we shall see, or may see, more of God's wisdom, power, and truth "then formerly wee have beene acquainted with." The situation was such that, for the moment, the model had no chance to be exhibited in England; Puritans could talk about it, theorize upon it, but they could not display it, could not prove that it would actually work. But if they had it set up in America—in a bare land, devoid of already established (and corrupt) institutions, empty of bishops and courtiers, where they could start *de novo*, and the eyes of the world were upon it—and if then it performed just as the saints had predicted of it, the Calvinist internationale would know exactly how to go about completing the already begun but temporarily stalled revolution in Europe.

When we look upon the enterprise from this point of view, the psychology of the second and third generations becomes more comprehensible. We realize that the migration was not sent upon its errand in order to found the United States of America, nor even the New England conscience. Actually, it would not perform its errand even when the colonists did erect a due form of government in church and state: what was further required in order for this mission to be a success was that the eyes of the world be kept fixed upon it in rapt attention. If the rest of the world, or at least of Protestantism, looked elsewhere, or turned to another

Puritanism and the End of the World

James F. Maclear, a professor of church history at the University of Minnesota in Duluth, writes in a 1975 article in the William and Mary Quarterly *that many Puritan settlers of the New World shared beliefs concerning eschatology—the study of events surrounding the end of the world as forecast in the Bible. They believed their migration was a step toward the time Christ would return to rule the world.*

Faith in the coming Christ and his promised government was held with peculiar intensity among Puritans of the migration age. Its basis lay in the developed Puritan "science" of eschatology that in turn rested on the usual Protestant historicist exegesis of prophetic scriptures, especially Daniel and Revelation. Identifying the sequential states through which the world must pass before the Last Judgment and observing contemporary turmoil, commentators commonly located their own age near the end of world history and, while expecting more tribulation and persecution, they also confidently awaited final divine judgments on oppressors of the church—notably the "Romish Antichrist" and the Turks. . . .

By the 1630s these themes were shaping a fervent millennial ideology in the English Puritan community, and there is reason to suppose that those Puritans who crossed the sea to Massachusetts held this faith in an especially vital form. The explanation lies partly in the colonists' predominant congregationalism, which sustained an eschatological dimension frequently overlooked. The "New England way" was not merely a polity. By its purity and faithfulness to God's word it was itself a sign of the approach of the millennium. The very gathering of the elect in objective holy communities anticipated the coming era when the saints would reign with the Lord. . . .

Preoccupation with the Last Things seems to have been a selective factor drawing many eschatologically sensitive Puritans to the New World.

model, or simply got distracted and forgot about New England, if the new land was left with a policy nobody in the great world of Europe wanted—then every success in fulfilling the terms of the covenant would become a diabolical measure of failure. If the due form of government were not everywhere to be saluted, what would New England have upon its hands? . . . How could a universal which turned out to be nothing but a provincial particular be called anything but a blunder or an abortion?

Losing the Audience

If an actor, playing the leading role in the greatest dramatic spectacle of the century, were to attire himself and put on his make-up, rehearse his lines, take a deep breath, and stride onto the stage, only to find the theater dark and empty, no spotlight working, and himself entirely alone, he would feel as did New England around 1650 or 1660. For in the 1640's, during the Civil Wars, the colonies, so to speak, lost their audience. First of all, there proved to be, deep in the Puritan movement, an irreconcilable split between the Presbyterian and Independent wings, wherefore no one system could be imposed upon England, and so the New England model was unserviceable. Secondly—most horrible to relate—the Independents, who in polity were carrying New England's banner and were supposed, in the schedule of history, to lead England into imitation of the colonial order, betrayed the sacred cause by yielding to the heresy of toleration. They actually welcomed Roger Williams, whom the leaders of the model had kicked out of Massachusetts so that his nonsense about liberty of conscience would not spoil the administrations of charity.

In other words, New England did not lie, did not falter; it made good everything Winthrop demanded—wonderfully good—and then found that its lesson was rejected by those choice spirits for whom the exertion had been made. By casting out Williams, Anne Hutchinson, and the Antinomians, along with an assortment of Gortonists and Anabaptists, into that cesspool then becoming known as Rhode Island, Winthrop, Dudley, and the clerical leaders showed Oliver Cromwell how he should go about governing England. Instead, he developed the utterly absurd theory that so long as a man made a good soldier in the New Model Army, it did not matter whether he was a Calvinist, an Antinomian, an Arminian, an Anabaptist or even—horror of horrors—a Socinian! . . .

Out of the New Model Army came the fantastic notion that a party struggling for power should proclaim that, once it captured the state, it would recognize the right of dissenters to disagree and to have their own worship, to hold their own opinions. Oliver Cromwell was so far gone in this idiocy as to became a dictator, in order to impose toleration by force! Amid this shambles, the errand of New England collapsed. There was nobody left at headquarters to whom reports could be sent.

Many a man has done a brave deed, been hailed as a public hero, had honors and ticker tape heaped upon him—and then had to live, day after day, in the ordinary routine, eating breakfast and brushing his teeth, in what seems protracted anticlimax. A couple may win their way to each other across insuperable obstacles, elope in a blaze of passion and glory—and then have to learn that life is a matter of buying the groceries and getting the laundry done. This sense of the meaning having gone out of life, that all adventures are over, that no great days and no heroism lie ahead, is particularly galling when it falls upon a son whose father once was the public hero or the great lover. He has to put up with the daily routine without ever having known at first hand the thrill of danger or the ecstasy of passion. True, he has his own hardships—clearing rocky pastures, hauling in the cod during a storm, fighting Indians in a swamp—but what are these compared with the magnificence of leading an exodus of saints to found a city on a hill, for the eyes of all the world to behold? He might wage a stout fight against the Indians, and one out of ten of his fellows might perish in the struggle, but the world was no longer interested. He would be reduced to writing accounts of himself and scheming to get a publisher in London, in a desperate effort to tell a heedless world, "Look, I exist!"

His greatest difficulty would be not the stones, storms, and Indians, but the problem of his identity. In something of this sort, I should like to suggest, consists the anxiety and torment that inform productions of the late seventeenth and early eighteenth centuries—and should I say, some thereafter? It appears most clearly in *Magnalia Christi Americana*, the work of that soul most tortured by the problem, Cotton Mather: "I write the Wonders of the Christian Religion, flying from the Depravations of Europe, to the American Strand." Thus he proudly begins, and at once trips over the acknowledgment that the founders had not simply fled from depraved Europe but had intended to redeem it. And so the book is full of lamentations over the declension of the children, who appear, page after page, in contrast to their mighty progenitors, about as profligate a lot as ever squandered a great inheritance.

And yet, the *Magnalia* is not an abject book; neither are the election sermons abject, nor is the inventory of sins offered by the synod of 1679. There is bewilderment, confusion, chagrin, but there is no surrender. A task has been assigned upon which the populace are in fact intensely engaged. But they are not sure any more for just whom they are working; they know they are moving, but they do not know where they are going. They seem still to be on an errand, but if they are no longer inferiors sent by the superior forces of the Reformation, to whom they should report, then their errand must be wholly of the second sort, something with a purpose and an intention sufficient unto itself. If so, what is it? If it be not the due form of government, civil and ecclesiastical, that they brought into being, how otherwise can it be described?

Meanings Below the Surface

The literature of self-condemnation must be read for meanings far below the surface, for meanings of which, we may be so rash as to surmise, the authors were not fully conscious, but by which they were troubled and goaded. They looked in vain to history for an explanation of themselves; more and more it appeared that the meaning was not to be found in theology, even with the help of the covenantal dialectic. Thereupon, these citizens found that they had no other place to search but within themselves—even though, at first sight, that repository appeared to be nothing but a sink of iniquity. Their errand having failed in the first sense of the term, they were left with the second, and required to fill it with meaning by themselves and out of themselves. Having failed to rivet the eyes of the world upon their city on the hill, they were left alone with America.

VIEWPOINT 2

"Had the founders of Massachusetts actually intended an overarching Errand, surely it would have been a persistent theme in their many explicit statements of purpose. ... But it was not."

The Puritans Did Not See Themselves as a Model for the World

Theodore Dwight Bozeman (1942-)

Theodore Dwight Bozeman is a professor of history and religion at the University of Iowa at Iowa City, specializing in the study of the role of religion in American history. He has written several books, including *Protestants in the Age of Science*. The following viewpoint is taken from his 1988 book *To Live Ancient Lives: The Primitivist Dimension in Puritanism*. Here Bozeman examines the essay by Perry Miller excerpted in the previous viewpoint. Miller had argued that the Puritans were motivated by the central and energizing vision of creating a true Christian society that would serve as a model for England and the rest of Europe. Bozeman reexamines primary sources of the time, including John Winthrop's famous *Arbella* sermon, and concludes that Miller's interpretation is wrong. The Puritans, Bozeman says, had a less grandiose motivation—simply escaping persecution and moving to a place where they could worship as they pleased. Miller's thesis is not supported by the evidence, Bozeman concludes.

Reprinted from *To Live Ancient Lives: The Primitive Dimension in Puritanism*, by Theodore Dwight Bozeman. Published for the Institute of Early American History and Culture, Williamsburg, Virginia. Copyright © 1988 by The University of North Carolina Press. Used by permission of the author and publisher.

No essay upon the colonial American experience has been more admired and influential than Perry Miller's "Errand into the Wilderness" (1952). There Miller presented an arresting explanation of the migration of the 1630s. The founders of Massachusetts, he had come to believe, were an "organized task force" embarked upon a world-saving mission. They had voyaged to America to create a model of Christian reformation that all England and Europe were to imitate. This was a strikingly new proposal. Earlier historians of the Great Migration knew nothing of a Puritan exemplary mission. Its rapid acceptance therefore marks a watershed in the scholarship. By the 1960s the founding Errand had made its way into the textbooks, and there it reigns today. Yet just here, in the virtually axiomatic authority this conception has attained, may be ample ground for reopening inquiry into the founders' intent.

As Sacvan Bercovitch has perceived, Miller's Errand into the Wilderness has "become influential in the wrong way"; its brilliantly devised argument has commanded such passive acceptance that little inquiry into the documentary basis has occurred. Yet scholars have not always understood the Errand in the same way. A reexamination of the issue properly begins with a look at the original formulation.

If Miller's essay is scrutinized for its statement and documentation of the Puritan Errand, some little-remarked features of the argument appear. First, Miller's main business was not to expound or substantiate the concept of a founding Errand, but, rather, to interpret the psychology of the second and third generations as manifested in the jeremiads. A brief exposition of the aims of the first generation was offered merely as required by the larger concern. Second, in defining the Errand, Miller made a seldom-appreciated distinction. The founders' aspiration, he held, is not reducible to a single statement of purpose; it embraced two distinct levels of meaning. In the first sense it meant the will to construct a covenanted community based, in John Winthrop's words, upon a due form of civil and ecclesiastical government. In this signification, the Errand meant the colonists' "actual business," their "conscious intention." Furthermore, it designated that intention as "an end in itself"; the founders were running the Errand on their own behalf, serving their own religious welfare. But, Miller proceeded, behind the explicit intention appeared a second, an "aim behind [the] aim" by which the colonists were seen "despatched for a further purpose."

That purpose was the creation of a "working model" of fully reformed Christendom "so that ultimately all Europe would imitate

New England." It also entailed the training of a civil and ecclesiastical leadership that eventually, following an anticipated Puritan triumph in the mother country, would return to govern England. And what was the status of this headier ambition in the colonists' consciousness? To this question Miller gave ambiguous answer. On the one hand he could suggest that the second meaning of Errand was fully conscious, collective, and overt: thus "Winthrop and his colleagues . . . went in order to work out that complete reformation which was not accomplished in England, but which would quickly be accomplished if only the saints back there had a working model to guide them." On the other hand, Miller deliberately contrasted this "aim behind the aim" with the "conscious intention," the "definite" aim, the "avowed end" of the Errand in the first sense. He identified only Winthrop, in his well-known invocation of a "Citty upon a Hill," as "fully conscious" of the further purpose. Neither in the essay of 1952 nor elsewhere did Miller cite other texts from the period 1629-1640 affirming a higher Errand. He described the expectation of a completed reformation and a return to England as an "unspoken assumption" entertained by the settlers only in their "heart of hearts." Clearly, at this level, we are left in uncertainty. Even should we grant Miller's interpretation of it, Winthrop's single text does not a grandiose theory make. We are here presented, not with a convincing demonstration that the founders were moved by world-redeeming purpose, but with an ambiguously formulated proposal obviously best regarded as a hypothesis in need of testing.

Both the subtlety and the ambiguity of Miller's formulation of the Errand are emphasized when we look at what others have made of it. Briefly, it is a story of how a minimally developed proposal, without substantial additional research, has been hardened into fact and then inflated well out of proportion to the original statement. . . .

Defining Puritanism

To an extraordinary degree, modern Puritan studies have been mired in definitional confusion and disagreement. It would be difficult to find anywhere a steadier flow of complaints that "the chief difficulty in writing about the Puritans . . . is one of definitions." In the absence of a broadly accepted concept of their Puritan differentia, it is comforting to believe that one can comprehend the motives driving the first immigrants to a far colony; and surely nothing has seemed more certain than their peculiar pretense to be embarked upon a conscious, explicit, collective, and overridingly important world mission. Such a mission, moreover, then can serve as the premise to a larger interpretation of the national past: The settlers' vision of an exemplary community "struck the keynote of American history."

About 1970, however, a restiveness with the conception of a founding mission became apparent. Researchers touching upon the migration and settlement often failed to discover evidence of a founding Errand, and in a few cases alternative hypotheses have been suggested: the settlers were primarily persecuted dissidents seeking sanctuary; they were social conservatives concerned primarily to rescue local liberties from the encroaching absolutism of Charles I; or they were in flight from an eschatological catastrophe soon to befall England. These studies do not converge upon a single line of attack, although most stress an exilic theme, but they do register a rising undercurrent of dissent from the ascription of a grandiose redemptive mission to Winthrop-era migrants. . . .

The interpretive prestige of the Errand into the Wilderness continued to run high among students of the Great Migration. It is, indeed, time to bring this construct under closer scrutiny: What and how numerous are the extant sources expressive of "reasons for settling"? Do they document a collective consecration to the fabulous, world-historical mission customarily assigned to the immigration of the 1630s?

The Founders' Agenda Reappraised

Students of American Puritanism readily will agree that the "most-quoted phrases of Puritan literature" are those of John Winthrop's lay sermon, "A Model of Christian Charity": "Men shall say of succeeding plantacions: the lord make it like that of New England: for . . . wee shall be as a Citty upon a Hill, the eies of all people are uppon us." This text, ritually cited in evidence for the Errand, is an obvious point of departure. What does this famed text signify, if considered in the whole context of the sermon? The argument of the "Model of Christian Charity" is clear enough; it is directed throughout to the presentation of a single and urgent thesis. Having pondered the difficulties of establishing a colony in unfamiliar, unsettled territory, Winthrop foresaw a time of deprivation and hardship. Necessities were apt to be in short supply for a time, and this circumstance would bear hard, perhaps intolerably, upon those of modest means. They, in turn, could scarcely then be held within the unity of purpose and effort required for the project's success; they might become sources of dangerous unrest. The purpose of Winthrop's sermon, therefore, was to urge "Christian charity"; his repeated theme was that a "community of perills calls for extraordinary liberallity." As in the primitive times, Christians now must subdue their possessive instincts and freely lend or share their goods, "abridg[ing them]selves of . . . superfluities, for the supply of others necessities." In this way, the community could go forward "knitt together" in pursuit of its chosen goals. It could develop a "due forme of Government both civill and ecclesiasticall" to the end that authentic Christianity might be realized "under the power and purity of . . . holy Ordinances."

Whose Vision?

Darrett B. Rutman has taught in the history department of the University of New Hampshire in Durham and has written extensively on Puritanism. His 1965 book Law and Authority in Colonial America *asserts that the ideals expressed by Puritan leaders on creating a perfect society were not necessarily shared by most settlers.*

That an ideal arrangement of society was visualized by some of the first comers to New England and that they contemplated realizing the ideal in the New World is patently obvious. One need only glance at Winthrop's "Modell of Christian Charity" to see it. But was the ideal uniquely Puritan? . . .

More importantly, was the ideal—so often expressed by the articulate few and commented upon by the intellectual historians—ever a reality in New England? Certainly conditions in America were not conducive to it. The very ideal contained a flaw, for while in England the social and religious covenant was an abstract principle to be toyed with by logicians, in New England it was, in town and church, transformed into practice. How does one convince the generality that the forms and personnel of authority are within its province, but that once established they are in God's domain and are to be honored as such? . . . Moreover, the transition from old to New England constituted a break in the social fabric familiar to the individual. In an English borough or village the individual located himself according to well-established social and political relationships, but these were no more. Family ties in New England during the early years were relatively few. Ties to the traditional elements of authority—vestrymen, churchwardens, manor stewards, borough councillors, justices-of-the-peace—had disappeared, to be created anew in the New England town, it is true, but such new relationships lacked the sanctity of long familiarity. And even when new ties existed, there was little stability in the New Englander's place in the social and political order. What mattered the regular assertion that God had ordained some to ride and some to walk when those who walked one day could, by virtue of the absence of traditional leaders, the presence of New World opportunities, and the application of their own diligence, ride another?

If a thesis about sharing love, together with a reminder of common ends, comprehends the essential message of the sermon, what are we to make of the author's proclamation that "wee shall be as a Citty upon a Hill, the eies of all people are uppon us"? As a preliminary it should be noted that the "Model" is only a single entry in a substantial corpus of writings. From the period of its first conception in 1629 to his death in 1649, the revered first governor of the Bay recorded his hopes for the Massachusetts project in a series of letters and more formal documents, including his extensive *History of New England*. Had his perception of the colony's mission actually revolved around the wish to create a beacon for the nations, as is routinely maintained, it is reasonable to expect that this ideal frequently and forcefully would come to expression in his written remains. What could be more disconcerting, therefore, than to find that the Bay project, except in the passing reference in the "Model," nowhere in the entire corpus is pictured as a redemptive city upon a hill, a light to the nations, or a decisive pattern for English, European, or worldwide reform?

If, however, for the purpose of the moment one concentrates upon the sermon itself, it will be perplexing to recall that Winthrop's reflections upon the "Citty upon a Hill" have become the "most quoted phrases of Puritan literature." They do not stand as climax or conclusion to Winthrop's principal arguments. They occur, instead, in passing, in the midst of a paragraph that commences with and proceeds to other and thematically more central matters. Judging from the evidence of the sermon itself, the famed text is nothing more than a momentary embellishment of the argument, a touch of rhetorical hyperbole rephrasing a popular biblical text (Matthew 5 :14).

To construe it as a charge to the settlers to function as a model to the nations, as "the hub of the universe, whose light and wisdom would radiate out in all directions" and change the course of history, ignores the plain meaning of Winthrop's formulation. He predicted that, if the covenant should be kept, God would "make us a prayse and glory, that men shall say of succeeding plantacions: the lord make it like that of New England." Of succeeding plantations! Significantly, the appeal is not to England, Europe, or "the world." He then continued: "Wee shall be as a Citty upon a Hill, the eies of all people are uppon us; soe that if wee shall deale falsely with our god in this worke . . . wee shall be made a story and a by-word through the world," to the discredit of the continuing Reformation. The projected impact upon "all people," in other words, presupposed the *failure* of New England's enterprise. Winthrop knew too well, in the words of a sympathetic English observer in 1632, that there were "a thousand eyes watchinge over you to pick a hole in your coats." There is, in sum, little in the "Model of Christian Charity" to support the conventional interpretation of Winthrop's most famous words. They would appear to be not only the most quoted but also the least understood in the Puritan literature.

But, it may be objected, did Miller not, and properly, intend his reading of the "Model" to be seen in the context of a larger body of literature produced by several apologists for the colonial project? And may not Winthrop's "Citty upon a Hill," if read accordingly, be seen as a play upon higher purposes generally assumed? In truth, at this point the hypothesis of an Errand becomes easiest to test. To a far greater extent than usually is recognized, the New England founders expounded, debated, clarified, and committed to paper their consciously held reasons for venturing to the New World. Perhaps the most commonly cited sources, after Winthrop's "Model," are John Cotton's farewell sermon to the first departing body of settlers for the Bay and two much later writings by Edward Johnson and Peter Bulkeley. But there are a host of other extant testimonies from members of the first New England generation and their close English associates, including at least eight laypersons, of "the reasons moving [them] to transplant themselves." In addition, there are no fewer than six more detailed tabulations of "reasons" compiled by John Winthrop, several pastors, and the anonymous author of *Good News from New-England*. A review of these data ought to yield the evidence for a conscious, explicit, collective, overriding, world-redeeming Errand.

Debating the Decision to Migrate

Descriptions of the Great Migration as impelled by a bold vision of the future tend to obscure the wavering, undecided attitude of many contemplating flight. The decision to depart from home and country often was taken, if at all, only after anxious and sometimes protracted debate. There were not only the expostulations of friendly critics to meet; of greater importance were the doubts and scruples of prospective emigrants themselves. Would it, for example, not be "a greate wronge to our owne country and church to take away the godly people" and thus increase the likelihood of covenantal judgment? Should not Christians "stay and suffer for Christ" in the teeth of worsening conditions? In the course of coping with such issues, men like Winthrop, Thomas Shepard, and Richard Mather were formulating what one historian has called a "casuistry of emigration," a body of often carefully wrought argument in which a wide variety of "arguments" and "considerations" found their place. It embodied the considerable effort of reflection and persuasion that would be expected of men who, so far from being seized by a high and clear sense of mission abroad, were tossed and restrained by a genuine ambivalence. And yet it also inventoried the conscious purposes of those who fought through ambivalence and elected, albeit in most cases reluctantly, to depart their homeland.

The absence of explicit appeal to an Errand in Winthrop's larger body of writing is the more telling, since he appears to have been the prime mover of an extensive effort by those initially engaged in the project to define, weigh, and refine "arguments for the plantation of New England." These were elaborated in several drafts of two distinct documents, "General Observations for the Plantation of New England" and "General Conclusions and Particular Considerations." Nowhere in all the literature of the Great Migration is there to be found a more detailed and considered justification of the removal from England. This material provides a perfectly clear profile of the mission visualized by Winthrop and his immediate colleagues.

Six major and repeated arguments readily may be identified. Four of these posit negative ends, of flight and escape from onerous conditions in England: overpopulation, economic distress, the corruption by anti-Puritan influences of schools and universities, and the hanging threat of God's covenantal punishment upon an unreformed land. Such considerations point plainly to New England as a *refuge* from adversity. There remain, however, two arguments delineating a positive function. First, the colony was to provide a Protestant "bullwarke" against the "kingdom of Antichrist which the Jesuites labour to reare" in North America; this would entail the Christianization of the native peoples. Second, the colony was to perform the additional service of "raysinge and upholdinge a particular Churche." These latter functions point to a conception of New England as a missionary enterprise dedicated—Winthrop says "chiefly"—to the "propagation of religion." Then, solely in the "General Conclusions and Particular Considerations," a seventh point appears: in light of God's impending judgment upon England, removal to a safe site would preserve covenantally faithful church members, that "they may be of better use to their mother Churche" later. They were to "returne after the storme" and presumably contribute to the restoration of true religion. "Refuge," then, and the "propagation of religion" in an unclaimed corner of the world as well as the preservation of saints to aid the eventual recovery of English Protestantism—these were the specific aims debated, refined, and affirmed by Winthrop and his associates as they pondered their dangerous undertaking, quelled doubts, and strove to rally enthusiasm. Other early statements of policy by officers of the Massachusetts Bay Company underscored the priority assigned to the establishment of right religion and to conversion of the natives, but otherwise added nothing new to Winthrop's seven points. The customarily alleged "overriding objective" is nowhere to be discerned.

A broad field of evidence is yet to be scanned. The remaining revelations of original purpose include reports of debates by clergy interested in the venture but concerned about biblical authorization, and numerous summaries of motives both before and after the fact. The record they furnish of the colonial mission as conceived by several founders readily can be inventoried under a few heads. Economic reasons were cited occasionally but not frequently, as were the "planting of the Gospel" in vacant parts, conversion of the Indians, and the desire to remain with emigrating "friends." John Dane's recollection, that he "bent [him]self to cum to nu ingland, thinking that I should be more fre here than thare [England]" from a young man's characteristic temptations, reminds us also of the presence of miscellaneous individual aspirations. Yet none of the above looms large in the total body of testimony. With overwhelming frequency, the data fall into two categories: the wish to secure a refuge and the determination to win "liberty of the Ordinances."

If the immigrants to New England were in fact a bold "vanguard" aggressively intent upon their exemplary Errand, it would be remarkable that a very large portion of their apologetic for the venture concentrated upon exilic themes. Ezekiel Rogers, a first-generation Massachusetts pastor and son-in-law of the great Richard Rogers struck the forlorn note clearly: they had chosen, he wrote in 1646, to become "poor Exiles of Christ, . . . God's Exiles." Not only Winthrop, as we have seen, and Ezekiel Rogers but also Thomas Hooker, Thomas Shepard, John Cotton, Richard Mather, John Allin, and others were prepared without a trace of reserve to describe their voyage as a flight from adversity. They identified, moreover, two separable incentives to flight: the imminent prospect of a divine judgment upon England and persecution for nonconformity. . . .

Threats of Persecution

It is now evident that any accounting of the founders' aims, any effort to view the Great Migration in their terms, must address a highly principled and obstinate resistance to hardening liturgical policy and the resulting threat of persecution. As with John Cotton, John Davenport, and Thomas Hooker, so with Charles Chauncy, Richard Mather, and Hugh Peter: animus against the increasingly ceremonial cast of English worship provided the ultimate motivation for flight to Massachusetts. By no means was that animus always the first precipitant, but it is a recurrent theme in the literature of the Great Migration. During a controversy in earliest Salem, Francis Higginson and Samuel Skelton declared that "they came away from the Common-Prayer and Ceremonies, and had suffered much for their Non-Conformity" on these points. About 1640 John Cotton reminded his Boston parishioners, "You have left your Trades, friends, Country, and have put your self upon a changeable and hazardous Journey because your Consciences could not submit to Ceremonies." Thomas Shepard and John Allin recollected vividly in the late 1640s the "time when humane Worship and inventions were growne to such an intolerable height, that the consciences of Gods saints . . . could no longer bear them"; since the immediate alternative was persecution, they chose "to fly into the Wildernesse from the face of the Dragon." About a decade later, John Eliot agreed: "The cause of our coming into New-England . . .

Religious vs. Secular Motivations

Everett Emerson, a professor of English at the University of Massachusetts in Amherst, discusses in his book Puritanism in America *the many reasons, not all of them religious, that people in England decided to migrate to Massachusetts.*

Secular-minded historians and Marxists are wont to argue that Puritanism had little to do with the beginnings of New England. Just as there were nonreligious reasons for being a Puritan, so there were admittedly several nonreligious reasons for leaving England. In the early years of the seventeenth century the old agrarian society disintegrated. The capitalist society that replaced it suffered in the beginning severe dislocations: economic depression marked the years 1619-1624, 1629-1631, and 1637-1640. There were plague years too, and bad harvests. In the strongly Puritan area of East Anglia, economic conditions reached crisis levels in 1629. . . .

The political situation in England in the 1620s and 1630s was another reason why some men sought to leave England. Soon after Charles I came to the throne he issued, in 1626, a letter to religious and secular leaders "to require and collect a loan for the King's use from persons able to lend." This letter, issued for what Charles called "reasons of state," infringed on the prerogatives of Parliament, and many men refused to furnish the money demanded. Among those who resisted the so-called benevolence and were consequently imprisoned were the Earl of Lincoln, a central figure in the creation of the Massachusetts Bay Company; Samuel Vassal and William Spurstow, who were among the original members of the Company; and William Coddington, who came to Massachusetts in 1630. This incident was only one of many that persuaded Englishmen, especially those sympathetic to Parliament and Puritanism, that the king was exceeding the proper limits of royal power. A constitutional crisis was clearly in the making.

Such conditions as these had much to do with the creation of the Massachusetts Bay Company. On the other hand, most, if not all, of its leaders were demonstrably Puritans, and it was at least in the name of religion that they left England.

[was] that we might be freed from the ceremonies and have liberty to enjoy all the pure ordinances of Christ . . . without . . . human additions and novelties.

The picture that emerges from a review of such materials is again one of flight from adversity, cast against a background of disaffection in which the issue of ceremonies occupied the most prominent place. Indisputably, the clergy held and pursued positive goals as well, but it cannot be sustained that "the migration was no retreat from Europe" or that "these were not . . . refugees seeking a promised land." "This was the situation," Cotton recalled in 1645, "that we [nonconforming clergy] either had to perish uselessly in prison or leave the country.". . .

If there is abundant evidence that the colonial venture was conceived negatively, as avoidance, flight, and asylum, even more evidence points to a positive conception, to a goal whose vividness and frequency of appearance in both clerical and lay testimony readily qualifies it as the overriding positive objective of the founders. "What was your end of coming hither?" Thomas Shepard asked his Newtown congregation sometime in the late 1630s. Shepard now wished to review with his auditors, including several of his former parishioners, their primary religious end within the colonial enterprise. It was, in a word, unobstructed use of the primitively instituted ordinances of Christian practice. In the many reports of original, explicit, and positive purpose left by articulate founders, including most of the prominent clergy, this—the "liberty of the ordinances"—was the incessantly repeated motif: "What came you into this Wilderness for? . . . You came . . . that you might have the Ordinances of God in his Churches rightly gathered." "Liberty" and "ordinances"— those interested in the purpose of the Puritan founders will find less in an elusive Errand and more in these two indubitable slogans of the early literature. . . .

Insofar as the "chief end" of the founders was expressed in such terms, this migration to Massachusetts takes on the dimension of a restorationist campaign. Thus, to give the biblical ordinances full play in the "free air of the new world" was indeed to fulfill at last the thwarted promise of the English Reformation, but this was not cast into the larger formula of an Errand to save the world or inaugurate the millennium. As in the texts cited above, the express wish is to have and to hold biblically certified practices. They were inestimably valuable in themselves, but their greater function within the history of Redemption was not immediately at issue. Further, the very context of thought within which the ordinances were understood focused attention *backward* toward the reinvoked drama of primitive Christianity. Before there could be any question of historical advance, there had to be a secure recovery of origins. Appreciation of that recovery, then, is vital to comprehending the first immigrants' religious purposes. Emigration meant freedom to come to terms with long-lost originals. The impulse was *revival*, directed to restoration and fulfilling enjoyment of forms ordained in the primal age.

Arrogant Apprehensions Disavowed

Had the founders of Massachusetts actually intended an overarching Errand, surely it would have been a persistent theme in their many explicit statements of purpose, and especially in the tabulations of "arguments" by Winthrop, Cotton, Thomas Shepard and Richard Mather, and others. But it was not. . . .

Consider the few texts in which founding figures style their colony as an exemplary "city," "light," or the like. At least two of these, from Johnson's *Wonder-Working Providence* and Peter Bulkeley's *Gospel-Covenant*, have been adduced as evidence for the Errand, but this construal suffers under critical examination. Edward Johnson, for instance, told the colonists they were "to be set as lights upon a Hill more obvious than the highest Mountaine." They were to "make choyce of the right, that all . . . Nations . . . who are soonly to submit to Christs Kingdome, may be followers of you." God "purposely pickt out this People for a patterne of purity and soundnesse." Yet, contrary to first impression, there is no persuasive evidence here for a founding Errand. *Wonder-Working Providence* was written in 1650-1651, a full decade after the Great Migration had come to an end. It interpreted the role of New England in light of the English Revolution and under the influence of the copious millennial speculation which that event had evoked. From this much altered standpoint, Johnson was ready to maintain that New England's Congregational establishments presented an influential spectacle of reformation to other nations as they were beginning to be marshaled into the millennial kingdom.

But as to the aims of the founders, the reader of Johnson's work will note the retrospective, contrived, and highly colored character of his introductory "Commission of the People of Christ shipped for New England"; for here alone he appears to suggest that the imagery of "lights upon a Hill" was ingredient to the first settlers' intention. In the more factual narratives that compose the bulk of the work, Johnson consistently portrays first intentions in other terms. He describes the immigrants' sober choice to flee fear and persecution and "take up a perpetuall banishment." While they proposed from afar to "pray without ceasing for England," their "chiefe errand," their "end of . . . coming hither," was to recover first forms. They would "worship the Lord in the purity of his Ordinances"; "purity in Religion" was what they had "spent their whole travel for." By 1650, working within a much-altered climate of opinion, Johnson moved to supplement the primitivist foundation with millennial concerns and to assign an undeniably historic mission to the Puritan colonies; but this revision cannot reasonably be taken as an account of original purpose.

In *Gospel-Covenant* (1646), Bulkeley warned his countrymen to "take heed . . . lest being now as a City upon an hill, which many seek unto, you be left like a Beacon upon the top of a mountain, desolate and forsaken." "Which many seek unto," however, suggests, not a center of radiating influence, but an attractive enterprise leading the way to itself. And note the flatly negative import of the "Beacon" imagery. The passage may reflect concern about the disturbing decline in immigration to New England after 1640. In a later passage Bulkeley again described the colonies as "a City set upon an hill," but now the point was, as in Winthrop's "Model," that "men . . . will cry shame upon us, if we walk contrary to the Covenant"—not their conversion by New England example. He did urge his hearers "so to walk, that this [covenantal obedience] may be our excellency and dignity among the Nations"; but nowhere did he describe New England's purpose as the creation of an exemplary city that would convert the world, or ascribe such an aim to the settlers of the previous decade.

Disclaimers of a World Mission

If it were otherwise, if indeed it was a sense of their catalytic role in the schedule of world redemption that had brought these Puritans across four thousand miles of ocean, we would not find them speaking with humility, even skepticism, about the exemplary function of their society. And yet at least six of the founders, including eminent clergy, openly discounted the world-redeeming pretension ascribed to them three centuries later. Roger Ludlow, describing in 1638 the "establish[ment of] the lord Jesus in his Kingly Throne" as "the en[d] of our Comminge into these westerne partes," also added a telling note: "Wee knowe that our profession will finde fewe frends upon the face of the earth." Only if one assumes the Errand will this appear a passing aberration. Seven years later, Richard Mather and William Tompson wrote a common letter of counsel to their old congregations in England. Pleased to offer advice as able, they yet wished to deny that they saw themselves "to be the only Prophets . . . able to give a word of counsel . . . such arrogant apprehensions are far from us." In Robert Middlekauff's apt commentary, "They did not want to be understood as posing as the representatives of a morally superior culture."

Even more interesting is a flat disclaimer issued by John Cotton about 1650. In one of his several debates with Roger Williams, Cotton denied that Bay Congregationalism was an immediately binding model for reform abroad: "It is an insolent phrase that savoureth of more arrogancy, then either we dare use, or allow in our selves or others, to seeme to make our [mode of] calling to the Ministry in *New-England*, a Rule, and patterne, and precedent to all the Churches of Christ throughout the world." About the same time, he was telling his Boston parishioners that for the foreseeable future it was unreasonable to expect England to adopt the Congregational way: "For [the] present, it is certaine [that] the Body of the Nation of England, is not Capable of Fellowship in Independent churches." Therefore, he advocated a flexible establishment providing Presbyterian (!) nurture for the larger portion of the citizenry. . . .

None of these assertions is incompatible with the conviction that Congregational Protestantism as worked out in New England was in fullest accord with New Testament direction or that, ideally, it should be universal practice. Cotton, for example, would allow variations on the point of "calling" only within the framework of the "consent of the Church," and he surely hoped that in due course England would submit to Congregationalism in all its details. Allin and Shepard merely recapitulated nonseparatist doctrine that established English churches were implicitly true churches and therefore not subject to the New England device of a new "gathering." But it is of greatest significance that, as if with one voice, these prominent figures insisted that they had come "not hither proudly to censure others, but to reforme our owne." Their state of mind corresponds to the Errand as defined in Miller's *first* sense; it is distinctly inhospitable to the crusading exemplarism usually associated with an Errand into the Wilderness. Least of all does it provide the originating instance of claims to an American national mission on behalf of the world. Such claims were to loom large in later history, but to find their progenitor in a Massachusetts City upon a Hill is to mistake the purposes of the 1630s.

For Discussion

Chapter One

1. Both John White and John Winthrop list several reasons for leaving England to come to the New World. How are their reasons similar? How are they different?

2. What attitudes and beliefs about the Indians are expressed in the viewpoints by White, Winthrop, and others? How do the Indians fit into the Puritans' vision?

3. What similarities and what differences do you discern in the sermons of John Robinson and John Winthrop to their people on the *Mayflower* and *Arbella*? Based on the viewpoints in this and other chapters, do you consider the differences between Pilgrims and Puritans to be fundamental ones? Why or why not?

4. Are equality and liberty, two important American values, featured in Winthrop's *Arbella* sermon describing his vision of a model society? How would you best describe the sermon?

5. Do William Stoughton and Increase Mather share the same beliefs concerning God's relationship with New England? Explain.

6. What motivations might Stoughton and Mather have for emphasizing the heroic nature of the early Puritan settlers? Do you think their perspective should be discounted? Why or why not?

7. Was Increase Mather correct in saying that the original Puritan settlers moved to New England "purely on a Religious account," and "did not propose to themselves worldly advantages"? Explain your answer.

Chapter Two

1. What "four particulars" was Roger Williams accused of by the Puritan authorities? Which of these does he spend the most time defending in his letter?

2. Why does John Cotton argue that Roger Williams in effect banished himself? Do you find his argument convincing? Why or why not?

3. What does Thomas Welde find so objectionable in the ideas expressed by Anne Hutchinson? What evidence does he cite to support the view that her ideas are wrong?

4. Do Winthrop's immigration regulations and his treatment of Anne Hutchinson conflict with his desire, expressed in his *Arbella* sermon, to create a loving community? How does Winthrop attempt to justify his actions? Does he succeed? Why or why not?

5. What objections does Henry Vane have to Winthrop's immigration restrictions? Keeping in mind that he is examining the issue from Puritan rather than modern sensibilities, do you think Vane successfully rebuts Winthrop's arguments on immigration? Explain.

6. John Cotton was Anne Hutchinson's favorite minister. He was accused of antinomianism and banished himself. How might this experience have affected his views and writings? Explain.

7. What accusations does Richard Saltonstall make about the Puritan colonies? Why might his status as a Puritan minister in England make those accusations especially jarring to Cotton and others?

8. Do the tone and content of Cotton's two viewpoints in this chapter vary? If so, why?

Chapter Three

1. Why does John Cotton believe that democracy is an inferior form of government? What does he use to defend his arguments?

2. On what basis does Robert Child claim that his rights and liberties are being violated? Why might the Puritan leaders have been especially sensitive to his charges (enough to detain him and thus delay his return to England)?

3. What differences exist in the accounts of John Winthrop and Robert Keayne concerning Winthrop's accusation that Keayne makes unfair profits? Why was Keayne not excommunicated, according to Winthrop? How does Keayne defend his actions?

4. In their viewpoints in this and other chapters, how do Winthrop and Cotton describe the relationship between church and state in the Puritan community? Are church and state the same for the Puritan leaders? If Puritan leaders had had their way, how might American government be different today?

5. What evidence does the Massachusetts General Court cite as proof of God's displeasure? Do you believe the Puritan population was as bad as the court seems to think? Why or why not?

6. How does William Bradford's membership in the separatist Plymouth Colony, rather than in Winthrop's Puritan colony affect his attitude toward the law and morality? Explain.

7. Which of the authors in this chapter rely heavily on the Bible for their arguments? Which of them do not? Do the disputes in this chapter reflect different degrees of referring to the Bible or different interpretations of the Bible? Explain.

Chapter Four

1. How does John Cotton justify taking land from the Indians? How does he rebut earlier arguments made by Roger Williams?

2. How does Roger Williams characterize the Indians? How do his descriptions correspond with those found elsewhere in this book?

3. Edward Johnson's viewpoint was written when the New England colonies were new and relatively unestablished. Samuel Sewall's viewpoint was written decades later when the colonies were firmly established and the threat of Indian warfare in New England was relatively small. How important do you believe these external conditions were to the different sentiments expressed about Indians in the viewpoints?

4. How does John Eliot compare the Indians and the English? What reasons does he give for optimism in missionary work?

5. How does Mary Rowlandson describe "praying Indians"? Does she imply or state any belief concerning missionary efforts among them? Explain.

6. In what ways does Mary Rowlandson reveal her Puritanism in her actions and thoughts during her captivity?

7. Which authors in this chapter do you believe express prejudice against the Indians? Do all of them have some form of racial, cultural, or religious prejudice? Explain.

Chapter Five

1. List the similarities you find in the viewpoints by Cotton Mather and Increase Mather. List the differences.

2. List the similarities in the viewpoints by Thomas Brattle and Robert Calef. List the differences.

3. Cotton Mather and Increase Mather make several recommendations regarding the prosecution of accused witches. Thomas Brattle describes several things he has observed in the prosecutions. Does Brattle observe the same things that the Mathers recommend? Do the Mathers' recommendations seem to you like reasonable ways to assess guilt? Explain. Do Brattle's criticisms seem reasonable? Explain.

4. Cotton Mather and his father Increase were both well-educated men interested in science as well as religion. Why do you sup-

pose they and other Puritans believed so strongly in witches and Satan's work in the world?

5. Thomas Brattle and Robert Calef condemned the witch trials at Salem. Was this because they did not believe in witches? Explain.

6. Viewpoints six and seven were each written by a group of prominent church leaders. Why do you suppose some religious leaders saw the devil's work in those very aspects of the Great Awakening that others found most promising?

7. From your own perspective, do you think the dramatic occurrences during the Great Awakening—the speaking in tongues, the personal experiences of God, and so on—are more likely to be true expressions of religious experience or charlatanry? List several reasons or examples to support your answer.

8. Which do you find more convincing—the excerpt from Jonathan Edwards or the one from Charles Chauncy? Why?

9. Based on your knowledge of Puritanism, does the Great Awakening seem to be a natural outgrowth of what came before it or a drastic change of direction? Explain.

Chapter Six

1. What importance does Perry Miller ascribe to events in England that affected the Puritans in America? Would Theodore Dwight Bozeman give such external events similar significance? Explain.

2. How do Miller and Bozeman differ in their analyses of John Winthrop's *Arbella* sermon? In your opinion, which historian has the more credible interpretation of the sermon? Why?

General

1. Which documents in this volume can be used to support the thesis that Puritanism contributed to the development of freedom and democracy in America? Which can be used to support the idea that Puritanism retarded the development of those values? Explain your choice.

2. Some of the documents reprinted in this book were written for specific audiences—English Puritans, voyaging settlers, future readers of history. Examine some of these documents to see whether they were written for an identifiable audience and describe how that audience might have affected the document's content.

3. Name three important values or ideas the Puritans brought with them to America from England. Were these ideas modi-

fied by experience in America? What factors in the American environment most contributed to changes within Puritanism?

4. Based on the readings in this volume, would you conclude that Puritanism has had a positive or negative impact on the history of America? Explain.

Chronology

1509	John Calvin, whose doctrine of predestination became the foundation of Puritanism, is born in Noyon, France.
1529	King Henry VIII breaks England's ties with the Catholic church over the pope's refusal to grant him a divorce from his Spanish wife.
1533	Calvin declares himself a Protestant.
1536	Calvin publishes his *Institutes of the Christian Religion.*
1553	Mary Tudor, daughter of Henry VIII, ascends the throne of England and returns England to Rome and Catholicism. Protestant reformers begin to flee to Europe.
1558	Elizabeth I becomes queen of England and Protestant exiles begin to return to England.
1563	The English government approves the Thirty-Nine Articles instituting some Protestant reforms but disappointing extremists who want to eliminate every vestige of Romanism from the Church of England.
1564	Calvin dies in Geneva, Switzerland.
1572	John Field, then the foremost leader of English Puritans, drafts the Admonition to Parliament, the first open declaration of Puritan demands.
1580	Robert Browne of Norwich is the first Puritan to advocate total separation from the Church of England.
1603	James I, the first of the Stuart monarchs, becomes king and quickly antagonizes the Puritans by asserting the divine right of kings.
1607	A group of English Puritans known as Separatists arrives in Amsterdam and eventually settles in Leyden in 1609.
1618	James I hands down his Declaration on Sports, a defense of games and village pastimes and a challenge to Puritans who oppose such activities.
1620	The first permanent settlement of English Puritans in New England is established at Plymouth by Separatists who draft the Mayflower Compact and who

will be known as Pilgrims.

1621   William Bradford is chosen as governor of Plymouth Plantation, and though he is never able to secure a royal charter for his Pilgrim community, he will govern successfully for a number of years without great interference from London.

1623   The Dorchester Company forms and establishes fishing settlements in New England.

1625   Charles I becomes king of England. His contempt for Parliament and assertion of monarchical authority as well as his apparent opposition to Puritan practices dismays Puritans.

1628   A charter is granted by the Council of New England to a group of Puritan merchants organized as the New England Company.

The Dorchester Company and some London merchants form the New England Company and send John Endecott to assume control of the Salem settlement.

1629   The New England Company reorganizes and receives a royal charter as the Massachusetts Bay Company; John Winthrop is selected by a "general vote and full consent" as the first governor of the colony.

Charles I dissolves Parliament.

1630   John Winthrop's group of Puritans, one thousand strong, establish Massachusetts Bay Colony. Unlike the Separatists in Plymouth, these Puritans continue to believe that the Church of England can be reformed.

One of John Winthrop's first acts is to levy a tax for the support of the two Puritan ministers then preaching in the young colony.

1631   The General Court (legislature) of Massachusetts Bay Colony opens freemanship (which includes the right to vote and hold public office) to all church members.

Roger Williams arrives in New England and is welcomed there because of his reputation as an eloquent preacher.

1633   The Reverend John Cotton arrives in Massachusetts. He will play a critical role in Puritan debates over what constitutes a Puritan church and a visible saint.

1635   The Reverend Richard Mather arrives in Massachusetts and begins a long line of Puritan ministers in the Mather family, including son Increase Mather and grandson Cotton Mather.

Thomas Hooker, minister of Cambridge, defies the Massachusetts government by leading his congregation westward and establishing the town of Hartford in Connecticut.

1636   Roger Williams is banished to Rhode Island for his extreme separatist views and for his criticism of Puritan treatment of neighboring Indian tribes.

Williams buys a tract of land from the Narragansett Indians and establishes the town of Providence.

The General Court limits freemanship to those persons who pass a new test for church membership, including direct testimony as to evidence of saving grace.

Harvard College, the first American college, is established by Puritan theologians and named for John Harvard, who had left his library and half his estate to the college.

1637   Anne Hutchinson is tried over the issue of her reliance on God's saving grace alone and her repudiation of the role of the Puritan minister. The trial will result in her conviction and banishment.

War breaks out between English settlers in the Connecticut Valley and the Pequot Indians. It ends with the virtual decimation of the Pequot tribe.

1638   The General Court rules that non-church members must be taxed to help pay for the preaching that might eventually lead to their conversion.

1639   The Fundamental Orders of Connecticut are adopted, creating a Puritan government in Connecticut similar to that in Massachusetts.

John Wheelwright, a disciple of Anne Hutchinson, leads some of his fellow dissenters to New Hampshire.

1640   The procedure for determining the status of a visible saint on the basis of testimony as to one's possession of saving grace is fully established in Massachusetts.

Charles I finally recalls Parliament and asks this body to levy new taxes to support his military ambitions.

1641   The calling of the Long Parliament brings Puritans into control of the English government.

The Body of Liberties is drafted and defines basic liberties for the Massachusetts Bay Colony.

1642   The English Civil War begins between the Cavaliers (supporters of the king) and the Roundheads (supporters of Parliament, who were largely Puritan). Puritan migration to America slows to a trickle.

1644 Roger Williams establishes the colony of Rhode Island with full freedom of worship for all faiths and no mandatory taxation in support of any religion.

1646 The General Court passes a law requiring everyone within a Puritan town to attend church services.

1648 A synod of Puritan clergy produces the *Cambridge Platform*, a declaration of principles on church government and discipline and endorsing the Congregationalist form of church order. Many view it as the high-water mark of clerical influence in New England.

1649 John Winthrop dies.

The Roundheads defeat the Cavaliers. Charles I is captured and beheaded.

The Society for the Propagation of the Gospel in New England is organized in England to help missionary efforts among the Indians.

1656 The first Quakers arrive in Massachusetts, where they are arrested and banished.

1658 English Puritans issue the Declaration of Savoy encouraging ministers to evangelize among the unconverted rather than confine themselves to reinforcing the faith among the membership.

1660 The Restoration begins in England. Puritan rule ends as Charles II ascends the throne. Some English Puritan leaders migrate to New England.

1662 The Half-Way Covenant is put in place, whereby the children and grandchildren of visible saints are granted partial church membership even though they had not had a conversion experience and the infusion of saving grace that would accompany it.

1667 The Reverend Solomon Stoddard of Northampton begins the practice of open communion, which invites full church membership without any attempt to discern evidence of saving grace.

1675 The General Court passes a statute titled "Provoking Evils," which seeks to identify and punish Puritan practices at odds with the founders of the colony.

1675-1676 King Philip's War rages across New England as various Puritan towns come under attack from Indians and Boston itself is threatened before the Wampanoags are defeated and their leader Metacomet (King Philip) is killed.

1676   A fire sweeps through Boston, providing Increase Mather with evidence of an angry God and giving him ammunition in his war against those Puritans he thinks too interested in living a life of pleasure.

1684   Massachusetts's 1629 colonial charter is abolished, leaving the colonial government with no legal authority.

1686   The Dominion of New England is created in London by James II to bring all of New England under a single royal governor and thereby eliminate the existing colonial assemblies.

1688   The Glorious Revolution takes place in England. William and Mary become joint sovereigns and the Catholic king, James II, flees to France. New Englanders, upon hearing of events in England, gather in a mob and drive Edmund Andros, the governor appointed by James II, from office. Andros is eventually imprisoned. The colonies regain former separate and legal status, except for Massachusetts, which remains without a charter.

1691   William and Mary grant Massachusetts a new charter. It restores some power to the General Court and incorporates Plymouth Colony within Massachusetts. It provides for a Royal Governor appointed by the Crown, however, and many of the colonies' former rights and liberties are lost.

1692   Nineteen residents of Salem, Massachusetts, are executed for witchcraft in the largest single episode of its kind in New England.

1696   Samuel Sewall, presiding judge at the Salem witch trials, confesses to his church that he was wrong in his judgments at the trials.

1701   Yale is founded in New Haven, Connecticut, by conservative Congregationalists who are unhappy with the growing religious liberalism at Harvard.

1706   Anne Putnam, one of the accusers at the Salem witch trials, recants her testimony and apologizes for doing great wrong while "deluded by Satan."

1711   The Massachusetts General Court reverses the judgments against the accused witches of Salem.

1727   An earthquake in New England seems to signal divine intervention against a society of Puritan backsliders.

1734 Jonathan Edwards, preeminent Puritan preacher, begins a series of influential sermons fusing rationalism and mysticism, initiating the Great Awakening in the New England.

1738 First visit of George Whitefield, often considered the greatest of the Great Awakening's itinerent preachers, to Georgia.

1739 Jonathan Edwards delivers a series of Great Awakening sermons over a period of thirty-nine weeks in an effort to impress upon his followers that all of them are but "sinners in the hands of an angry God."

George Whitefield preaches to gatherings of six thousand and more in the Philadelphia area. In the next two years, he travels from Maine to Georgia, arousing enthusiastic fervor in thousands of listeners.

1743 Charles Chauncy's important sermon *Seasonable Thoughts on the State of Religion in New England* clearly shows the division growing within the Puritan faith between the New Lights (who supported the Great Awakening) and the Old Lights (who did not).

1746 The College of New Jersey (later known as Princeton) is founded by clergy who have been imbued with the ideas and emotions of the Great Awakening.

1748 Jonathan Edwards, grandson of Solomon Stoddard and his successor at Northampton, announces that he can no longer admit candidates to full church membership without proof of saving grace.

1775 Various Massachusetts leaders of the American Revolution seek to call the colony's citizens back to the Spartan life of the early Puritans in mounting their war against England.

Annotated Bibliography

Bernard Bailyn, *The New England Merchants in the Seventeenth Century*. Cambridge, MA: Harvard University Press, 1955. A study that argues that the merchant class was more important than the clergy in shaping the Puritan world of the seventeenth century.

Emory Battis, *Saints and Sectarians*. Chapel Hill: University of North Carolina Press, 1962. A study of the trial of Anne Hutchinson that concludes that much of her support came from the commercial community.

Sacvan Bercovitch, *The American Jeremiad*. Madison: University of Wisconsin Press, 1978. Ranging from the Puritans to the Civil War, this volume defines the Puritan sermon known as the jeremiad in literary, historical, and anthropological terms.

Sacvan Bercovitch, *The Puritan Origins of the American Self*. New Haven, CT: Yale University Press, 1975. A highly technical, densely written exploration of a single text, John Cotton's "Life of John Winthrop."

Paul Boyer and Stephen Nissenbaum, *Salem Possessed*. Cambridge, MA: Harvard University Press, 1974. A sociological study of the background and conduct of the Salem witch trials, emphasizing the class divisions within the Salem community.

William Bradford, *Of Plymouth Plantation 1620-1647*. Samuel Eliot Morison, ed. New York: Alfred A. Knopf, 1959. One of the more accessible editions of the famous journal kept by the longtime governor of Plymouth Colony.

Francis J. Bremer, *The Puritan Experiment*. New York: St. Martin's Press, 1976. A general introductory history of the American Puritans.

Samuel Brockunier, *The Irrepressible Democrat*. New York: Ronald Press, 1940. A thorough, scholarly biography of Roger Williams, which neither praises nor blames him but is sympathetic.

Timothy Breen, *Character of the Good Ruler*. New Haven, CT: Yale University Press, 1970. A history of seventeenth-century Puritan political ideas that contends that the "good leader" was being increasingly defined in secular terms.

Carl Bridenbaugh, *Cities in the Wilderness*. New York: Ronald Press, 1938. A history of the first century of urban life in the colonies; provides much information on the city of Boston.

J. M. Bumstead, ed., *The Great Awakening: The Beginnings of Evangelical Pietism in America*. Waltham, MA: Blaisdell Publishing/Ginn & Company, 1970. A concise collection of documents from the Great Awakening, providing the reader with the essence of the thought of the time.

B. R. Burg, *Richard Mather of Dorchester*. Lexington: University of Kentucky Press, 1976. A study that illuminates the struggles of the first generation of Puritans as they defined their religious practices in the soil of the New World.

George Lincoln Burr, ed., *Narratives of the Witchcraft Cases, 1648-1706*. New York: Barnes & Noble, 1914. An excellent collection of primary sources from some of the leading participants in and observers of the Salem witchcraft cases.

Richard L. Bushman, ed., *The Great Awakening*. New York: Atheneum, 1970. Interesting collection of documents relating to the religious revival of 1740-45.

John Canup, *Out of the Wilderness*. Middletown, CT: Wesleyan University Press, 1990. A cultural history of Puritanism and how Puritan thought was shaped by American surroundings.

Charles Cohen, *God's Caress*. New York: Oxford University Press, 1986. A psychological study of the nature and evolution of the Puritan conversion experience.

Patrick Collinson, *The Elizabethan Puritan Movement*. Berkeley: University of California Press, 1967. A study that stresses the laity's importance in defining Puritanism; focuses on leaders, organization, and divisions rather than theology.

William Cronon, *Changes in the Land: Indians, Colonists, and the Ecology of New England*. New York: Hill and Wang, 1983. A study that seeks to explain how the farming practices and commercial enterprises of the early English colonists helped destroy the forest habitat of New England.

Claire Cross, *Church and People, 1450-1660*. London: Humanities Press, 1976. A history tracing the laity's struggle to gain control of English Protestantism and the resulting religious pluralism within England.

Andrew Delbanco, *The Puritan Ordeal*. Cambridge, MA: Harvard University Press, 1989. Less a history of ideas than a history of feelings as experienced by the first generation of Puritans in the New World.

John Demos, *Entertaining Satan*. New York: Oxford University Press, 1982. A history of witchcraft in the New World that places this phenomenon in an international context.

John Demos, *Little Commonwealth*. New York: Oxford University Press, 1970. A history of the physical setting of daily life in Puritan New England, with special emphasis on styles of housing, furniture, and clothes.

Richard Dunn, *Puritans and Yankees*. New York: Norton, 1971. A history of Puritanism that provides a less generous assessment of John Winthrop than can be found in Edmund S. Morgan's biography of the founding father of the Massachusetts Bay Colony.

Emory Elliott, *Power and the Pulpit in Puritan New England*. Princeton, NJ: Princeton University Press, 1975. An intriguing psychological analysis of Puritan ministerial rhetoric.

Everett Emerson, ed., *Letters from New England*. Amherst: University of Massachusetts Press, 1976. A collection of letters written by Puritan settlers of New England between 1629 and 1638.

Edwin Scott Gaustad, *The Great Awakening in New England*. New York: Harper & Brothers, 1957. A well-documented and readable history of this exciting time in New England religious history.

Charles George and Katherine George, *The Protestant Mind of the English Reformation*. Princeton, NJ: Princeton University Press, 1961. An exhaustive study of English Protestantism that contends that Puritans did not really exist, because the ideas generally attributed to Puritans were in fact shared by most English Protestants.

C. C. Goen, ed., *The Works of Jonathan Edwards: The Great Awakening*. New Haven, CT: Yale University Press, 1972. One of a series of volumes collecting the works of the great preacher Jonathan Edwards. This volume includes a thoughtful introduction by the editor as well as many of Edwards's writings from the 1730s and 1740s.

Philip Gura, *A Glimpse of Sion's Glory: Puritan Radicalism in New England, 1620-1660*. Middletown, CT: Wesleyan University Press, 1984. A history of religious dissenters, including Separatists, Baptists, and Quakers. All lived under the rule of one-time dissenters who achieved a position of authority and who grew more authoritarian in the process of contending with their own dissenters.

David Hall, *The Antinomian Controversy, 1636-1638*. Middletown, CT: Wesleyan University Press, 1968. A documentary history of the Antinomian controversy. It contains several of John Cotton's writings in defense of Anne Hutchinson, John Winthrop's account of the controversy, and the records of Hutchinson's court examination and church trial.

David Hall, *The Faithful Shepherd: A History of the New England Ministry in the Seventeenth Century*. Chapel Hill: University of North Carolina Press, 1972. An examination of the social and economic conditions facing New England ministers as they were Americanized; based on extensive personal records of many ministers.

Michael Hall, *The Last Puritan*. Middletown, CT: Wesleyan University Press, 1988. A comprehensive, well-illustrated, and well-written biography of Increase Mather.

William Haller, *The Rise of Puritanism*. New York: Columbia University Press, 1938. A study of Puritanism, combining literature, history, and sociology.

Charles Hambrick-Stowe, *The Practice of Piety*. Chapel Hill: University of North Carolina Press, 1982. A study of the Puritan conversion experience that argues that conversion was an ongoing reality rather than a single event.

Alan Heimert, *Religion and the American Mind*. Cambridge, MA: Harvard University Press, 1966. A history of the Great Awakening. The author argues that the religious enthusiasm generated during that era had a direct impact on the coming of the American Revolution.

Alan Heimert and Andrew Delbanco, eds., *The Puritans in America: A Narrative Anthology*. Cambridge, MA: Harvard University Press, 1985. An anthology of writings by and about American Puritans, dating from 1622 to 1725.

Alan Heimert and Perry Miller, eds., *The Great Awakening*. Indianapolis: Bobbs-Merrill, 1967. Excellent collection of writings from the time of the Great Awakening as well as documents leading up to and developing out of the movement.

Christopher Hill, *Society and Puritanism in Pre-Revolutionary England*. New York: Oxford University Press, 1967. A study that argues that the critical sphere of Puritan activity was located among middling artisans who were anxious to become commercial capitalists.

Francis Jennings, *The Invasion of America*. Chapel Hill: University of North Carolina Press, 1975. A history of Puritan-native American relations that attacks the myth of white superiority.

M. J. A. Jones, *Congregational Commonwealths: Connecticut, 1632-1662*. Middletown, CT: Wesleyan University Press, 1968. A thorough interpretation of the Fundamental Orders of Connecticut and a somewhat cynical view of its purported liberalism in matters of church membership and political power.

Marshall Knappen, *Tudor Puritanism*. Chicago: University of Chicago Press, 1939. A study of the various divisions within English Puritanism on the eve of the colonization of the New World.

George Langdon, *Pilgrim Colony*. New Haven, CT: Yale University Press, 1966. A history of New Plymouth from its founding to 1691 and its absorption into Massachusetts Bay Colony.

Douglas Leach, *Flintlock and Tomahawk: New England in King Philip's War*. New York: Macmillan, 1958. An entertaining, but still scholarly military history of the first real war on the American continent. It presents a well-rounded picture of the war, showing how it deeply affected civilian populations on both sides.

Thomas Leverenz, *The Language of Puritan Feeling*. New Brunswick, NJ: Rutgers University Press, 1980. A study of Puritanism as a response to the perceived chaos and corruption of English society in the late sixteenth century.

David Levin, ed., *What Happened in Salem?* New York: Twayne Publishers, 1950. A collection of original documents from the time of the Salem witchcraft trials. It includes trial records as well as the writings of Cotton and Increase Mather, Thomas Brattle, and others.

Kenneth A. Lockridge, *A New England Town—The First Hundred Years: Dedham, Massachusetts, 1636-1736*. Expanded ed. New York: W.W. Norton & Company, 1985. A thorough examination of a typical Puritan community.

David S. Lovejoy, *The Glorious Revolution in America*. New York: Harper and Row, 1972. A study tracing the effect of English politics on the American colonies after the restoration of the monarchy in 1660 through the aftermath of the Glorious Revolution of 1688 which was much welcomed in New England.

David S. Lovejoy, ed., *Religious Enthusiasm and the Great Awakening*. Englewood Cliffs, NJ: Prentice-Hall, 1969. Collection of abbreviated writings from the time of the Great Awakening.

Paul Lucas, *Valley of Discord*. Hanover, NH: University Press of New England, 1976. A comprehensive history of the conflict between Presbyterians and Congregationalists in seventeenth-century New England.

Michael McGiffert, ed., *Puritanism and the American Experience*. Reading,

MA: Addison-Wesley, 1969. Primary sources and historical essays examine how the experiences of the Puritans in America shaped their ideas.

William McLoughlin, *New England Dissent, 1630-1833*. Cambridge, MA: Harvard University Press, 1971. A history of two centuries of religious dissent focusing on the Baptists, but including material on a variety of dissenters to the Puritan orthodoxy.

Robert Middlekauf, *The Mathers*. New York: Oxford University Press, 1971. A revisionist history of the Mather family that humanizes three intellectual giants of Puritanism, Richard, Increase, and Cotton Mather.

Perry Miller, *Errand into the Wilderness*. Cambridge, MA: Harvard University Press, 1956. A series of essays and addresses on Puritans, Quakers, and Congregationalists, as well as on such important New England leaders as Thomas Hooker and Jonathan Edwards.

Perry Miller, *Jonathan Edwards*. New York: Sloane, 1949. A biography that shows its subject as not just a preacher but as the foremost philosopher of his era.

Perry Miller, *The New England Mind: From Colony to Province*. Cambridge, MA: Harvard University Press, 1953. A history of colonial Massachusetts from Richard Mather's farewell sermon of 1657 to Jonathan Edwards's Harvard lectures of 1731.

Perry Miller, *The New England Mind: The Seventeenth Century*. New York: Macmillan, 1939. A study of Puritans that emphasizes that these were normal people who wanted to prosper and enjoy life, but their intellectual and theological outlook set them apart from others.

Perry Miller, *Orthodoxy in Massachusetts*. Cambridge, MA: Harvard University Press, 1933. A study of Puritanism from its English background to 1648; pays special attention to the development of Congregationalism.

Perry Miller, *Roger Williams: His Contribution to the American Tradition*. Indianapolis: Bobbs-Merrill, 1953. A biography analyzing the theological basis for Williams's argument that the state had no authority in religious matters.

Perry Miller and Thomas H. Johnson, eds., *The Puritans*. New York: Harper & Row, 1963. The classic twentieth-century collection of Puritan writings originally published in 1938.

Edmund S. Morgan, *The Puritan Dilemma*. Boston: Little Brown, 1958. A fascinating biography of John Winthrop and his struggle over how to live a good and moral life in a world his Puritan theology told him was often less than good and moral.

Edmund S. Morgan, *The Puritan Family*. Boston: The Trustees of the Public Library, 1944. A study of the Puritan family as an agent of discipline and character development. It also examines the relationship between Puritan ideas and Puritan practices.

Edmund S. Morgan, *Roger Williams: The Church and the State*. New York: Norton, 1967. A brief biography of the banished Puritan, stressing the symmetry of the ideas behind his zealotry and polemics.

Edmund S. Morgan, *Visible Saints*. Ithaca, NY: Cornell University Press, 1963. A study of the evolving debate within Puritanism over how inclusive or exclusive membership in the church ought to be.

Edmund S. Morgan, ed., *The Founding of Massachusetts: Historians and Their Sources*. Indianapolis: Bobbs-Merrill, 1964. A collection of primary sources and historiographical writings focusing on the early years of the Massachusetts Bay Colony.

Edmund S. Morgan, ed. *Puritan Political Ideas*. Indianapolis: Bobbs-Merrill, 1965. An anthology of Puritan writings on government and society, dating from English works prior to the American migration up to Puritan-influenced writings on the American Revolution.

Samuel Eliot Morison, *Builders of the Bay Colony*. Boston: Houghton Mifflin, 1930. Biographical sketches of some of the leaders of early Massachusetts, including John Winthrop, Robert Child, John Eliot, and Anne Bradstreet.

Samuel Eliot Morison, *The Founding of Harvard College*. Cambridge, MA: Harvard University Press, 1935. A celebratory, but nonetheless vivid and fascinating, history of the early years of the first college to be founded by Europeans in the New World.

Geoffrey Nuttall, *The Holy Spirit in Puritan Faith*. New York: Oxford University Press, 1946. An intellectual history of the Puritan theology of religious experience during the course of the English revolution.

Thomas Parker, *John Calvin*. Philadelphia: Westminster Press, 1975. A biography of the founding father of Puritanism that portrays him as a hero, and also as a religious leader not always in control of his followers.

Irwin H. Polishook, ed., *Roger Williams, John Cotton, and Religious Freedom*. Englewood Cliffs, NJ: Prentice Hall, 1967. A collection of the writings of Williams, Cotton, and others on religious tolerance in the New England colonies.

Robert Pope, *The Half-Way Covenant: Church Membership in Puritan New England*. Princeton, NJ: Princeton University Press, 1969. A history of a fifteen-year debate that culminated in the Half-Way Covenant of 1662, which the author argues was a rational, even natural way for the Puritans to adapt to changing circumstances.

Amanda Porterfield, *Female Piety in Puritan New England*. New York: Oxford University Press, 1992. Examines images of female piety and how it affected Puritan ideas of worship, marriage, and family.

Sumner Chilton Powell, *Puritan Village: The Formation of a New England Town*. Middletown, CT: Wesleyan University Press, 1963. A closely examined social history of the town of Sudbury, Massachusetts, that seeks to reveal Puritan life.

Records of Salem Witchcraft. Roxbury, MA: W. Elliot Woodward, 1864. Copies of many of the original documents from the Salem witchcraft trials.

Richard Reinitz, ed., *Tensions in American Puritanism*. New York: John Wiley and Sons, 1970. A collection of primary source and historical writings focusing on issues that divided the American Puritans.

Peter Lockwood Rumsey, *Acts of God and the People, 1620-1730*. Ann Arbor: UMI Press, 1986. An examination of the Puritans' ideas on divine providence and how these ideas affected the Salem witch trials and other actions.

Darrett B. Rutman, *American Puritanism*. Philadelphia: Lippincott, 1970. A study that tries to bridge the gap between Puritan ideas and social reality and treats the Puritan religion as a gift from the preachers to their congregations.

Darrett B. Rutman, *Winthrop's Boston*. Chapel Hill: University of North Carolina Press, 1965. A study contrasting the ideals of the founder of the Massachusetts Bay Colony, circa 1630, with the pragmatic, commercial reality of a more settled community at the time of his death in 1649.

Darrett B. Rutman, ed., *The Great Awakening: Event and Exegesis*. New York: John Wiley, 1970. A good collection of documents from the time of the Great Awakening and several twentieth-century essays discussing that event in the context of American history.

Neal Salisbury, *Manitou and Providence: Indians, Europeans, and the Making of New England*. New York: Oxford University Press, 1982. A solid ethnohistory that analyzes the native American population before European contact and discusses the cultural interaction of the first half-century of contact between the two worlds.

Charles M. Segal and David C. Stinebeck, *Puritans, Indians, and Manifest Destiny*. New York: G.P. Putnam's Sons, 1977. A documentary history of Puritan/Indian relations; generally is critical of the Puritans.

George Selement, *Keepers in the Vineyard*. Lanham, MD: University Press of America, 1984. A study of Puritan ministers that argues that they did not form an elite removed from the daily life of their followers.

Harold Selesky, *War and Society in Colonial Connecticut*. New Haven, CT: Yale University Press, 1990. An example of the new military history that stresses the lives of the ordinary people who went to war rather than their leaders.

Frank Shuffelton, *Thomas Hooker, 1586-1647*. Princeton, NJ: Princeton University Press, 1977. A biography that tries to relate Hooker's writings to his religious and political activities and stresses his role in the controversies involving Anne Hutchinson and Roger Williams.

Kenneth Silverman, *The Life and Times of Cotton Mather*. New York: Harper and Row, 1984. It presents Cotton Mather as an American phenomenon and the first truly American author as well as an early liberal on such subjects as ecumenism, parenting, and pacifism.

Richard Slotkin and James K. Folsom, eds., *So Dreadful a Judgment: Puritan Responses to King Philip's War, 1676-1677*. Middletown, CT: Wesleyan University Press, 1978. A collection of Puritan writings concerning the conflict, including sermons, poems, and captivity narratives.

David Stannard, *The Puritan Way of Death*. New York: Oxford University Press, 1977. A study that argues that the Puritans faced death fearfully because they saw themselves powerless to bring about their personal salvation.

Marion L. Starkey, *The Devil in Massachusetts: A Modern Inquiry into the Salem Witch Trials*. New York: Alfred A. Knopf, 1949. An interesting and readable discussion of the trials and their aftermath, including detailed notes on sources; emphasizes the role of psychology in the study of history.

W. K. B. Stoever, *A Faire and Easie Way to Heaven*. Middletown, CT: Wesleyan University Press, 1978. A careful study of Puritan dogmatics and theology with a special emphasis on the Antinomian controversy of 1636-1638 and the Antinomians' assertion against obedience to human authority.

Harry Stout, *The New England Soul*. New York: Oxford University Press, 1986. A study of Puritan sermons from 1630 to the American Revolution that tries to relate the Puritan view of liberty to the coming of that revolution.

Ann Taves, ed., *Religion and Domestic Violence in Early New England: The Memoirs of Abigail Abbot Bailey*. Bloomington: Indiana University Press, 1989. An annotated edition of a journal kept by a Puritan wife and mother who was a victim of domestic abuse.

Alden T. Vaughan, *New England Frontier*. Boston: Little Brown, 1965. A history of the first half-century of contact between the Puritans and native Americans; sympathetic to the Puritans.

Alden T. Vaughan, ed., *The Puritan Tradition in America 1620-1730*. Columbia: University of South Carolina Press, 1972. Extensive collection of Puritan documents.

Alden T. Vaughan and Edward W. Clark, eds., *Puritans Among the Indians*. Cambridge, MA: Belknap Press/Harvard University Press, 1981. An anthology of captivity narratives, the highly popular accounts of Puritans who had been held captive by Indians.

Alden T. Vaughan and Francis J. Bremer, eds., *Puritan New England: Essays on Religion, Society, and Culture*. New York: St. Martin's Press, 1977. A collection of articles by historians on Puritanism and its cultural development in America.

R. E. Wall, *Massachusetts Bay: The Crucial Decade, 1640-1650*. New Haven, CT: Yale University Press, 1972. A detailed study of the internal and external difficulties facing the colony during its first decade.

Dewey Wallace, *Puritans and Predestination*. Chapel Hill: University of North Carolina Press, 1982. A study seeking to establish the centrality of the theology of grace in English Protestant thought.

George M. Waller, ed., *Puritanism in Early America*. 2nd ed. Lexington, MA: D.C. Heath, 1973. An anthology of both Puritan and historiographical writing.

Michael Walzer, *The Revolution of the Saints*. Cambridge, MA: Harvard University Press, 1965. A history of Puritanism which argues that it became essentially a political movement bent on disciplining individuals to achieve the Puritan goal of an ordered community.

Francois Wendel, *Calvin: The Origins and Development of His Religious Thought*. London: Collins, 1963. A study of John Calvin's theology.

J. William T. Youngs, *God's Messengers: Religious Leadership in Colonial New England, 1700-1775*. Baltimore: Johns Hopkins University Press, 1976. A study of Congregational ministers and their efforts to regain influence in an increasingly secular world.

Larzer Ziff, *The Career of John Cotton*. Princeton, NJ: Princeton University Press, 1962. More intellectual history than biography, this is a study of

Cotton's search for a middle ground in the debate between Antinomians and Arminians.

Larzer Ziff, *Puritanism in America*. New York: Viking Press, 1973. A history of seventeenth-century Puritanism emphasizing its literary and cultural dimensions.

Michael Zuckerman, *Peaceable Kingdoms*. New York: Alfred A. Knopf, 1970. An analysis of the Puritan town, the real concern of which was community and order rather than individual freedoms.

Index

Algonquin Indians, 170
Allin, John, 277, 278, 282
America
  Dutch colony in, 31
  natural resources in, 31
  see also New England
American Congregational churches,
  115
Anabaptists (Baptists), 113, 114, 118-
  119, 266
Antinomians
  destroying Puritan community,
    82-91
  follow the spirit of God, 92-104
  religious revival and, 218-219, 223,
    226
  religious tolerance and, 105, 113,
    118-119
aristocracy, Puritans and, 124, 127
Arminianism, 219, 223, 227, 266
Assembly of Pastors of Churches in
  New England, 218

Baptists. *See* Anabaptists
Barker, William, 197
Belknap, Jeremy, 213
Bozeman, Theodore Dwight, 269
Bradford, William, 153, 257, 258
Brattle, Thomas, 200, 213
Bremer, Francis J.
  on Puritans settling New England,
    44
  on Roger Williams, 71
Bridge, John, 37
Brockwell, Charles, 248
Bulkeley, Peter, 59, 275, 280-281
Burroughs, George, 212

Calef, Robert, 213
Calvinists, 229, 264
Cambridge Platform of 1648, 115
Chauncy, Charles, 242, 277
Child, Robert, 129
Christianity
  in New England
    decline of, 63-66
    revival of
      is false, 225-228, 244
      must be judged appropriately,
        229-241
      offers hope, 218-224
      zealotry should be avoided, 242-

250
  native Americans and, 28, 31, 33, 40,
    171-176, 276
  New England colonies would
    benefit from, 35-43, 276
  primitive zeal in, 233-234
  Puritans' rules and, 45-49
Church of England
  corruption of, 35, 36, 38
  membership in, 134
  persecution and, 37, 277-279
  reformation of, 44, 48, 134, 263-267,
    270, 279
  separation from, 48, 52, 78, 257
Clarke, John, 114, 116
Congregationalists, 115, 119, 192, 260,
  282
Connecticut General Court, 149
Cotton, John, 37, 192
  Antinomians and, 82, 92-93, 98
  business practices, 138-139
  debates with Roger Williams, 71-74,
    75-81, 160-162, 281-282
  political leadership, 123
  reasons for migration, 275, 277-279
  religious tolerance and, 115
  treatment of native Americans,
    160-162
Crandall, John, 114
Cromwell, Oliver, 110, 266
Cushman, Robert, 30

Dailey, Barbara Ritter
  on Antinomians, 92-93
Dane, John, 277
Danforth, Samuel, 256, 257, 261, 263
Davenport, John, 277
democracy, Puritans and, 124, 127
devil, 194, 204, 209-211, 216
Dorchester Company, 28
Dudley, Thomas
  Antinomians and, 92, 98-102
  government and, 128
  religious tolerance and, 113, 118

Edwards, Jonathan, 229, 242
Eliot, John, 170, 178, 278-279
Emerson, Everett, 278
Endecott, John, 114
England
  government in, 110, 112, 130-131
  King Charles I, 110, 272, 278

land patent for Puritans, 72, 76-77,
130-131
  are legal, 160-162
King Charles II, 110
King Philip's War, 168, 169, 177, 182-
187, 261
Puritans in
  civil war and, 110, 112, 131, 258,
266
  government and, 129, 131
  religious tolerance and, 112, 117,
118, 259, 266

Finley, Samuel, 237
Folsom, James K.
  on Puritans and native Americans,
178
Foster, Ann, 197

Gortonists, 266
government, Puritans and, 124-128,
129-135
Great Awakening
  as mere enthusiasm, 243-244
  as the work of God, 240-241
  beginnings of, 229, 235
  behavior during, 227, 244-246, 248
  Bible should be guide, 247-249
  determining good and bad, 232-241
  human nature and, 232-237
  offers errors in religious thinking,
225-228, 244
  offers hope of religious revival, 218-
224
  reformation of sinners and, 221, 237-
240
  religious fervor should be praised,
229-241
  religious zealotry should be avoided,
242-250
  scriptures and, 231-232
Great Migration
  reasons for, 258-268, 272, 275-282

Hale, John, 197
Heimert, Alan, on Roger Williams, 70
Higginson, Francis, 48, 277
Higginson, John, 256
Holmes, Obadiah, 114, 116, 117
Hooker, Thomas, 37, 64, 87, 124, 257,
277
Hutchinson, Anne
  Antinomian beliefs of, 92-93
  creates dissension in Puritan
community, 83, 88-91, 105, 110
  death of, 90-91, 93
  excommunication and banishment

of, 82, 84, 87, 93, 103-104, 266
  trial of, 93-104
Indians. See native Americans
Ireland, immigrants to, 32

Jesuits
  in New England, 36, 276
Johnson, Edward, 165, 275, 280-281

Keayne, Robert
  business practices in New England
condemned, 136-139
  defended, 140-145
King Charles I, 110, 272, 278
  land patent for Puritans, 72, 76-77,
130-131
  are legal, 160-162
King Charles II, 110
King Philip's War, 168, 169, 177,
182-187, 261
Kyles, John, 183

Leonard, Nathaniel, 221
Lord Say and Seale, 123-124
Ludlow, Roger, 281

Maclear, James F., 265
Massachusetts Bay Colony, 28, 35
  Antinomians caused dissent in, 82-
91
  con, 92-104
  banishment from, 70, 82, 93, 133
  government in
    leadership restricted to church
members, 123-128
    should be lifted, 129-135
    should be liberalized, 130-135
    voting rights in, 132
  immigration to
    should be restricted, 105-109
    con, 110-111
  making a profit harms community,
136-139, 151
    con, 140-145
  reasons for settlement, 28-34, 35-43,
258-268, 275-282
  stricter laws are needed, 146-152
    con, 153-155
  worship required in, 123, 134, 148-
149, 259
Massachusetts Bay Company, 28, 44,
263, 276, 278
Massachusetts General Court
  Antinomians and, 84-87, 93-104
  banishment of Roger Williams by,
71, 72, 77
  Baptists and, 114

immigration to Massachusetts and, 105-106, 111
  on government, 129-130, 132
    stricter laws needed, 146-152
  Roger Williams' letter to, 163-164
Mather, Cotton
  family of, 62
  on witches, 192-199, 208, 213
  reasons for immigration, 267
Mather, Increase
  family of, 62, 192
  sermons of, 169, 226, 256
    on reformation, 261-262
  witchcraft trials and, 208-212, 213
Mather, Richard, 62, 192, 208
  family of, 62, 192, 208
  reasons for immigration, 275, 277, 281
Mayflower, 52-53, 54
Mayflower Compact, 53, 54
Miller, Perry, 255, 259, 269, 270-271, 282
ministers
  itinerant, 226, 242
  persecution of, 37
  rules for, 223, 226
miracles, Puritan definition of, 193
Mohegan Indians, 164, 165
monarchy, Puritans and, 124, 127
Morgan, Edmund S.
  on New England politics, 129-130, 146

Narragansett Indians, 71, 78, 132, 161, 163
native Americans
  Algonquins, 170
  as savages, 179-186
  attacks on Puritans, 146, 164, 177, 179-180
  captive's view of, 177-187
  conversion to Christianity
    as missionaries, 168, 169, 171
    is impossible, 177-178
    would benefit, 28, 31, 33, 40, 171-176, 276
  creation of laws, 173
  educating the children, 174-175
  English can civilize, 31-32, 39, 171-176
  killing of is justified by God, 165-167
  kindness to captives, 178, 181-182, 183-184, 187
  land ownership and, 39, 71, 79, 160, 161
  land purchased from, 78, 161
  Long Islanders, 164

missionary's view of, 170-176
Mohegans, 164, 165
Narragansetts, 71, 78, 132, 161, 163
Pequots, 164, 165
plague and, 30, 39, 161, 172
Puritan treatment of
  as justified, 160-162
    con, 163-164
reservations for, 169-173
should be treated charitably, 168-169
Tarentines, 31
welcomed the English, 161, 164
New England
  colonies in
    as unsafe, 41-43
    farming in, 29, 31
    fishing opportunities in, 29, 31
    health and, 29
    objections to, 32-34
    practical benefits of, 28-34
    Puritan vision for, 44-51
    religious dissent in, 62
      Antinomians and, 82-91, 92-104, 266
    Separatist vision for, 52-56
    shipping industry and, 31
    would serve true Christian church, 35-43, 276
  failure of colonies in, 41
  God has blessed, 57-61
    con, 62-66, 256, 261-262
  land patents for
    are legal, 77, 130-131, 160-162
    con, 72, 76
  right to settle land, 39
  sedition in, 71, 77-78, 80-81
    Antinomians and, 88, 93
  see also Massachusetts Bay Colony; Plymouth Colony
Noyes, Nicholas, 155

Oakes, Urian, 256

Pastors of the Churches in the Province of Massachusetts Bay, 225
Pequot Indians, 164, 165
Pequot Wars, 163-164, 165
Peter, Hugh, 277
Phips, Sir William, 205, 208
Pilgrims
  affiliation with Congregationalists, 192
  founding of Plymouth Colony by, 52
  Mayflower Compact and, 54
  motivation of, 257-258
Plymouth Colony
  founding of, 30, 52

purpose of, 257-258
religious tolerance in, 153
Presbyterians, 119, 266, 282
Puritans
    aristocracy and, 124, 127
    as reformationists, 44, 48, 263-267,
        270, 279
    attacks on native Americans, 163,
        165
    democracy and, 124, 127
    end of the world and, 265
    God's mission for, 50-51, 61, 66,
        258-259
    God's punishment of, 146-147
    government and, 124-128, 129-135
    in England, 70, 105
        civil war and, 110, 112, 131, 258,
            266
        government and, 129, 131
        religious tolerance and, 112, 117,
            118, 259, 266
    laws governing behavior
        attending worship, 148-149
        authority and, 150-151
        avoiding Quakers, 148
        cursing, 149-150
        drinking and taverns, 150, 152
        hair and clothes, 147-148
        idleness, 151
        single people and, 152
        youth and, 149, 152
    miracles, as defined by, 193
    monarchy and, 124, 127
    New England community must be
        preserved, 105-109
    on justice and mercy, 45-47
    on love, 47-48
    on wealth and poverty, 45, 258, 272
    proper business conduct of, 136-139,
        140-145
    punishment and, 148-152
        does not improve behavior, 154
    reasons for migration, 28-34, 35-43,
        258-268, 275-282
    religious intolerance of, 259-260, 266
        Antinomians and, 82-83, 92-93, 105
        are not too intolerant, 115-119
        Roger Williams and, 70, 77-78
        should be more tolerant, 113-114
    restricting immigration to
        community
        is just, 105-109
        is unjust, 110-111
    saw themselves as model for the
        world, 255-268
        con, 269-282
    separation of church and state, 71,

73, 79-80, 111
        is not necessary, 123-128
    sexual behavior and, 154
    social classes and, 45, 258, 273
    special covenant with God, 50-51,
        57-60, 259-260, 263
        punishment for failing, 261, 264,
            276
    treatment of native Americans
        is justified, 160-162
    vision for new colony, 44-51

Quakers
    behavior of, 244-245
    Puritans must avoid, 148

religion
    revival of
        fervor should be praised, 229-241
        is false, 225-228, 244
        proof of, 220-222, 231-232
    true nature of, 250
Rhode Island
    Antinomians settle, 90, 93
    founding of, 71, 163
    religious tolerance in, 153, 266
Robinson, John, 52
Rogers, Ezekiel, 277
Rogers, Richard, 277
Rowlandson, Joseph, 177
Rowlandson, Mary, 177
Rutman, Darrett B., 273

Salem witch trials, 168
    see also witchcraft, trials for
Saltonstall, Richard, 112, 115
Savoy Confession of Faith, 169
Seekers, 113, 118-119
Separatists
    history of, 52, 257, 263
    Anne Hutchinson and, 102
    Puritans and, 48
    vision for new colony, 52-56
Sewall, Samuel, 168
Shepard, Thomas, 64, 256
    reasons for leaving England, 37, 275,
        277-279, 282
Skelton, Samuel, 277
Slotkin, Richard
    on Puritans and native Americans,
        178
Socinians, 266
Stoughton, William, 57, 256, 261

Tarentine Indians, 31

Vane, Henry, 98, 105, 110,

Waller, George M.
  on Puritan politics, 126
Ward, Nathaniel, 117
wars
  English civil war, 110, 112, 131, 258,
    266
  native Americans and
    King Philip's War, 168, 169, 177,
      182-187, 261
    Pequot Wars, 163-164, 165
Welde, Thomas, 82, 170
Wheelwright, John
  Antinomians and, 82, 93, 94, 99
White, John, 28, 35
Williams, Roger
  banishment of, 163, 266
    was justified, 75-81, 109
    con, 70-74
  debates with John Cotton, 70-74, 75,
    163-164, 281-282
  on treatment of native Americans,
    163-164
Winthrop, John, 59, 62
  on Antinomians, 84
  on authority, 126
  on business practices, 136-139
  on government, 128, 130,
    259-260
  on immigration to Massachusetts,
    105, 110
  Puritan vision for new colony, 44-51,
    257, 258-266, 270-275
  reasons for migration to New
    England, 35-43, 258-266, 275-276
  sermon preached on board *Arbella*,
    44, 138, 258, 262, 269, 272-275

trial of Anne Hutchinson and, 92,
    93-104
witchcraft
  accusations of, 201-203, 204, 205,
    206-207
  in Europe, 196-197
  opposes God, 196
  possession and, 198
  proof of, 194-195, 205-207, 209,
    210-211
  Puritan definition of, 193
  trials for
    end of, 205, 208
    executions and, 205
    judges', methods, 201-203
    jurors repent, 215
    opposition to, 200-207, 213-217
    reflect lack of faith in God, 213-217
    should proceed cautiously, 208-212
witches
  confessions of, 195-197, 203-205, 206,
    211
  devil's influence and, 194, 204,
    209-211, 216-217
  evil spirits and, 193-194, 203
  evil works of, 193, 196-197, 198
  must repent, 198-199
  punishment of, 196, 205, 209
  should be condemned, 192-199
  unfair prosecution of, 197, 200-207
Witter, William, 114
women
  marriage and, 125, 126
  position in the Puritan community,
    93, 94, 96-98